MEMORY
AND DELIVERY

Transmitting and Transforming Knowledge and Culture in Liberal Arts Education for the Future

---

Selected Proceedings from the Fifteenth Annual Conference of the Association for Core Texts and Courses
Memphis, Tennessee
April 17–19, 2009

Edited by

Richard Dagger
Christopher Metress
J. Scott Lee

University Press of America,® Inc.
Lanham · Boulder · New York · Toronto · Plymouth, UK

Copyright © 2016 by
University Press of America,® Inc.
4501 Forbes Boulevard
Suite 200
Lanham, Maryland 20706
UPA Acquisitions Department (301) 459-3366

10 Thornbury Road
Plymouth PL6 7PP
United Kingdom

Library of Congress Control Number: 2015960101
ISBN: 978-0-7618-6731-9 (paperback : alk. paper)
eISBN: 978-0-7618-6732-6

Table of Contents

Introduction

Richard Dagger, Christopher Metress, and J. Scott Lee   vii

Plenary Addresses

Whither Philosophy?
Richard Kamber   3

The Cunning of Tradition
Wilfred M. McClay   13

Of the Wings of Atalanta—Meaning and Dualism in DuBois, Morrison,
and Historically Black, Liberal Arts Education
Grant D. Venerable   23

Platonic Forms as a Model of Modern Physics: Confessions of an
Experimental Physicist
Steven Turley   31

Liberal Education and the Liberal Arts

Liberal Education: Transmitting Knowledge through Texts
Molly Brigid Flynn   49

Why Should Science Majors Waste Their Time on Great Books
James J. Donovan   55

Medieval Political Philosophy, Christianity, and the Liberal Arts
Benjamin Smith   61

Thinking about Thinking about Justice: The Abolition of Man and
Reflections on Education
Storm Bailey   65

The Futility of Escaping the Mind: Invisible Man and a Liberal Education
David Dolence   69

An Exemplary Model of Core Text Education:
Kuhn's Structure of Scientific Revolutions as a Paradigm Provider
Bryan Johnson   73

Memory and the Classical Heritage

Homer and the Duty of Remembrance
Karl Schudt   79

Justius Lipsius and the Re-Invention of Stoicism
Andrew Terjesen   83

"Literaturizing" Life: Reading and Misreading Honor in Petronius' *Satyricon*
Michael J. Mordine   89

Hobbes's Thucydides and Homer: Translation as Political Thought
Laurie M. Johnson Bagby   95

"But I Did Not Love Only Him": Helping Students Discern
Platonic Values in Sense and Sensibility
Steven Epley   103

Freedom and Happiness from the Renaissance to Modernity

The Originality of Pico's Oration
Neil G. Robertson   111

Death and Core Tradition in a Polish Renaissance Lament
James Roney   117

Freedom and Its Limits: Moliere's *Don Juan* as Free-Thinker
Diane Fourny   121

Freedom and Coercion in Locke's Treatment of Religion and Politics
Thomas Powers   127

Ambition, Happiness, and Adam Smith's *The Theory of Moral Sentiments*
Edward J. Harpham   131

Camus's *The Fall:* Remembering the "Great Books" in Light of
Modernity's Fall
Christopher E. Baldwin   137

Work, Leisure, and the *Vita Contemplativa*—Pieper's Leisure: The Basis
of Culture
Terry Hall   141

Transmitting and Transforming through Core Texts

Teaching the Reformation through Luther's Galatians
Jarrett A. Carty   149

Galileo's *Two New Sciences* and the Quantification of Motion
Brian P. Schwartz   153

Satire as a Means of Transmitting and Transforming Knowledge and Culture
Lyndall Nairn   159

Memory, Invention, and Delivery in *Middlemarch*
Mark E. Thomas   165

"Recalling now the obscure shapes, the echoes, the sounds and sights after
their sorts": Whitman's Poetics of Memory in "Out of the Cradle Endlessly
Rocking"
Brian Nowlin   171

The Burning Deck: Elizabeth Bishop's Modern Parable
David Southward   177

Introduction

The fifteenth annual ACTC conference, hosted by Rhodes College in Memphis in the spring of 2009, evoked classical rhetoric as a means for discussing the intersections between the study of core texts and their impact upon our knowledge and culture. Core texts themselves are a form of memory, whose images, arguments, and ideas are discovered and invented anew in each generation and delivered by unique programs at our institutions. The papers collected in this volume represent some of the conference's best reflections on which traditions and futures are being offered by these unique programs and their carefully selected core texts.

Certainly, Cicero, one of the founders of classical rhetoric, had little doubt about what the past offered to his civilization:

> To me ... it does not seem possible that a mute and voiceless wisdom could have turned human beings suddenly from their habits and introduced them to different patterns of life... After cities had been established, how could it have been brought to pass that humans should learn to keep faith and observe justice, and become accustomed to obey others voluntarily, and believe not only that they must work for the common good but even sacrifice life itself, unless humans had been able by eloquence to persuade their fellows of what they had invented by reason? (*De Inventione* I.ii.3)

Cicero is speaking about the necessity of discourse to harmonious cultural life, about how institutions provide the infrastructure for the transmission of values that hold human beings together, about how without human construction we would never have the means to use our thoughts and our language to build a better world. But are discourse, cultural life, institutions, values, arts and sciences, thought and language still important to the world's and each tradition's way of life for the future? Perhaps this question is wrapped up in another: Are core texts still important for the future?

Since our 2009 conference, it has become exceedingly clear that our citizens, our scientists, our artists, and our business leaders, as well as all those working in education or social programs, would benefit from the historical, ethical, literary, and philosophic perspective provided by a core text, liberal arts education. Undoubtedly, our universities and colleges do a fine job of training specialists and offering a seemingly endless choice of curricular opportunities. But specialization and endless choice each lead to isolation: the former to the isolation of community where one group, discipline, corporation or association runs its discourse without having to take into account the presumed, inexpert failings of outsiders; the latter to the isolation of individuals, where, though individuals have some insights into many corners of the world, they have no means nor practice to connect islands of isolated learning. The challenge here is to bridge the gap between individuals who have isolated knowledge spread throughout the world and bodies of discourse which seem concentrated on one aspect of the world. Fortunately, where core text curricula exist or are in development, there is a way to bridge this gap, for core text curricula offer to students, professors, and institutions an opportunity to change the future by thinking with the widest possible coordination of texts, cultures, and ideas. Core texts would seem to offer us a discourse of connection, a way out of the isolation.

However, the discourse of connection is not without problems. In this age of globalism and diversity, no one can operate in an isolated sphere or tradition. Whether we come from specific religious, political, linguistic, ethnic, racial, or cultural traditions, our traditions are meeting other traditions, and we must communicate. Certainly, our individual traditions are worth preserving, but along with preservation of the old there must be communication with the new. But which new traditions, and how many? Thus, the discourse of connection that is fostered by core text programs also presents those programs with perhaps their greatest challenge. Against the isolation of specialization and endless curricular choice, core texts promise connection, but what if those connections promise to be so endless that we never find firm footing within any single system of meaning? How do we think about these problems of communication that are, now, inevitable? How do we develop and transmit images, arguments and ideas that we hold to be precious, while at the same time moving into the future to discover something different and of deep worth?

The discourse of connection brings with it other difficulties as well. One of the glaring ironies of the contemporary world is that while we read more words than any other generation in history, less substantive content is being communicated than ever before. Liberal arts, core text curricula have an important role in transforming communications, and in ACTC there are signs of their renewal on college campuses. Behind these movements is an understanding that the liberal arts and core texts not only touch all of our lives, but that they may deeply affect what we know and how we think.

But exactly how might the resources of disciplines, traditions, and cultures be connected to the past and future by our texts, programs, and teaching? What do we do when we do not, at least at first, share the same memory? There can be little doubt that we need shared memory and, in light of recent events, perhaps those institutions outside of the core text sphere have begun to see the value of possessing a common cultural discourse. What is in doubt, because it is so little taught, is by what means we are to evaluate, judge, and decide for the future about such things as concerned Cicero when we are no longer operating in an isolated sphere or tradition. How do the secular and religious reach out to each other? How do the traditions of East and

West meet? No longer are the sciences, social sciences, humanities, and fine arts distinct realms, hermetically sealed from each other. What shall their future interaction be?

For this, it appears, our core text curricular programs are leaders in inventing new approaches, new selections of traditions, new ways of teaching for the future. Through the traditions of the past, our students may look to the building of different forms of government, to the founding of different forms of religion, to the inventive explorations of literature, drama, poetry, and fine arts, and to the world revolutions wrought by each of these and science as well. Our students and programs can bring the rich resources of distinctive traditions and texts to the agora of world traditions that is the 21st century.

By convening a conference on Memory, Invention, and Delivery, ACTC sought to engage a series of important questions about the past, present, and future of core text, liberal arts education. The papers collected in this volume engage different questions about that past, present, and future, and they certainly represent a wide array of approaches and offer a diverse set of conclusions. However, all of these essays share a common faith that a core text, liberal arts education provides students and faculty with the best space for thinking about these questions, as well the insight to understand the importance of such questions. A combination of plenary and panel presentations, the papers are divided into five categories. In the first category are the plenary addresses. As they did when delivered in Memphis in 2009, these addresses provide an overview of the major themes of the conference. The pieces by Richard Kamber and Wilfred M. McClay ask large questions about trends in the liberal arts, and they make a strong case for the sustaining power of tradition for both the academy and the world at large. Grant D. Venerable and Steven Turley do the same by exploring specific traditions: for Venerable, it is the liberal arts tradition found in Historically Black Colleges; for Turley, it is the often-unacknowledged intersection of philosophy and physics. The provocative insights of these plenary addresses are played out again and again in the papers that follow. In section two, the papers directly engage questions of liberal education and the liberal arts. Molly Brigid Flynn, James J. Donovan, and Benjamin Smith do so by reflecting on the value of liberal learning to students across the disciplines, each making a strong case for how this kind of learning promotes a conversation that is vital to our culture. As in the previous section, these essays are followed by papers that take a more specific focus. For Storm Bailey, David Dolence and Bryan Johnson, individual core texts can provide students with models for thinking about their own intellectual journeys, thereby encouraging the kind of self-reflection that is essentially to any sustained conversation with others. Section three takes as its focus the classical heritage and its legacy. Karl Schudt, Andrew Terjesen and Michael J. Mordine each deal directly with a specific text from that heritage, while Laurie M. Johnson Bagby and Steven Epley explore the presence of classical works in writers who have inherited that tradition. A common theme of memory and invention threads through each of these essays, and when read together they raise interesting questions about the transmission (and perhaps, "mis-transmission") of ideas through time. The fourth section highlights the themes of freedom and happiness. Treating figures as varied as Pico, Kochanowski,

Moliere, Locke, Smith, Camus, and Pieper, these essays address questions essential to human flourishing: how may we express sorrow, what are the limits to our freedom, when may we coerce others, should our ambitions rule us, how do we create meaning, what is the value of work? As Aristotle reminds us, we all wish to flourish, and Neil G. Robertson, James Roney, Diane Fourny, Thomas Powers, Edward J. Harpham, Christopher E. Baldwin, and Terry Hall remind us how varied are the ways of flourishing. In the final section of this volume, six conference participants address how specific core texts provide models for transmitting and transforming knowledge. For Jarrett A. Carty and Brian P. Schwartz, Luther and Galileo provide the texts. For Lyndall Nairn, Mark E. Thomas, and David Southward, it is George Eliot, Walt Whitman and Elizabeth Bishop. This section is a fitting end to a collection of papers from a conference devoted to exploring how core text courses and program create a stimulating conversation enriched by the traditions of the past while open to the possibilities of the future.

Finally, of course, we want to thank the readers and assistant editors who have helped us to complete this project. Without their assistance, this collection would not have come to fruition. We received many fine submissions, more than we could possibly publish in any one volume. We relied heavily on the judgment of our readers, who provided us with detailed responses, and did so in a timely and generous manner while juggling other duties and responsibilities. These readers include David Alvis (University of West Florida), Vince Brewton (University of North Alabama), Kathleen Burk (University of Dallas), Jamie Cromartie (Richard Stockton College), Betsy Dobbins (Samford University), William Donahue (Saint John's College, Santa Fe), Anne Marie Flanagan (University of the Sciences), Bryan Johnson (Samford University), Lisa Manter (St. Mary's College of California), Donald G. Marshall (Pepperdine University), Al Martin (Benedictine University), Richard Myers (St. Thomas University), Lyndall Nairn (Lynchburg College), James Roney (Juniatta College), Barbara Stone (Shimer College), Jason Wallace (Samford University), and Anne Wiles (James Madison University). In addition, Jean-Marie Kauth and Peg Kelley provided valuable copy editing and layout work. It has been a pleasure working with each of these individuals, and we hope that you will enjoy reading these proceedings as much as we enjoyed compiling them. If core texts are indeed a form of memory, whose images, arguments, and ideas are discovered and invented anew in each generation, then this volume assures us that many individuals and institutions remain committed to delivering that memory to another generation of students.

Richard Dagger
Christopher Metress
J. Scott Lee

Plenary Addresses

Whither Philosophy?

Richard Kamber
The College of New Jersey

Fifty years ago C.P. Snow gave a lecture at Cambridge University entitled "The Two Cultures."[1] The gist of that lecture was that a wide and worrisome gap had developed in Western society between the sciences and the humanities. During and after World War II Snow had helped conduct interviews of thousands of British scientists and engineers. When he asked his subject what books they had read, their typical reply was: "I've *tried* a bit of Dickens" (Snow 12). Humanists, he had discovered through less structured encounters, were equally ignorant when it came to science. He surmised that they had about as much insight into modern physics as their Neolithic ancestors (15). Snow put much of the blame for this gap on overspecialization in education. He worried that the house of Western culture had become so deeply divided that it was losing its capacity to keep pace with Russia and China and to "think with wisdom" in a world of accelerating social change where the rich "live precariously among the poor" (50).

Today the gap between the sciences and the humanities is wider than ever, and the troubles of the world have grown more complicated. (I sometimes long for the predictable rivalries of the Cold War.) Our collective capacity "to think with wisdom" is no greater than it was fifty years ago, and education has done little to make scientists more appreciative of the humanities or humanists more conversant with the sciences.

Still there are a few bright spots. The Association for Core Texts and Courses (ACTC), I am proud to say, ran a successful three-year curriculum and faculty development project on Bridging the Gap between the Humanities and Sciences, and is now applying for a new twelve-month grant. I am also pleased to see that a number of the presentations at this conference deal with texts in science and mathematics. One of the strengths of ACTC is that it invites each of us to apply the scholarly tools we bring from own disciplines to the rich materials afforded by core texts for the express purpose of building bridges with scholars from other fields. We build these bridges at a modest cost, and they are never "bridges to nowhere." As the new President of ACTC, I am eager to see us continue our leadership in bringing scientists and humanists closer together. I will have more to say about this and other expressions of ACTC's mission toward the end of my talk, but first I want to focus on a "two cultures" problem that is peculiar to my own discipline, philosophy.

When non-philosophers think about philosophy they tend to think of it as the *history* of philosophy. They think of it as a succession of eminent philosophers—along, of course, with the theories those philosophers developed, the texts they wrote, and the movements they inspired. Socrates, Plato, and Aristotle are frequent favorites. After that, the lists vary according to taste and background, but there are some philosophers who seem never to get on these popular lists. I have found, for example, that a good way to kill conversations with non-philosophers is to ask what they think of Willlard Quine or Saul Kripke. Since Quine and Kripke are among the most influential American philosophers of the past fifty years, there is reason to wonder why they are not better known outside of philosophy.

One reason for their extramural obscurity is suggested by an imperious quip attributed to Quine. He is credited with saying: "There are two kinds of philosophers, those who are interested in the history of philosophy and those who are interested in philosophy." What is intimated here is that the history of philosophy is not really philosophy and that those who pursue it are not really philosophers. Quine knew full well that philosophy departments were expected to conduct research and teach classes in the history of philosophy, but he did not think that service of that kind had much to do with the proper business of philosophy—working out solutions to philosophical problems like "What is there?" and "What can we know?" In other words, he saw two cultures *within* philosophy: a can-do culture akin to mathematics and science, and a can-teach culture akin to the humanities.

As a humanist and historian of philosophy I am tempted to dismiss Quine's dichotomy as false. I am ready to point out that philosophy, unlike the natural sciences, is the custodian of its own history. Astrophysicists do not think it is their task to write histories of astrophysics. They relegate that task to historians of science—a branch of learning that belongs to the humanities. Philosophers, on the other hand, are jealous guardians of this duty and, thus, of their own footing in the humanities. I am also disposed to argue that every chapter in the history of philosophy is an experiment from which we can learn valuable lessons. I am wont to insist that retelling the story of philosophy can be a powerful way of doing and critiquing philosophy. But these objections may miss a deeper point. Perhaps Quine's dichotomy should be construed, not as an imperious quip, but as a provocative way of raising an Aristotelian question about the *telos*—the *good*—of philosophy. Is the *telos* of philosophy to solve problems in the manner of the natural sciences, or is it to produce a rich succession of inspiring texts and ideas?

The answer I would like to give is "Both!" Unfortunately, both alternatives face significant difficulties. The first alternative is compromised by the fact that philosophers have not succeeded in 2500 years in reaching agreement on the solution to a single, major philosophical problem by means of philosophical methods or argument. Scientists, by contrast, have enjoyed spectacular success in reaching *provisional* agreement on a wide range of problems and changing the face of the world with technological applications. I emphasize the word *provisional,* for agreement in science is always subject to revision when new evidence warrants. If you had asked astrophysicists twelve ago what the universe is made of, they would have said "matter and energy" and referred you to the "standard model" of particles and forces (plus gravity) to describe the details. Today, most astrophysicists will tell you that that ordinary matter and energy make up only about 5% of what there is. The rest, they now say, is *dark* matter and *dark* energy—elusive stuff whose origin and characteristics remain largely unknown. Again, this is provisional knowledge, but it is the best answer we can get now, because it fits the relevant data better than any previous answer. To page back in the history of science for an answer one finds more congenial or inspiring—say, fire, earth, air, and water—would be foolishness.

The case with philosophy is very different. If you ask philosophers "What is there?" you will get a multitude of competing answers—including the answer, "it is experienced as self-evident"[2] and Quine's deflationary analysis, "to be is to be the value of a bound variable" (15). What you will not get is consensus, provisional or otherwise. Plato complained that the quarrels of philosophers discredited the search for wisdom (*Republic* VII, 539b-c). Two thousand years later, Descartes drew an even bleaker picture and set out to fix it: "As to philosophy," he wrote, "it [has] been cultivated for many centuries by men of the most outstanding ability, and that none the less there is not a single thing of which it treats which is not still in dispute, and nothing therefore, which is free from doubt" (98).

Until a few decades ago most philosophers nurtured the hope that a revolution in methodology or reforms in standards of practice could change this picture. Ludwig Wittgenstein, whom Bertrand Russell accused of having "the pride of Lucifer," claimed in 1921 to have "found, on all essential points, the final solution of the problems [of philosophy]" (Wittgenstein 5). Eleven years later, the English pragmatist F.C.S. Schiller predicted that if philosophers selected for their "open-mindedness, honesty, and good temper" were brought together for "thorough and systematic discussion" under conditions that encouraged mutual understanding and the working out of differences, "they could clear up and clear away a majority of the questions which cast a slur on Philosophy in considerably less than . . . five to ten years" (Schiller 14). Philosophers today are far more skeptical about the chances for philosophical consensus. Few remain confident that agreement on the major problems will ever be achieved, and some declare openly that philosophical problems are unsolvable (Putnam 9) or at least unsolvable for human brains (McGinn).

Given philosophers' failure to reach agreement for 2500 years and the erosion of hope that this will someday change, the second alternative seems all the more appealing. If the *telos* of philosophy is to produce a rich succession of inspiring texts and ideas, then it may be a plus that the ingenious worldviews and critical insights that philosophers have developed over the centuries don't converge. Aristotle's teleological worldview fell from favor a long time ago, but it remains a majestically coherent way of thinking about ourselves and the world we inhabit. Berkeley's arguments that one cannot prove the existence of material substances have never been decisively refuted—not even by Samuel Johnson's petulant kicking of a rock. But practically no one today concurs with Berkeley's conclusion that all that exists are minds and ideas.

Seen from this angle, the beauty of philosophy is very much like the beauty of poetry.

I don't share Milton's theology—though I am sometimes tempted to believe that Satan invented gunpowder—but I am happy to share the world he envisioned. Milton's world is a kind of refuge, a place where the ways of God and the woes of man are united in poetic intelligibility. Sometimes I like to slip into Kafka's world, a nightmarish warren where earnest people strive in vain to get on with their lives in the face of hopeless odds and cosmic silence. (Kafka consoles me for having to commute on the New Jersey Turnpike.) I also like to roam Joyce's Dublin where microcosm becomes macrocosm and the mundane is transfigured into the mythic. Each of these worlds is remarkable in its own right, but it would be foolish to ask which represents the consensus of poets or the best answer to date in light of relevant evidence.

So why not treat philosophy the same way? Jean-Paul Sartre is among my favorite philosophers. At a time when other philosophers were trying to dissolve the problem of consciousness by reducing it to something else, Sartre put it at the center of his philosophy. In his most important work, *Being and Nothingness*, he called consciousness "Nothingness" (*le Néant*) to emphasize that it is a non-substantial being that can exist only as a revelation of something other than itself. What flows from this is a rich worldview that includes, among other things, a radical theory of free will and an original framework for psychoanalysis. Sartre's world is as atheistic and pessimistic as Milton's is theistic and hopeful. He closes the main body of *Being and Nothingness* with these words: "Thus the passion of man is the opposite of that of Christ, for man loses himself as man so that God can be born. But the idea of God is contradictory, and we lose ourselves in vain. Man is a useless passion" (Sartre 708).

Now, as much as I admire the gritty originality of Sartre's picture of the world, I find it unconvincing in many respects. I doubt the usefulness of treating consciousness as its own kind of being. I am not convinced that human beings have as much free will as Sartre claimed. I find his psychoanalytic theory naïve. I don't think the concept of God is contradictory. And I believe the pessimism of *Being of Nothingness* had more to do with the temper of the times—the darkest days of World War II—than with anything basic to Sartre's understanding of the human condition. Sartre himself confirmed this by turning his pessimism into optimism after the liberation of Paris.[3] Today the gloominess of Sartre's writing before 1945 is more likely to elicit smiles than shudders. Perhaps, nothing illustrates this more cheerfully than Danny Shanahan's 1991 *New Yorker* cartoon "The Letters of Jean-Paul Sartre to his Mother." A stocky Madame Sartre stands before an empty rural mailbox. A balloon shows us her thoughts: "*Sacre bleu!* Again with the nothingness, and on my birthday, yet!"

I have talked about Sartre in some detail as a way of illustrating my own comfort with looking at philosophy through the lens of history and appreciating the power and originality of individual philosophers without worrying about consensus on the solution to philosophical problems. I must confess that I have been looking at philosophy this way for a long time. I started college as a physics major, but after causing a nasty explosion in a chemistry lab, I was counseled to seek a major in which I was likely to do less harm. Philosophy seemed a safe haven, especially if one stuck to the task of studying and teaching the ideas of eminent philosophers rather trying to solve philosophical problems.

As the years went by, I realized that you can take the lad out the lab but you can't take the lab out of the lad. I never lost my interest in science or my reservations about the capacity of philosophy to secure knowledge of the world through methods independent of empirical research. Luckily, my style as a teacher was to celebrate what was best in each philosophical text, and my duties as a dean insulated me from thinking very deeply about anything. But things began to unravel several years ago, when I started to write a book called *Why Philosophers Can't Agree*. It occurred to me that my historical outlook embodied a historical distortion. One may treat philosophers like Plato, Aristotle, and Descartes as akin to great poets, but that is not how they saw themselves. They wanted to answer philosophical questions and to do so in ways that would be persuasive to anyone who was willing and able to follow their arguments. In essence, they agreed with Quine that the *telos* of philosophy was to solve its problems rather than to celebrate its history.

So the second alternative cannot stand on its own. In order to do justice to the history of philosophy, we need to acknowledge the priority that nearly all celebrated philosophers have given to problem-solving and try to explain why they have failed to reach agreement. My own explanation for the persistence of philosophical disagreement has multiple facets, but I shall mention only two. One is that philosophers often strive to acquire knowledge with characteristics that may be impossible for humans to obtain: knowledge that is categorical, essentialistic, and necessarily true. Another facet is that philosophers lack a process for discarding theories.

Stephen Jay Gould, who was both a biologist *and* a historian of biology, observed that "Science advances primarily by replacement, not by addition. If the barrel is always full, then the rotten apples must be discarded before better ones can be added" (322). Scientists, unlike philosophers, rely on the testing of empirical predictions extracted from their theories to help them reach agreement on what theories to discard. The process is sometimes messy, and its implementation varies from one science to another, but it works surprisingly well. Philosophers are not blind to their lack of a comparable discarding process. They joke among themselves about the dean who was chiding the physics department for spending too much money on laboratory equipment. "Why can't you be more like the math department?" she asked. "All they ask for are pencils, paper, and wastebaskets. Or, better yet, why can't you be like the philosophy department? All they ask for are pencils and paper."

Philosophers generally rely on reasoning and intuition to debate the relative superiority of philosophical theories, but they have never succeeded in developing a process that commands consensus on which theories should be removed from the apple barrel of provisional knowledge and tossed into the wastebasket of history. Perhaps, the closest they come is tacit agreement that some theories are no longer interesting.

Is my explanation surprising? For many philosophers today it may seem little more than a confirmation of the truism that philosophy isn't science. But the methodological chasm between philosophy and science, now so familiar to us, is the culmination of a fissure that was still being formed a century ago. It is worth noting that over twenty-five percent of Aristotle's extant writings are biological treatises and that they are heavily empirical in content. Descartes, who was best known in his own day as a mathematician and physicist, dissected animal carcasses to study the interaction of brains and bodies. The arch-experimentalist Robert Boyle wrote essays on moral philosophy. David Hume subtitled his *Treatise of Human Nature*: "*Being an Attempt to Introduce the Experimental Method of Reasoning into Moral Subjects.*" Had Kant died before he wrote the *Critique of Pure Reason*, his most original work would have been his essays in astronomy. Adam Smith was influential as an ethicist, and John Stuart Mill as an economist. William James was trained as a medical doctor and helped to found modern psychology. His celebrated treatise *The Principles of Psychology* (1890) was used as a textbook in *both* psychology and philosophy classes.

Is consensus in philosophy possible? I believe philosophers could achieve agreement on at least some of their major problems, if they were willing to formulate theories that yielded predictions as testable as those in science. How this might work in practice has barely been explored, but promising steps have been suggested by a new movement called experimental philosophy.[4] Philosophers often appeal to intuitions as critical links in their arguments, but they seldom explain what intuitions are or why we should rely on them. Experimental philosophy borrows techniques from experimental psychology to gather systematic data on philosophically interesting intuitions, such as what counts as knowledge or under what circumstances a person is morally responsible. It takes armchair pronouncements about what is "obvious to all" or "natural to believe" and tests them against the reported intuitions of actual subjects. It sets up experiments that are designed to discover whether variations in intuitions correlate with contingencies such as a subject's cultural, linguistic, or socio-economic background.

One of the fringe benefits of experimental philosophy is that it lends itself to student participation. In the fall of 2009, I asked the students in my freshman seminar on *Morality, Mind, and Free Will* to join me in developing a survey designed to test John Stuart Mill's thesis on qualitatively superior pleasures. In *Utilitarianism*, Mill contends it is better to be a dissatisfied human than a satisfied pig, a dissatisfied Socrates than a satisfied fool. In defense of this thesis he cites the "unquestionable fact" (Mill 12) that those who have experienced both prefer the higher to the lower. He says: "no intelligent human being would consent to be a fool, no instructed person would be an ignoramus, no person of feeling and conscience would be selfish and base, even though they should be persuaded that the fool, the dunce, or the rascal is better satisfied with his lot than they are with theirs" (12-13). But are these alleged universal preferences really "unquestionable"? My students and I found that 18% of the subjects who responded to our survey indicated they would rather be "a satisfied pig" than a "dissatisfied human"; 20% a "satisfied fool" rather than a "dissatisfied Socrates"; 23% a "satisfied but uneducated person" rather than a "dissatisfied but educated person." Interestingly, only 6% indicated they would rather be a "satisfied person who is selfish and base" rather than a "dissatisfied person of feeling and conscience."

An intriguing question for me is whether philosophers would be willing to let their theories be discarded, if those theories yielded false predictions about the intuitions of appropriate subjects. Would an aesthetician be willing give up a theory of art if it turned out that artists and art professionals had intuitions incompatible with the theory? Clive Bell argued that William Powell Frith's popular painting *The Railway Station* was not art because it lacked "significant form." Would Bell have been willing to give up his theory if painters, museum curators, and art historians found Firth's painting to be a work of art? (I included Frith's painting in my 2010 survey on "What is art?" and found that 97% identified it as art.[5])

There is considerable interest at present in the naturalization of philosophy and a spirited debate growing about the fruitfulness or futility of seeking wisdom from an armchair. Many philosophers shrink from trading the autonomy of philosophy for the promise of gaining science-like agreement as a Faustian bargain that is likely to imperil the soul of their discipline. But I think they overlook the riskiness that has always attended originality in philosophy and underestimate the toughness of philosophy's soul. At the very least, an earnest effort to bridge the methodological gap between science and philosophy would be a thrilling experiment. Although not all experiments are successful—that's why we call them experiments—this one might open a new chapter in the history of philosophy and help draw cognitive scientists into areas of fruitful collaboration with philosophers.

You now know something about my work as a philosopher, but what about my hopes for the work of ACTC? Let me begin by affirming the mission that ACTC has forged for itself over the past fifteen years. As a founding member of ACTC's advisory board, I have had the privilege of working closely with the two presidents who preceded me, Steve Zelnick and Phil Sloan. Steve and Phil are among the ablest people I have ever known, and their contributions to ACTC have been remarkable. Steve presided over the birth of ACTC and its growth from a local consortium to an international organization. Phil presided over the maturation of ACTC into a multifaceted liberal arts organization that commands respect across North America and beyond. Scott Lee, our Executive Director, has served ACTC throughout its history with unstinting dedication, boundless energy, and admirable ingenuity.

Their leadership backed by the enthusiastic support of the board, volunteers, and general membership has enabled ACTC to establish a unique place among academic associations and to offer services of a kind and quality that cannot be found elsewhere. We serve two kinds of members: individual and institutional. Our individual membership—some 300 strong—is drawn from faculty members and deans across the entire spectrum of higher education college. Our institutional members now number 68 and include research universities, four-year colleges, comprehensive institutions, and community colleges. Our reach is international. We have long benefitted from the leadership of both Canadian and U.S. members. We now have the honor of counting the Universidad Tecnológica de Bolívar among our members and having two representatives from Chiao-tung University in Taiwan at this conference. In June 2009, Scott will be addressing the Chinese University in Hong Kong and participating in a general education workshop with six other Hong Kong universities.

Our greatest challenge in the immediate future will be to sustain our success. The worldwide recession has led to deep cuts in academic budgets, and many educational associations are struggling with diminished support and shrinking attendance at their meetings. It is indicative of our strength that this conference is so well attended, but we can't take this success for granted. To ensure that conference attendance continues to be strong, we will need to reach out to new constituencies and increase the visibility of our conferences activities. You and I know that our annual conference provides a unique forum for scholars in virtually every field to share and compare substantive ideas formed in response to common readings, but we need to ensure that others know it as well. Eventually, I would like to see our membership climb to 400.

We also need to build bridges of mutual cooperation with other associations and to expand the circle of institutions that support ACTC. We need to take the lead in helping institutions learn from one another how to construct successful core text programs. Our "Webliography" project will put a wealth of such information online, but it is through our programs and workshops we are most likely to foster institutional change. In coming months Scott and I will be writing you to ask for your advice and assistance. If you prefer, you can reach us by using the email address on the ACTC website or by writing directly to me at The College of New Jersey. My email address is rkamber@tcnj.edu

Why is all this worth doing? Why does the work of ACTC really matter? It is worth doing, in the first place, because it is a particularly fine way of living the examined life. It is worth doing because the use of core texts can be an especially effective way of helping students to become liberally educated. It is worth doing because a liberal education is an eminently practical education. Unlike C. P. Snow, I have not said much about the drawbacks of an overspecialized and *il*liberal education, but a moment's reflection should make some of those drawbacks obvious. How can we expect financial executives to behave responsibly when they turn a blind eye to economic history and can't (or won't) recognize a bubble that is about to blow sky high. How we can expect the citizens we educate and the governments they elect to "think with wisdom" about turmoil in the Islamic world, if they know nothing of the religion, cultures, and history of that world? How can we expect our graduates to exercise good judgments about energy conservation or environmental protection if they lack basic scientific and technological knowledge? Of course, specialization is indispensable to the functioning of a modern society, but it needs to be leavened with liberal learning if we are to grasp the problems of our time in historical perspective and solve them with a sense of proportion.

Notes

1. It was delivered as the Rede Lecture on May 7, 1959.
2. See Roy A. Clouser, *The Myth of Religious Neutrality.*
3. His best known repudiation of his pessimistic assessment of the human condi-

tion was a lecture he gave at the Club Maintenant on October 28, 1945 under the title "Existentialism is a Humanism." That lecture was published a few months later and has since become a classic in the history of existentialism. See Jean-Paul Sartre, *Existentialism is a Humanism.*

4. For an excellent overview of experimental philosophy, see Joshua Knobe and Shaun Nichols, *Experimental Philosophy*. For an engaging introduction that puts experimental philosophy in historical context, see Kwame Anthony Appiah, *Experiments in Ethics.*

5. A summary and analysis of the results of my 2010 "What Is Art?" surveys under the title "Experimental Philosophy of Art" is scheduled for publication in *The Journal of Aesthetics and Art Criticism.*

Works Cited

Appiah, Kwame Anthony. *Experiments in Ethics.* Cambridge, MA: Harvard UP, 2008.

Clouser, Roy A. *The Myth of Religious Neutrality.* Notre Dame: University of Notre Dame P, 2005.

Descartes René. *Descartes: Philosophical Writing, Discourse on Method.* Trans. Norman Kemp Smith. New York: Random House, 1958.

Gould, Stephen Jay. *The Mismeasure of Man.* New York: W. W. Norton, 1981.

Knobe, Joshua and Shaun Nichols. *Experimental Philosophy.* Oxford: Oxford UP, 2008.

McGinn, Colin. *Problems in Philosophy.* Oxford: Blackwell, 1993.

Mill, John Stuart. *Utilitarianism.* Ed. Oskar Piest. New York: The Liberal Arts Press, 1957.

Putnam, Hilary. *Realism with a Human Face.* Cambridge, MA: Harvard UP, 1990.

Quine, Willard V. O. "On What There Is." In *From a Logical Point of View.* 2nd Ed. New York: Harper & Row, 1963.

Sartre, Jean-Paul. Sartre, *Existentialism Is a Humanism.* Trans. Carol Macomber. New Haven, CT: Yale UP, 2007.

———. *L'être et le néant: Essai d'ontologie phénoménologique.* Paris: Librairie Gallimard, 1943.

Schiller, F.C.S. *Must Philosophers Disagree? And Other Essays in Philosophy.* London: Macmillan, 1934.

Snow, C.P. "The Two Cultures." In *The Two Cultures and A Second Look.* Cambridge: Cambridge UP, 1964.

Wittgenstein, Ludwig. *Tractatus Logico-Philosophicus.* Trans. D. F. Pears and B. F. McGuiness. London: Routledge & Kegan Paul, 1961.

The Cunning of Tradition:
Plenary Address Presented to the Fifteenth Annual Conference,
Association for Core Texts and Courses

Wilfred M. McClay
University of Tennessee at Chattanooga

My title is a play on words, a famous term used by the German philosopher G.W.F. Hegel in his *Lectures on the Philosophy of History*. There Hegel spoke of "the cunning of reason," by which term he meant to denote the uncanny way that History manages to channel and direct men's irrational passions toward the realization of rational ends. Or so he claimed. As he would express the idea in his lofty and inscrutable argot, these passions become the means by which the World Spirit realizes the Universal Idea. Or one can put it more simply: Reason triumphs in History precisely through the unconscious workings of *un*reason. As in the eighteenth-century vision of an "invisible hand" that insensibly produces general good out of the uncoordinated transactions of countless self-interested individuals, so did Hegel believe that History itself thrives on the existence of some such inherent spontaneous order, a happy if ironic twist at the very center of History.

Or so Hegel argued. But two can play at this game. Anyone who knows the terrible and bloody history of the twentieth century, with its unequalled wars, massacres, displacements, and despoliations, might be tempted to propose that Hegel had it precisely *reversed*, and that History is instead plagued by something like "the cunning of unreason," which sees to it that all the fabulous productions of modern science and technology have served only to escalate the danger, violence, and anxiety with which humans must live, and to render the human prospect itself ever more vulnerable.

But we need not resolve that particular struggle today. My own remarks play off of Hegel's words in a different way. I want to propose that there is something like a "cunning of tradition," and that a deepened awareness of that "cunning" and its potential uses is an essential tool for all of us as educators, particularly when we find ourselves swimming against the anti-traditional currents of our culture and our educational establishment. It may be that the underlying reality is less bleak than we realize, meaning that the presence of tradition is something much more persistent and pervasive in our lives than we are aware.

But we have to be fully aware of the issues involved, which is why, in contrast to Hegel, I argue here for the value of a *self-conscious* appropriation of tradition—even of what Jaroslav Pelikan called, in his wonderful book of that title, a *vindication* of tradition. Yes, tradition is cunning, no doubt about it, but not so cunning as to be able to do its job well without watchful help. We should not labor under the illusion that traditions that have been self-consciously sustained, preserved, revived, and adapted are somehow no longer worthy of the name. This is a false purism. But we are nonetheless left with a complicated task, full of peril and paradox, in seeking clarity about tradition's proper place.

Let me then, at the outset, suggest three paradoxes regarding tradition that will help us order our inquiry and guide our path. If these sound a bit vatic and obscure at this point, that is merely to pique your interest. I promise to give an explanation of each of them in the course of my remarks today. But now the three paradoxes:

First, the past is in some respects younger than the present.

Second, tradition is always an essential element in the effort to overturn tradition.

Third, it is in the act of adapting a tradition that we are most faithful to its fundamental character.

Let me begin our inquiry with the word "tradition" itself. It's a term that contains worlds within itself, and manages to retain a profound ambivalence toward the very thing it signifies. That ambivalence is evident early in the word's history. The word "tradition" comes from the Latin *traditio*, and before that from the past participle of the verb *tradere*, which means "to deliver," in the sense of carrying something across, from one place to another. But it also means, and this seems to be the more primary meaning, "to surrender" or "to betray." In other words, although the word seems consistently to refer to the act of "carrying across," it can convey more than one sense of the concept. It not only means "to hand down," but also "to hand over."

Indeed, the more negative meaning of "tradition" as a "surrender" or "betrayal" seems to have come earliest in the word's history, and the more benign meaning of "handing down" customs, stories, and beliefs—the meaning that now seems our chief association with the word—seems to have been a later modification. There are other words deriving from the same root that are still in circulation, and have retained elements of the more negative meaning. For example, we still may use the verb "to traduce" to complain of an act of verbal defamation, or to call someone a "traitor."

This amazingly versatile common root is what made possible the famous Italian pun, *Traduttore, traditore!*—literally, "Translator, Betrayer!"—the translator, meaning one who takes it as his or her task to "carry across" the linguistic lines, is a traitor to, or betrayer of, the thing he translates. You also can readily see the word's ambivalent meaning reflected in the Latin translations of certain very familiar passages in the Greek New Testament. Mark 15:15 speaks of Jesus being "handed over"—*tradidit*—to be crucified; but in Matthew 11:27, Jesus says that all things have been "handed over"—*tradita*—to him by his Father. Even there, the Janus-faced quality of that common root is preserved, a clear sign that it is a singularly cunning word that we are dealing with here.

So, although there is a certain warm and comfortable feeling that attaches to the word "tradition," the word also contains many countercurrents, especially in modern America, where the sense of tradition as a betrayal of human potential is especially strong. Think, for example, of the works of Ralph Waldo Emerson, who began his *Nature* with the following cry:

> The foregoing generations beheld God and nature face to face; we, through their eyes. Why should not we also enjoy an original relation to the universe? Why should we not have a poetry and philosophy of insight and not of tradition, and a religion by revelation to us, and not the history of theirs?... The sun shines today also. There is more wool and flax in the fields. There are new lands, new men, new thoughts. Let us demand our own works and laws and worship. (7)

When Emerson later divided our nation's intellectual history between "the party of memory" and "the party of hope," there was little doubt which he believed was to be preferred.

Or if Emerson is too highbrow for you, then consider the words of the great anti–historical philosopher of history, industrialist Henry Ford. I have to admit that I've always rather liked his description of history as "one damned thing after another," which perhaps has unrealized potential for Calvinist historians. But his cruder, and better–known, words are probably closer to expressing the strain of anti-traditionalism in the American outlook: "History is more or less bunk. It's tradition. We don't want tradition. We want to live in the present, and the only history that is worth a tinker's damn is the history we make today."

Or consider the tensions in the great musical drama *Fiddler on the Roof*. Tevye the milkman, a lovably ineffectual spokesman for the authority of Jewish "tradition," has been portrayed by actors speaking not only English, French, Russian, and German, but Japanese, Turkish, and Chinese. Apparently, you don't even have to be Judeo–Christian to love the story, for its appeal seems to be frankly archetypal rather than historical. At its core, it is a parable of modernization, of the breakdown of shtetl life and the emigration to America, the mythic land of the future.

While the life of the shtetl is lovingly portrayed, with its wonderfully colorful array of human types, on the crucial issue separating the traditional order from the modern one—the issue of arranged marriages, and more generally, the importance of romantic love and mutual consent in marriage—it leaves us in no doubt that the old order did not stand a chance. When Tevye rejects his daughter who dares to elope with a non-Jew, and treats her as if she were dead, we see him as monstrously inhuman. Such rigidity seems almost of a piece with the brutal Czarist pogroms that finally drive these Russian Jews to seek freedom and peace in America. The oft–repeated refrain of the song "Tradition!" with which the musical so brightly begins has become subdued and plaintive, almost a dirge, by the end. On Broadway, tradition seems not to have a chance.

Ambivalence about tradition is also an inherent feature of the Christian faith. The Christian gospel is about new birth, about the making of a new man in the crucible of conversion—about the washing away of sin, the canceling of debt, the negating of the weight of the past, the annulling of the condemning power of the Law in favor of the redeeming and renewing power of the Spirit.

This is by no means exclusive to Protestantism, but is intrinsic to the faith as a whole. One of the chief elements of Jesus' radicalism is his constant criticism of the religious establishment of his day, not only for its pride and impiety, and its self-serving disregard for the plain meaning of Scripture, but for its exaggerated reverence for its own *traditions*. Again and again he defied social convention, often by showing concern for the very people who were normally despised or marginalized by respectable society. He spoke to women in public. He showed special solicitude for children, a countercultural gesture in a Roman-dominated world that calmly accepted such horrors as infanticide and the deliberate abandonment of unwanted children. He associated with prostitutes and lepers, and even allowed them to touch him.

He demonstrated repeatedly his disdain for particular human customs, and he did so because he wanted to expose those who mistook the authority of tradition for the authority of the word and will of God. "Why," asked the Pharisees and teachers of the Law, "do your disciples break the tradition of the elders?" Jesus fires back with a question of his own: "Why do you break the command of God for the sake of your tradition?" (Matthew 15:2). No matter how venerable, the traditions had no authority of their own, unless they were clearly in line with the more primary authority of God's word.

So anti-traditionalism is strong in American culture, strong in the culturally dominant religious faiths—and it's also strong in the scholarly world. As for "tradition" in its stronger sense, the authoritative sense given it by Tevye and others, we modern historians are trained to distrust it profoundly, and treat it as guilty unless proven innocent. The invocation of "tradition" is routinely regarded as an act of rank mystification, and the likely stalking-horse for some nefarious political purpose, some lurking act of domination or exploitation. For a long time now, historians have treated the work of Eric Hobsbawm and his anthology *The Invention of Tradition* as something approaching Holy Writ, and the mention of it is guaranteed to certify oneself as a deep thinker, a critical mind, a properly educated person who is not rube enough to be taken in by nationalist sentimentalities and packaged nostalgia. The underlying spirit of modern historical scholarship places a high premium on debunking, and the assault on tradition is an inevitable concomitant of that spirit.

Then there is the fact of our living in a technologically, socially, and economically dynamic society, where the rhythm of constant change, institutionalized in what we interestingly call "the fashion industry," is often our only constant. It is the inevitable tendency of a consumer culture, with its relentless drive toward fluidity and mutability, to encourage the constant erasure of memory to make room for new desires, new markets, new purchases. The result is that memory itself, always a mutable thing, is lost or debased in the process. Tradition not only cramps the human spirit; it can be bad for the economy.

So the suspicion of tradition is, as it were, over-determined in American life, both in terms of the general culture and in so many of the particulars of that culture, some of which—but not all of which—are admirable. I'm reminded, in an ironic way, of the famous words at the end of F. Scott Fitzgerald's *The Great Gatsby*, in which the title character's hunger for possibility, symbolized by the green light at the end of Daisy's pier, is shown to be futile: "So we beat on," Fitzgerald intoned, "boats against the current, borne back ceaselessly into the past" (189; Ch. 9). Beautiful words. Yet we would seem to have the *opposite* problem, especially as historians. No matter how hard we try to make sustaining contact with the past, we are ceaselessly borne back into the present. Our culture, our faith, our professional training—all seem to conspire in keeping the past at arm's length.

But Fitzgerald had it right, perhaps without entirely realizing it. For Jay Gatsby's desire was not really for the future. It was a yearning for the recovery of the past. He longed for a restoration and fulfillment of his romance with Daisy, the goal to which he had dedicated his whole life, and his entire personal makeover. It was an unworthy goal, pursued by unworthy means, and that's a big part of what the book is about. But my point, and perhaps some part of Fitzgerald's too, is that the human longing for sustaining contact with the past is not something that can be willed away. In fact, it can become the core around which a worthy human life is organized.

We sometimes think of the past as nothing more than antique curiosities on a shelf, statuettes of marble and amber whose moments of living reality have passed. But that is not necessarily so. Sometimes the past can be far more vital and life-giving than the present, precisely because contact with it frees us from the prison of the immediate and the familiar, a world cluttered and smudged by too many human fingerprints, and brings us closer to the beginnings of things.

The word "archaic" is generally used as a pejorative in our speech. But it comes from the Greek *arche*, which refers not only to the antiquity of things but to their foundational character. They are first not only in time, but in principle. *En arche en ho logos*, begins St. John's Gospel: In the beginning was the Word. This is not merely a beginning in the sense of a starting point. It is a usage that reflects the endless abundance of these ancient terms, for an *arche* is the deep spring from which all else emanates. And there is profound mystery, for the *arche* is a cause, not an effect.

Our fresh encounter with first things can be startling, precisely because the very means by which we are nourished become unfamiliar with the passage of time. Consider our reaction to another of the oldest artifacts of our civilization, the Homeric epics. We often fail to grasp their power. The great journalist Rebecca West and her husband described their encounter in the 1930s with remote Yugoslav tribesmen who still sang and recited oral epics in the Homeric fashion. These bards recounted actions that "must have been made a million million million times since the world began," but that in each new telling seemed "absolutely fresh" (1044). Thus, when one reads in the *Iliad* of a man drawing a bow or raising a sword, "it is," West wrote, "as if the dew of the world's morning lay undisturbed on what he did" (1044). Far from being old and dead, the past draws life from its closeness to the origins of things.

It is in that sense, then, that old books are younger than new ones. This is why old books can be so full of new life. This is why these books speak to us across gulfs of time and space—of language and culture—of race, class, and gender—without the aid of scholarly busybodies or other anointed experts, and have things to tell us that surpass even the wisdom of the New York *Times* op-ed page—or the Fox News channel—precisely because they could bring us the news that really matters, the "news" of the human condition, the news that the newspapers neglect to print. They bring us an electric feeling of genuine connection, across space and time to others, who have shared our human condition. That is the meaning behind the words of T. S. Eliot, "The communication of the dead is tongued with fire beyond the language of the living" ("Little Gidding," ll. 49-51).

I see some of this same electricity operating in the rediscovery by many young people today of the virtues of the most ancient religious rites and liturgies. Such practices are, precisely because of their antiquity, free of the taint of commodification. Such young people describe to me an oceanic feeling in the presence of these forms of worship, because they are productions so old which have passed through so many hands that they no longer bear any of the specific fingerprints or intentionalities of any particular individuals who handled them in the past.

This perspective challenges our modern romantic myths of creativity as involving throwing off of the old—Emerson, for example, who comes to look like an over-simplifier of what is in fact a very complex interplay between old and new, past and present. More on-target, I think, are these words of T.S. Eliot from his essay "Tradition and the Individual Talent." To be sure, at the outset Eliot seems entirely sympathetic to Emerson's concerns:

> Yet if the only form of tradition, of handing down, consisted in fol-
> lowing the ways of the immediate generation before us in a blind
> or timid adherence to its successes, "tradition" should positively
> be discouraged. We have seen many such simple currents soon lost
> in the sand; and novelty is better than repetition. (38)

But then he continues, and takes a very different turn:

> Tradition is a matter of much wider significance. It cannot be in-
> herited, and if you want it you must obtain it by great labor. It
> involves, in the first place, the historical sense, which we may call
> nearly indispensable to anyone who would continue to be a poet
> beyond his twenty-fifth year; and the historical sense involves a
> perception, not only of the pastness of the past, but of its pres-
> ence; the historical sense compels a man to write not merely with
> his own generation in his bones, but with a feeling that the whole
> of the literature of Europe from Homer and within it the whole of
> the literature of his own country has a simultaneous existence and
> composes a simultaneous order. This historical sense, which is a
> sense of the timeless as well as of the temporal and of the timeless
> and of the temporal together, is what makes a writer traditional.

And it is at the same time what makes a writer most acutely conscious of his place in time, of his own contemporaneity. (38)

No poet, no artist of any art, has his complete meaning alone. His significance, his
appreciation is the appreciation of his relation to the dead poets and artists.

Emerson was wrong—the party of memory and the party of hope are the *same* party.
Or as Edmund Burke once put it, with admirable lucidity, "People will not look forward to posterity who never look backward to their ancestors."

So we need a better way to look at tradition—not as the quintessence of hide-
boundness, but as a means by which we free ourselves from the tyranny of the
present, with its peculiar obsessions, anxieties, and other forms of cognitive impris-
onment. We need to be mature enough to recognize that disenchantment is itself a
form of enchantment, and that debunking, however necessary it may be at times, is
an activity that ultimately leads nowhere.

Of course, the condition in which we find ourselves is partly due to the characteristic deformations of contemporary academic life. It is by endless cycles of cutting
and slashing, revising and revisioning, "neo"ing and "post"ing, interrogating and all
the rest of the tedious professional jargon, that reputations are made, empires are
built, careers are jumpstarted, and—not to put too fine a point on it—tenure is won
and promotion secured. The dynamic of revisionism, a dynamic of churning, inces-
sant novelty, serves the cause of academic careerism far more than it does the cause
of political correctness, either of the left or the right. And such careerism and specialization has the effect of stamping out an appreciative sense of the past. ACTC is,
I think, an organization that bears admirable witness to the possibility of a different
way, and long may it prosper.

There also is something ultimately self-contradictory and self-defeating about
the Emersonian–Fordist belief that tradition is a pernicious inhibiting force that can
and should be overcome. As the philosopher Alasdair MacIntyre has argued compel-
lingly, much of the intellectual activity that we value is *constituted* by tradition—
meaning that it exists within discursive traditions that are no less indispensable for
being unacknowledged as such. Again, tradition demonstrates its cunning ways. The
most vital traditions, in his view, are traditions of *argument*, in which a whole series
of debates, disagreements, visions, and revisions are constituted around a certain
set of assertions, perspectives, and questions. It is a misunderstanding, in this view,
to see tradition as an inert body of propositions and customs passed along intact
from one generation to the next. Tradition is the necessary medium—institutional,
linguistic, social, cultural—within which fruitful intellectual and cultural activity is
rendered possible. It is not just a chest of treasures, but also a web of debates: a cunning web.

MacIntyre makes the point that radical anti-traditionalism is just as unintelli-
gible as radical individualism, and for exactly the same reasons. Just as a baby cannot
rear itself in isolation, so an argument cannot find voice without drawing on an enormous armory of resources that are the gift of the past. And he is right, too, to insist
that tradition is not static. There is a difference between tradition and traditionalism,
a difference that Jaroslav Pelikan—to whose wonderful little book *The Vindication*

of Tradition I referred before—has expressed unforgettably in its pages: "Tradition is the living faith of the dead, traditionalism is the dead faith of the living. And it is traditionalism that gives tradition such a bad name." In Pelikan's view, the distinction between "tradition" and "insight" that Emerson made is not sustainable.

A "leap of progress" is not a standing broad jump, which begins at the line of where we are now; it is a running broad jump through where we have been to where we go next. The growth of insight—in science, in the arts, in philosophy and theology—has not come through progressively sloughing off more and more of tradition, as though insight would be purest and deepest when it has finally freed itself of the dead past. It simply has not worked that way in the history of the tradition, and it does not work that way now. By including the dead in the circle of discourse, we enrich the quality of the conversation. Of course we do not listen only to the dead, nor are we a tape recording of the tradition. That really would be the dead faith of the living, not the living faith of the dead. But we do acquire the insight for which Emerson was pleading when we learn to interact creatively with the tradition which he was denouncing.

And Pelikan concludes with a charge, taken from Goethe:

> What you have as heritage,
> Take now as task;
> For thus you will make it your own. (82)

The acknowledgment of tradition does not absolve us of the need to think for ourselves, and build things of our own. Instead, it helps us to recognize the work we are meant to do. Our heritage *is* our task. We cannot undertake the task without the benefit of the heritage. But it is by doing our task that we can come into the full possession of that heritage—thereby perpetuating the tradition as something living, rather than something moribund—and thereby making it possible for us to have a free and full relationship with the heritage, like that of a child who has fully grown up.

Let me illustrate these abstractions by reference to a poem, an extraordinary poem, by the American poet Dana Gioia. It is called "Planting a Sequoia," and it describes just that. But it is also an enactment of a tradition, with the very kind of twist and adaptation that makes traditions live on, and makes them ever more vital. Gioia is an American of Sicilian descent, and relates in the poem a Sicilian custom, followed by his own father, of planting an olive or fig tree upon the birth of a first son, along with a piece of the discarded umbilical cord. The poem depicts a reenactment of that tradition—but with a difference. For Gioia's own son had died tragically of Sudden Infant Death Syndrome.

> All afternoon my brothers and I have worked in the orchard,
> Digging this hole, laying you into it, carefully packing the soil.
> Rain blackened the horizon, but cold winds kept it over the Pacific,
> And the sky above us stayed the dull gray
> Of an old year coming to an end.
> In Sicily a father plants a tree to celebrate his first son's birth—
> An olive or a fig tree—a sign that the earth has one more life to bear.

I would have done the same, proudly laying new stock into my father's orchard,
A green sapling rising among the twisted apple boughs,
A promise of new fruit in other autumns.

But today we kneel in the cold planting you, our native giant,
Defying the practical custom of our fathers,
Wrapping in your roots a lock of hair, a piece of an infant's birth cord,
All that remains above earth of a first–born son,
A few stray atoms brought back to the elements.
We will give you what we can—our labor and our soil,
Water drawn from the earth when the skies fail,
Nights scented with the ocean fog, days softened by the circuit of bees,
We plant you in the corner of the grove, bathed in western light,
A slender shoot against the sunset.

And when our family is no more, all of his unborn brothers dead,
Every niece and nephew scattered, the house torn down,
His mother's beauty ashes in the air,
I want you to stand among strangers, all young and ephemeral to you,
Silently keeping the secret of your birth.

There are far too many things to be said about this poem. I offer but a single observation. What Gioia has done here, both in the poem itself and in the act that the poem describes, is a luminous and haunting lesson in both the permanence and the adaptability of tradition. He has kept faith with his heritage. But he also has made it his own. And instead of planting a "practical" tree that will be productive within the range of his lifetime, he chose to plant a thin slip of a mighty tree, a tree whose lifetime will be measured in millennia—and whose full majesty and mature fruitfulness will never be seen by anyone now alive, or in any context that we can now imagine.

Such a noble gesture draws on tradition to defy death and fend off meaninglessness, and to transcend the confining spirit of our age. Despair is held at bay by the greater dignity of simple affirmation, of keeping faith with what one has loved.

The act being described is clearly an iteration of a very old tradition. The kind of archaic tradition on which the dew of the world's morning still seems to rest. And that is not the only such tradition being alluded to. It also looks backward to the Hebrew Bible, to Isaiah 65:

> Behold, I will create new heavens and a new earth; the former things will not be remembered, nor will they come to mind.... I will create Jerusalem to be a delight and its people a joy. I will rejoice over Jerusalem and take delight in my people; the sound of weeping and of crying will be heard in it no more. Never again will there be in it an infant who lives but a few days, or an old man who does not live out his years.... They will build houses and dwell in them; they will plant vineyards and eat their fruit. No longer will they build houses and others live in them, or plant and others eat. For as the days of a tree, so will be the days of my people; my chosen ones will long enjoy the works of their hands. They will not toil in vain or

bear children doomed to misfortune; for they will be a people blessed by the Lord, they and their descendants with them. (Isaiah 65:17–23)

Gioia's poem looks back at two traditions, then, the Sicilian tradition and the messianic Biblical one. The traditions are an essential part of his effort to find meaning in these tragic events. But he adapts the tradition to his own use, and offers something new. There could be no better example of the gift that the cunning of tradition offers us.

Works Cited

Bible: The New International Version. Zondervan Ebooks, 2008.

Burke, Edmund. "Reflections on The Revolution in France, 1791." *Internet Modern History Sourcebook.* Ed. Paul Halsall. Aug 1997. <http://www.fordham.edu/halsall/mod/1791burke.html> Accessed January 5, 2011.

Eliot, T. S. "Little Gidding." *Four Quartets.* Orlando: Harcourt, 1943.

———. "Tradition and the Individual Talent." *Selected Prose of T. S. Eliot.* Ed. Frank Kermode. Orlando: Harcourt, 1975.

Emerson, Ralph Waldo. *Nature.* Boston: James Munroe, 1849.

Fitzgerald, F. Scott. *The Great Gatsby.* New York: Scribner, 1999.

Ford, Henry. *Columbia Dictionary of Quotations.* Ed. Robert Andrews. New York: Columbia UP, 1993.

Gioia, Dana. "Planting a Sequoia." *The Gods of Winter: Poems.* Minneapolis: Graywolf Press, 1991.

Hegel, G.W.F. *Lectures on the Philosophy of History.* Cambridge Studies in the History and Theory of Politics. Cambridge, UK: Cambridge UP, 1981.

Hobsbawm, Eric and Terence Ranger, eds. *The Invention of Tradition.* Cambridge, UK: Cambridge UP, 1992.

Pelikan, Jaroslav. *Vindication of Tradition: The 1983 Jefferson Lecture in the Humanities.* New Haven: Yale UP, 1986.

West, Rebecca. *Black Lamb and Grey Falcon: A Journey through Yugoslavia.* London: Viking Press, 1941.

Of the Wings of Atalanta— Meaning and Dualism in DuBois, Morrison, and Historically Black, Liberal Arts Education

Grant D. Venerable, II
Lincoln University of Pennsylvania

PROLOGUE

I quote here excerpts from the essay, "Of the Wings of Atalanta" in *The Souls of Black Folks* by W.E.B. DuBois:

> South of the North, yet north of the South, lies the City of a Hundred Hills, peering out from the shadows of the past into the promise of the future...she lay gray and still on the crimson soil of Georgia.

Perhaps Atlanta was not christened for the winged maiden...[but] you know the tale—how swarthy Atalanta, tall and wild, would marry only him who out-raced her; and how the wily Hippomenes laid three apples of gold in the way. She fled like a shadow, paused, startled over the first apple, but even as he stretched his hand, fled again; hovered over the second, then, slipping from his hot grasp, flew over river, vale, and hill; but as she lingered over the third, his arms fell round her, and looking on each other, the blazing passion of their love profaned the sanctuary of Love; and they were cursed. If Atlanta be not named for Atalanta, she ought to have been.

> Atalanta is not the first or the last maiden whom greed of gold has led to defile the temple of Love;... [In] all our Nation's striving is not the Gospel of Work befouled by the Gospel of Pay?

The hundred hills of Atlanta are not all crowned with factories. On one, toward the west, the setting sun throws three buildings in bold relief against the sky.... and in the midst, half hidden in ivy, a larger building, boldly graceful, sparingly decorated, and with one low spire. It is a restful group.... There I live, and there I hear from day to day the low hum of restful life. In winter's twilight, when the red sun glows, I can see the dark figures pass between the halls to the music of the night-bell.... In the morning, when the sun is golden, the clang of the day-bell brings the hurry and laughter of three hundred young hearts from hall and street, and from the city below.... The riddle of existence is the college curriculum that was laid before the Pharaohs, that was taught in the groves by Plato, that formed the *trivium* and the *quadrivium*, and is today laid before the freedmen's sons by Atlanta University.

> The vision of life that rises before these dark eyes has in it nothing mean or selfish. Not at Oxford or at Leipzig, not at Yale or Columbia, is there an air of higher resolve or more unfettered striving.... The function of the University is not simply to teach bread-winning, or to furnish teachers for the public schools or to be a center of polite society; it is, above all, to be the organ of that fine adjustment between real life and the growing knowledge of life, an adjustment which forms the secret of civilization. (63-4)

DUALISM IN DUBOIS AND THE LIBERAL ARTS

The core text I have just read from was taken from an essay, Of the Wings of Atalanta, from the *Souls of Black Folks* first published by W.E.B. DuBois in 1903. I want to begin the conversation with the relevance of DuBois to the practical and fiscal reality which all of us inhabit in 2009. I refer to recent headlines in the Chronicle of Higher Education that leaped right off the page: 1) Overstimulated Science and 2) Big Campaigns Feel Downturn's Drag. In the first, some university presidents worry that a sudden influx of federal stimulus money for scientific research could have a downside. When the money runs out, young scholars brought on board with stimulus funds could find themselves out of work. In the second case, it is a very real worry that the financial downturn will adversely affect an institution's ability to build endowment. But DuBois conveys his view of the function of the university *as the organ of that fine adjustment between real life and the growing knowledge of life.* If that is so, then the Chronicle headlines are answered and so is the secret process through which we reach the judgments implied in the articles and how the dualistic constructs we learned prefigure our judgments. True to the prevailing paradigm of linear dualism rooted in fear, everything becomes a zero-sum game. This drives a politics based on fear of *not enough.* DuBois was right. Let us consider the first example, economic over-stimulation. If money runs out, young scholars are out of work. The dualistic polarity here is work and its opposite, out of work or not work. But is out of work the only conclusion? In a liberal arts context, it is not. In a historically black college liberal arts context, it most certainly is not, or the HBCU (historically black college or university) founded in the 1800s and eternally facing a nearly hand-to-mouth existence would not still exist. So why is "out of work" not the only pole at the opposite end of the polarity work-not work? It is because the liberal arts and the HBCU contexts afford a deeper reservoir of intellectual options than a simplistic dualism rooted in fear.

A liberal arts context always poses possibilities beyond opposites. Because of the virtually hard-wired-in-the-brain philosophical heritage of African complementary dualism, the opposite of a thing is never necessarily its opposite, but always its complementary "not thing." Even the celebrated Dead White Male (DWM) thinkers were imbued with a very human awareness of thing and not-thing, and you are probably thinking of such eminent DWMs as Kant, Hegel, Marx, James, and Freud and those more recent scientific philosophers Clerk Maxwell with his thermodynamic demons, Heisenberg and his inversely uncertain variables, Schrodinger and his weird cats, DeBroglie, and Einstein himself. Well, of course, we know this kind of complementary dualistic thinking was something that African societies actually enshrined in their complex cosmologies for tens of thousands of years, and all of modern science is rooted in such a three-part dualism of thing, not-thing, and the membrane interface that separates, yet joins, thing and not-thing. That is what DuBois was really referencing when he stated that the function of the university is, above all, to be the organ of that fine adjustment (the membrane interface) that separates, yet joins, real life (as thing) with the growing knowledge of life (as not-thing). In the complementary dualistic universe of African cosmology, the opposite of work is not-work or the *idea of work*, which can sometimes include but is never limited to its opposite. Thus, not-work as the *idea of work*, is much larger than work itself. And not-fundraising is the idea of fundraising and need not become a literal inability to raise funds in a time of fiscal crisis.

Now, I've said it all. I've made my point; we can all go home. Except, it might be useful to connect a few dots to reinforce the point.

THE DUALITY OF THING AND NOT-THINGNESS

Let us then behold some of the most influential *thing-not-thing* pairings of the day: The complementary equivalence of mass and energy where the *speed of light* is the *interfacial membrane* that mediates between mass-thingness and energy-no-thingness; time and space where *gravity* is the interfacial membrane; and the dual wave-particle thing-not-thing nature of matter where the photon is the interfacial membrane. And finally we have our wondrous human skin that enwraps our physical bodies which serves as the amazing, sometimes troubling (depending on what color it is), interfacial membrane between self and everything that is not-self.

Armed with a thorough grounding in the liberal arts, we avoid the folly of self-incarceration in simplistic opposites, the kind of reasoning that says if no funding, no work; if no work, lessened possibility for survival and fulfillment. And by reincorporating the complementary dualism of African thought which shows up most often in the pedagogy of historically black educational settings, we can deepen the liberal arts program and create something now much needed in the American educational condition. This has figured in to the challenge that President Barack Obama met and dealt with at the recent G-20 summit in London. I speak here of skill at handling duality and paradoxical complexities that was lost, perhaps inadvertently, perhaps not, when in 1954 the Supreme Court announced its Brown v. Board of Education decision. While the ultimate effect of this decision was the dismantling of race as an inimical social construct, its immediate effect was to promote a false desegregation of the races through the firing and displacement of the Negro teachers and principals, a critical mass of whom were skilled exponents of African complementary dualistic thought. But fortunately, it could not be divorced from African-American literature.

Now let us recall that fascinating passage from Toni Morrison's novel *Song of Solomon* in which the insurance agent announces his suicide in advance as a "flight" from the top of his little yellow house situated on Mains Avenue:

Town maps registered the street as Mains Avenue, but the only colored doctor in the city had lived and died on that street, and when he moved there in 1896 his patients took to calling the street, which none of them lived in or near, *Doctor Street*. Later, when other Negroes moved there, and when the postal service became a popular means of transferring messages among them, envelopes from Louisiana, Virginia, Alabama, and Georgia began to arrive addressed to people at house numbers on Doctor Street.... Then in 1918, when colored men were being drafted, a few gave their address at the recruitment office as Doctor Street. In that way, the name acquired a quasi-official status. But not for long. Some of the city legislators, whose concern for appropriate names and the city's landmarks was the principal part of their political life, saw to it that "Doctor Street" was never used in any official capacity. And since they knew that only Southside residents kept it up, they had notices posted in the stores, barbershops, and restaurants in that part of the city saying that the avenue running northerly and southerly from Shore Road fronting the lake...had always been and would always be known as Mains Avenue and not Doctor Street.

> It was a genuinely clarifying public notice because it gave Southside residents a way to keep their memories alive and please the city legislators as well. They called it *Not* Doctor Street. (9-10)

African Knowledge Systems and
Binary Opposition in Morrison

In a powerful literacy device, Morrison chose an in-your-face disclosure of the complementary character of African *thing-not-thing dualism*. She drew a sharp distinction between white and black cultural habits in the town by having the city legislators so steeped in their quite culturally linear dualism that they couldn't see what was coming. While this sort of dualism exists to varying degrees in all human societies across the earth, anyone who has ever followed the neotenous Michael Jackson and his culture of "bad" or the hip-hop culture of "high-fiving" and "fist-bumping" realizes how pronounced complementary, binary opposition is in African American culture. I remember vivid examples from my own upbringing.

Outsiders to the black middle class community would have thought that "Eighth and Towne" was a minor intersection of city streets. It was and it wasn't, because it was both. For every church-going soul in pre-1960s Central Los Angeles, it referred to the much-revered First African Methodist Episcopal Church located at Eighth Street and Towne Avenue. In my childhood that is all I ever remember hearing it called. It was the occasion for no little excitement in our Westside home whenever my Mother would alert us kids that our Aunt Neosho and Uncle Bill had invited us to go with them for Sunday services at "Eighth and Towne," because Eighth and Towne had a great choir and a real pipe organ. So total was the impact in my mind of the dualism that I never truly grasped until I was an adult that Eighth and Towne was only the cultural "not-thing" idea behind the First AME Church and therefore connoted the entire religious, musical, and neighborhood cultural heritage of that historic edifice. Furthermore, the tradition was so enduring that when the Church moved to its present location in the 1970s to Sugar Hill at 22nd and Harvard Streets (on the former site, by the way, of my great uncle's Moorish villa), it was still referred to by folk who knew it "when," as Eighth and Towne.

My reference to Not Doctor Street in Toni Morrison and the Eighth and Towne-First AME Church dualisms is intended to provide some perspective on how duality is handled in two culturally distinct knowledge system traditions, the European and the African. These were traditions that evolved in unique ways after more than 300 years of incubation in the Petrie dish of a British colony in the process of becoming the American nation. The whole meaning underlying Black Studies and the HBCU draws upon African cultural vestiges in the shaping of a unique African-American culture. It is a culture that evidences a self-conscious handling of dualism, a mental awareness found in all cultural traditions, but handled in distinct, environmentally influenced ways across those traditions. In my view, this is the minimum, irreducible prerequisite for possession of a knowledge system. The writings of Morrison and DuBois alone offer evidence in abundance for such a view.

However, the historical subtext of an HBCU education is rooted in mental processes giving every appearance of contradiction and paradox—when two things that cannot be together (due to their mutually opposing differences) must be harmoniously together to maintain the integrity of a higher unity. We could be talking about a two-party democratic system. We could be talking about the challenge of human friendship and corporate mergers. We could be talking about the process of the ongoing entropy increase of the physical universe—co-existing with the local entropy decrease around a living organism capable of dissipating its accumulation of entropic disorder.

That is why liberal arts education is so important, because it does more than liberate the mind. A liberated mind ensures that the brain system can avert the entropic buildup of disorder. Clearly, the end of learning is the thermodynamic definition of death in both the cellular and the mental domains. The end of learning is the end of processing the relentless informational inflows of daily existence in a way that reorders, reorganizes, and refreshes the mind to reframe and resolve any issue that challenges the learner—even preparing college students for jobs that do not yet exist. That is the practical side of a good liberal arts education. It is what I did when I began to teach chemistry in the University of California in a way that was considered by less liberal arts-minded colleagues as too far removed from the traditional lecture approach for their comfort. As a consequence I took the opportunity I was given to go elsewhere.

THE VOCATIONAL IMPLICATIONS OF BLACK STUDIES
AND LIBERAL ARTS EDUCATION

The anxiety I felt in departing so quickly gave way to an exciting exercise in dissipation, not the self-polluting kind, but the thermodynamic kind in which I dissipated a buildup of disorder in my existence. My mind as brain-computer began to re-sort, re-order, and re-organize my holistic constructs of chemistry, which assumed a form more akin to the binary oppositions found in a Toni Morrison novel than to the canonical approaches to teaching science. I envisioned their application as an innovative basis for the design and manufacture of microchips and office automation systems. And so I was off to see the Wizard of the new Oz, Silicon Valley industry just over the Santa Cruz Mountains from Monterey Bay. And there I spent nearly a decade in entrepreneurial activity before my re-entry to academe at San Francisco State University as a Lecturer in Black Studies focusing on science and civilization.

En route to San Francisco State, I enjoyed eclectic vocations ranging from high-tech consulting to tending wine bars in the Sonoma wine country, adjunct teaching, and making ends meet as a typist and file clerk for a major vineyard and then for the municipal water district of Oakland (CA). Along the way, I chased Alice's proverbial rabbit in Wonderland into an interdisciplinary time warp as I refined a liberal arts approach to teaching science and mathematics, published my first widely distributed book (*The Paradox of the Silicon Savior—Charting the Reformation of the High-Tech Super-State*), and invented algorithms for the design of high-technology systems. This kind of experience, I would submit, uncovers not only the tell-tale footprint of a liberal arts education, but also a historically African-American attitude toward education: not too surprising as I am the product of two well-respected liberal arts research universities (UCLA and Chicago). And, just as importantly, I am the product of elders and ancestors who were students or teachers in and the academic associates of founders, presidents, and professors of such celebrated HBCU's as Atlanta U, Central State, Florida A&M, Howard, Hampton, Huston-Tilotson, both Lincolns (MO and PA), Tuskegee, Wilberforce, and Wiley (the setting for the film The Great Debaters).

One rarely ever hears of such panoply of apparent binary contradictions. But it cuts to the core of what William Edward Burghardt "W.E.B." DuBois apprehended and wrote about under the rubric of "double consciousness"—a minority people which simultaneously inhabits its own localized world of lived experience and the demands of the majority culture to which it finds itself subject. And, of course, it cuts to the core of DuBois's essays on the meaning of what he called the "Negro University" and what I call a culturally African knowledge system—a decidedly holistic approach to education grounded in those universals of mind reflected in the fundamental ideas of mathematics. But minority group members of any marginalized minority who survive and succeed are *forced* to become intellectual "universalists"—while the majority remain culturally "privileged" or "deprived" (depending on one's viewpoint) for not necessarily having to develop a dual consciousness, unless forced to do so on account of other circumstances—as, for example, did the truly great scholars in the European intellectual tradition. DuBois early on pointed out that every great academic tradition has a cultural origin in some part of the world.

When Black Studies burst upon the scene in 1967 at San Francisco State College, there was widespread condemnation from culturally conservative quarters that accused the College of trading the traditional curriculum based on the DWM icons of Western Civilization for racial, "feel-good" instruction. There was no ability, really, to understand DuBois's observation about the psycho-cultural tenets of a higher education. This does not mean that Black Studies in the 1960s through 1980s was a methodologically mature discipline, because it wasn't. However, it was no less valid in its beginnings than the once-upon-a-time possibly even more heretical, fledgling disciplines of Chemistry, Sociology, Business Education, and American Studies, when they, too, invaded American academic space in their respective times of appearance after 1870. Furthermore, aspiring collegians today have countless choices in the multifaceted medium of college education. Witness the import of a Talmudic immersion at Brandeis, Yeshiva, or, indeed, the University of Chicago itself (with its transplanted German research model). Witness the appeal of Puritan-founded Harvard and Presbyterian-founded Princeton and Lincoln; Congregational Church-founded Yale and UC Berkeley, Methodist-founded Emory; and Caltech founded by what we now know as the Unitarian-Universalist Church. We must also mention those Roman Catholic academic powerhouses from St Joseph's University not far from Lincoln University (PA) to Notre Dame, the College of St. Mary, and those notorious "Left Coast" Jesuit strongholds at the Universities of Santa Clara and San Francisco. And many others.

Those who view the idea of historically African-American liberal arts education rooted in an African knowledge system as ironic or metaphorical need only look to Wayne C. Booth, one of the great literary thinkers who engaged, baffled, regaled, teased, cajoled, and thrilled generations of University of Chicago students. I did not have the opportunity to study with Booth as my doctoral studies in chemistry amply filled my time in Kent-Jones Hall and the Argonne National Laboratory. My treasured connection to the Humanities was through John Hope Franklin, who held the Manley Chair in a History Department filled with such luminaries as William McNeill, Daniel Boorstin, and Hannah Holborn Gray (who later succeeded to the Chicago presidency). Keen of mind, quick-witted, and kindly in manner, John Hope and his wife Aurelia welcomed me, a young chemist, into their inner circle of young historians. It was much later that I finally met up with Wayne Booth in the last few years of his life when I attended his lecture on *irony* during an annual alumni week and engaged a correspondence with him. In the presence of suspected ironies, he asked, "How does a reader or listener recognize the kind of statement which requires the rejection (or acceptance) of its 'clear' and 'obvious' meaning? And how does any reader know where to stop, once he has embarked on the hazardous and exhilarating path of rejecting (or accepting) 'what the words say' and reconstructing 'what the author means?'"

In the case of "African Knowledge System" and "Historically Black Liberal Arts Education," I actually mean the terms quite literally and not ironically. Delaying acceptance of that literal meaning leaves one blinded by the discredited assertions of the past 200 years that flowed from the pens and mouths of individuals who offered specious measurements to create a racial totem pole that inversely correlated dark skin complexion and the ability to perform complex mental operations.

EPILOGUE—HUMAN INHERITANCE OF DUALISM

I have often speculated about how it was that I had acquired an innate sense of *complementary dualism* and the three-part structured *whole* of thing, not-thing, and the membrane interface between. How did my father Grant, Sr. come by his deep sense of complementarity in mathematics, if not from his grade-school educated father, who was but an infant in 1867, a year before DuBois was born? How does someone so close to the devastating episode of human group slavery, still retain the ontological rudiments of the ancestral group? How did DuBois, who was among the first of the race to obtain a Harvard Ph.D. in 1895? How did my father, who was the first of the race to graduate from the California Institute of Technology in 1932; how did he actualize a formal, academic grasp of the mental structures in mathematics and engineering? However it came about, the structured whole lived quietly within the deep mental structure of the African people, even as they were packed into the cargo holds of the slave ships. They, in turn, transmitted it from generation to generation, without being privy, we suppose, to the formalisms of modern algebra and the calculus of limits. So what did the ancestors teach their children from one generation to the next? While I must defer these questions to another time, I surmise that the answer lies in a context not unrelated to Noam Chomsky's universal grammar. As the dualistic structure of the whole is intrinsic to African mythology and culture, one would expect African families to handle their infants and children in a way that activates key cognitive structures in the brain. These structures are then prerequisites for an "innate" sense of knowing complementary wholeness, which lurks behind the scenes throughout modern science and in the poetic words of DuBois with which I now conclude:

> The Wings of Atalanta are the coming universities of the South. They alone can bear the maiden past the temptation of the golden fruit.... [So] let us build the Southern University—William and Mary, Trinity, Georgia, Texas, Tulane, Vanderbilt, and the others—fit to live; let us build too, the Negro universities: Fisk, Howard, and Atlanta.... Teach workers to work, a wise saying;... Teach thinkers to think, a needed knowledge in a day of loose and careless logic; and they whose lot is gravest must have the carefulest training to think aright.... And the final product of our training must be neither psychologist nor a brickmason, but a [whole person.]

> When night falls on the City of a Hundred Hills, a wind gathers itself from the seas and comes murmuring westward. And at its bidding, the smoke of the drowsy factories sweeps down upon the mighty city and covers it like a pall, while yonder at the University the stars twinkle above Stone Hall. And they say that yon gray mist is the tunic of Atalanta pausing over her golden apples. Fly, my maiden, fly, for yonder comes Hippomenes. (DuBois, 66)

While DuBois used the term "man," and probably more or less generically, had he written this essay today, I suspect he would have used *whole person*, which seemed to be the point of his writing in 1903.

Works Cited

DuBois, W.E.B. "Of the Wings of Atalanta." In *The Souls of Black Folks*. San Diego: Icon Classics, 2008.

Morrison, Toni. *Song of Solomon*. New York: Vintage, 2004.

Platonic Forms as a Model of Modern Physics: Confessions of an Experimental Physicist

Steven Turley
Brigham Young University
Plenary Speaker, ACTC Conference, April 18, 2009

INTRODUCTION

I agreed to this opportunity to write about how core texts have influenced my scientific research with both enthusiasm and trepidation. The enthusiasm was a result of my strong interest in the integration of ideas from all of the liberal arts to enhance our perspectives of each field individually. My two academic honors which mean the most to me are named after wonderful examples of this integration, Alcuin of York and Karl G. Maeser.

Alcuin, with whom some of you may be familiar, was an English scholar invited by Charlemagne to take a role in reestablishing significant scholarship in his empire. Alcuin strove to expand the education of capable clergy and lay people in the monastery schools to include a solid classical education going beyond the simple narrow ability to read the scriptures. He argued that a facility to understand reasoning and symbolism from a broad education would greatly expand the abilities of his students to deeply understand the scriptures and other ideas needed to improve the kingdom.

Maeser, the founding principal of the academy that has evolved into Brigham Young University is probably less well-known in this audience. Maeser was a remarkable German scholar who left a comfortable and respected academic position in Germany to join the early Mormon settlers in Utah. With typical German rigor and efficiency he established a normal school in Provo Utah where, at various times, he taught theology, rhetoric, mathematics, languages, music, gymnastics, and science. His students included a future United States Supreme Court justice, a future United

States senator, future state and community leaders, future church leaders, and future educators and scholars. Many of these remarked on how Maeser's broad education and strong moral teachings proved foundational in their later accomplishments.

Carrying the name of these two personal heroes in the awards I've received, I've felt particularly obligated to myself be an example of the integration of insights from many disciplines. My fear in presenting this talk is that I am not a specialist in most of these fields. I hope, however, that as I share how I've used ideas from classical works in philosophy and literature in my scientific research, it may help those of you who *are* experts in those fields to benefit from my perspective in how I've found them useful in areas where I *am* an expert.

As I pondered Scott Lee's invitation to discuss how ideas from the classics have affected my work as an experimental physicist, I was drawn to the idea of Platonic Forms as a model for modern physics. In particular, Plato's allegory of the cave is an apt symbol of how my physics colleagues and I investigate physical reality. To illustrate these connections, I will start by explaining the idea of cross sections in physics and how most physics experiments can be cast into this language. I've had the good fortune to be involved in a wide variety of kinds of physics research, so I'll use examples from a number of different areas.

As a brief reminder, in Book VII of the Republic, Plato introduces the allegory of the cave to illuminate the process of learning about nature. Plato asks us through the voice of Socrates to imagine human beings in an underground dwelling with a long entrance serving as its source of illumination. He tells us these people have been in the cave since birth and constrained by bonds so that they are prevented from viewing the light from the entrance directly, but rather can only see the shadows from images cast on the wall in front of them. These shadows are created by people carrying statues of men and other animals made out of a variety of materials. The people in the cave can hear sounds, as if from some of the statues, which are uttered by men as they carry them across the light source. Plato makes the point that the people in the cave would infer that these shadows of reality (in fact, the shadows of representations of reality) would seem like reality to the people in the cave. He then asks the reader to consider the experience of someone released from the cave and able to eventually experience a more direct reality outside the cave. He also considered what would happen as this person returned to the cave and the likelihood that his perception would be considered to be flawed by his companions in the cave who hadn't experienced what he had outside the cave.

CROSS SECTIONS

The idea of measuring a cross section in physics can probably best be understood by an analogy. Imagine you were in a dark room and told there was an object with an unknown shape in the center of a room. You are given a rifle that you could fire at will while the lights are off. Before the lights are turned back on, the target is removed. You then have the opportunity to examine the holes in the wall left by bullets that missed or struck the target. From the patterns in the wall, you try to infer the size and shape of the object you couldn't see.

The problem may not be as difficult as you would imagine at first. For instance, the bullets that didn't strike the target would go straight ahead from your rifle to the back wall. Bullets that hit the target would be deflected off at other angles. There won't be any bullets in the area directly behind the target, where the target shields the wall and produces a shadow, similar to the ones seen by the men in Plato's cave. If a lot of bullets are deflected, the target must have had a large cross sectional area. Furthermore, with some geometry, you can deduce a lot about the shape of the target from the pattern of deflected bullets on the wall. You might even knock off a piece of the target and embed it in the wall of the room. That would give you additional valuable information about the nature of the target.

This kind of discovery of information about otherwise invisible objects is quite similar to techniques used in medical imaging. Simple x-ray pictures show the shadows of bones and internal organs based on the difference in how x-rays are absorbed by different materials in the body. Similar images can be derived using the shadows from ultrasonic sound waves in sonograms. Magnetic resonance imaging takes advantage of how the nuclei of various elements respond to radio waves in a magnetic field. Each of these "shadows" gives us views of interior body parts otherwise invisible without invasive surgery. Just as with the men in Plato's cave, multiple perspectives using different angles give us a variety of views which allow even better two-dimensional or three-dimensional reconstructions using computer-aided tomography (or CAT) scans.

The "bullets" and "targets" I've used in my physics experiments are also similar to the ones in the analogy of the dark room. The idea of a shadow from the cross section of a target has come up frequently in multiple areas of research. I will give examples from shadows I've seen in nuclear physics, radar computations, and extreme ultraviolet optics. I'll follow with extensions to how I see physics "knowledge" in general as inferences of Platonic forms from observation and reason.

I will use the idea of a shadow, the region where the probe beam is blocked, interchangeably with the idea of a cross section, which is more correctly how the probe beams are deflected by the target. I will also not distinguish between cases where I detect the reflected or modified probe beams and cases where part of the original target itself is what's detected.

NUCLEAR PHYSICS

In my PhD research, I studied the position and velocity distributions of protons inside the nucleus of ^{16}O nuclei. These are the most common nuclei of oxygen atoms, being ones with eight protons and eight neutrons. These particles are much too small to be "seen" in the normal sense by visible light. In that sense, these provide great prototypical examples of things physicists "see" by their shadows rather than seeing them directly.

The experiment was done by creating a beam of high-energy light particles called gamma rays. Although Plato probably didn't think of it this way, the light from the sun producing shadows in the cave was made of many different wavelengths. Semitransparent objects would have been able to cast shadows and reflections with different

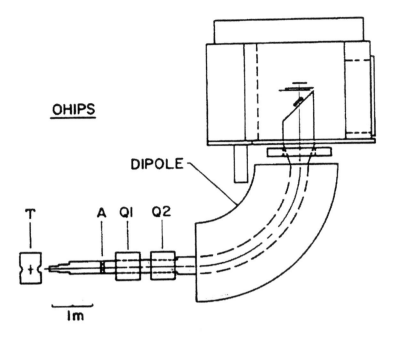

Figure 1. Nuclear physics magnetic spectrometer

colors depending on how they responded to the different wavelengths in the sunlight. Likewise, my gamma ray beam had a spectrum of wavelengths associated with it, each capable of producing different responses by the protons in the ^{16}O nucleus.

When the gamma rays hit my sample containing ^{16}O atoms, various particles were ejected, including protons and particles called deuterons, which consist of a proton and neutron bound together.

Figure 1 is a schematic diagram of the magnets and detectors used to collect the particles ejected from the target. The stand labeled "T" is where the target was located. The aperture labeled "A" was to select just the particles coming from the target at a particular angle. The two magnets labeled "Q1" and "Q2" focused the emerging particles in the vertical and horizontal directions. The large magnet labeled "DIPOLE" spread the particles out according to their momentum. By measuring where these particles hit the position sensitive detector at the top of the magnet, I was then able to make a precise determination of their momentum and energy when they left the target.

There were two types of detectors on top of the dipole, as shown in Figure 2.

The detector labeled VDCX was the position detector I alluded to earlier. It could track the position and direction of high-energy charged particles passing through it by sensing the location of the ionization tracks they left behind. (This is in essence the shadow left by the particles as they passed through the detector.) The four detectors labeled S0, S1, S2, and S3 were plastic scintillators. Particles passing through those detectors would lose energy in each one, converting some of that energy into

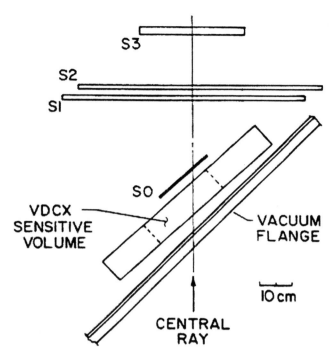

Figure 2. Nuclear physics detectors

light pulses, which could be sensed by photo detectors. (This was another example of their shadow.)

In nuclear physics experiments, the detectors can be fired by many kinds of particles, including random spontaneous background noise. In order to distinguish real protons passing through the detectors from random signals and other kinds of particles, I looked for correlated signals in each of the detectors and characteristic energy loss in the plastic scintillators.

For example, Figure 3 shows the correlated signals seen in the plastic scintillator S3 on the vertical axis along with the same signal in the position detector on the horizontal axis. I have marked the region where the particles would have passed through the bottom scintillator S0, thus losing additional energy that the others didn't. From these kinds of plots, I was able to isolate protons from the deuterons coming through the dipole magnet with the same momentum.

As a side note, this is the same kind of detection scheme used (on a much grander scale) in the ATLAS detector coming online this summer at the Large Hadron Collider in CERN. In that case, physicists will be looking for signatures of an important building block in matter called the Higgs Boson and possibly other new particles.

Don't get overwhelmed by all of the details. However, please notice how I was able to learn a lot about the protons in the ^{16}O nucleus by carefully looking at many aspects of its shadow within the cave of this experiment. Using many detectors, beam

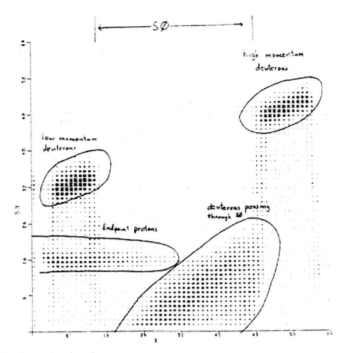

Figure 3. Nuclear physics data cuts

energies, and angles I was able to get a good picture of the pattern of ejected protons from the nucleus. An example of this pattern, or "cross section," is shown in Figure 4.

It shows the measured cross section as a function of the angle of the ejected protons. Also plotted are three existing theoretical predictions of what these cross sections would be. While these calculations were somewhat close (though not very close) to the data that existed before my measurements, this experiment showed that they were grossly inadequate for this expanded angular range.

Since that time, there have been significant advances in our ability to calculate the momentum and energy of protons in nuclei for the energies I was considering here. I assume that theorists would be able to do a much better job of reproducing my 1983 data.

The important point I would like to make is that this experiment is particles by their cross sections. We detect their distribution (often through rather involved processes) in their interactions with beams and then compare those distributions to computations from theories based on fundamental principles. When there is agreement between the measurements and theories, it adds credence to the methodologies employed in the calculations. In other words, we look at the shadows of these objects on our cave wall and infer properties of the original objects by how well we can predict the shadows and reflections we would expect to see.

One of the projects I worked on at Hughes Research Laboratories was comput-

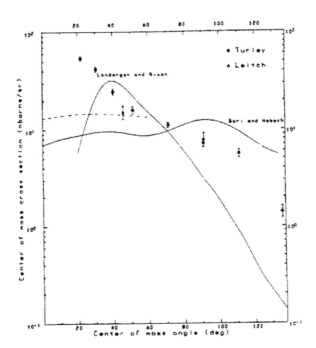

Figure 4. Comparison of data with experiment

ing the radar cross sections of various objects. Many of these objects were designed to have shadows in the cave of enemy radar detectors which looked very different from the actual object. Published reports in open literature say that a B2 bomber looks more like a bug than a large bomber when seen on radar.

However, even stealthy objects like the B2 bomber are not totally immune to detection. There is a sophisticated radar technology called bistatic radar which has the transmitting and receiving antennas for the radar located in different locations. This is like being able to see the shadows of the object in Plato's cave from a number of different perspectives. Under these conditions, it is much easier to determine the real shape of the plane than when limited to a single angle akin to Plato's long narrow cave entrance.

EXTREME ULTRAVIOLET OPTICS

My current research is in the area of extreme ultraviolet optics. We learn a lot about the properties of thin films of materials by looking at how they reflect and absorb light with wavelengths in between the ultraviolet wavelengths that cause sun burn and skin cancer and the x-ray wavelengths used for medical and dental imaging.

Using an intense beam from the Advanced Light Source at the Lawrence Berkeley National Laboratory, we measure the reflection and transmission of extreme ultraviolet light incident on thin films of various materials. From this, we are able to infer optical properties of the materials, the thickness of the films, and the

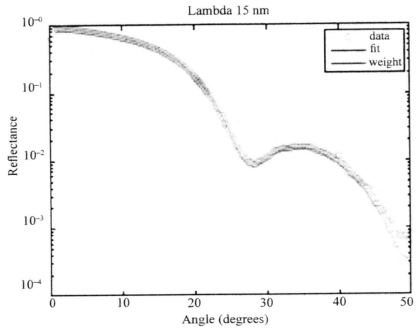

Figure 5. Extreme ultraviolet optics data and fit

roughness of the film surfaces. Figure 5 shows an example of the data and theoretical fit from a recent measurement. When we use a single sample and a single measurement technique, we are often deceived as to these values, much like the men in Plato's cave. In practice we use many angles, wavelengths, surfaces, and films. This gives us a better picture of the properties of our materials.

OTHER EXAMPLES

This same idea of looking at the shadows and reflections of objects is seen in other applications. The kinds of XUV optics we develop can be used to observe the shadows or reflections of components in cells too small to see with visible light, to take movies of Earth's magnetic field, or to image the interior of stars. Geologists locate oil deposits and study the Earth's interior by detecting how sound waves and earthquakes are absorbed and deflected as they travel through the Earth. Buried explosives can be located and diffused using reflected signals from ground-penetrating radar. I've used carefully tuned lasers to detect the elemental composition of plasmas in rocket engines using electric fields to eject high-energy ions to generate thrust.

PHYSICS RESEARCH

By now, I hope I've convinced you that much of what we do in experimental physics is akin to what the men experience in Plato's cave. We try to avoid the kinds of deceptions possible with them by essentially using multiple caves with many different perspectives looking at the same objects. However, the fact remains that we most often are looking at shadows of the objects we study, rather than sensing them directly. If, in many cases, we're forced to live with interpreting the shadows in Plato's cave, what protections do we have as physicists against the kind of deceptions imposed on Plato's allegorical prisoners?

I will present a mixed answer to this question. In a number of areas, we can look at our shadows using multiple probes and multiple angles. As I've mentioned earlier, this is akin to looking at Plato's shadows from multiple perspectives. This essentially unchains the prisoners. I saw a wonderful example of how this works in an exhibit of Walter Wick's work at BYU's Museum of Art. A wonderful example of how this works can be seen in Warner Wick's book *Optical Tricks*.

Somewhat like an Escher drawing, the impossible geometry in the number and shape of photographed columns in a seemingly ancient Roman forum is possible because Wick limits our view to a single angle and perspective by forcing us to see the scene through his camera lens. If you stare at the picture in the book, it is impossible to tell if you are looking at an arch or three columns. Using a different perspective and angle another picture in Wick's book shows that it is easier to see the "true" nature of these objects and the illusions he creates.

In most developed areas of physics, we have looked at our shadows under so many circumstances and from so many sides; it is hard to imagine a "real" world that is fundamentally different from the one we see in our measurements. Within the realm of the physical world, our modern "Forms" are the foundational laws and symmetries we see in the universe.

These symmetries, such as invariance of physical law with respect to translation in position, motion in time, or rotation, give rise to universally conserved quantities like mass-energy and linear and angular momentum.

QUANTUM MECHANICS

One area of modern physics where we are on less certain metaphysical ground is the field of quantum mechanics. Here, Platonic Forms and their generalization in process philosophy give us a language to discuss important foundational questions.

Quantum mechanics is the branch of physics that deals with interactions of systems generally the size of atoms and smaller. Under these conditions, we are forced to abandon the deterministic predictions of classical Newtonian physics and deal in probabilities.

This world of the small, where I've done much of my professional research, is eerily different from the experiences we have in the everyday world of the relatively large. At this length scale, objects have both particle-like and wave-like properties. We see an electron simultaneously traverse two separate and distinct paths. Particles traverse barriers that are energetically impossible for them to climb. Objects can be in a mixture of contradictory states that remain unresolvable until a measurement is made.

The nuclear physics measurements I discussed earlier fall exactly into this class. When I say I measured the momentum and position of the protons in the nucleus, I was actually measuring the probability that they had this momentum and position. In fact, there was a non-zero probability of measuring any number of momenta and positions. The momenta I was measuring in particular were some of the least likely ones to see. In addition to this probability, the proton itself was really a combination of particles. A quite prominent feature in the cross section was due to the possibility the proton had of being a very different particle called the Delta[1232] particle during the process of the interaction.

Einstein was so perplexed by the unordered chaos introduced by such a system that he believed until his death that the apparent randomness of these measurements was due to some hidden attributes these particles possessed, which we had yet to discover. In other words, the particles themselves were really behaving in a deterministic matter, but in a way that depended on circumstances we were unable to measure. In the language of Plato's cave, Einstein was asserting that our constrained ability to see in the cave blocked our capacity to sense other aspects of the true objects casting shadows on the cave wall.

For decades, Einstein's arguments appeared to be irrefutable by the observational tools of physics. It wasn't until shortly after his death that John Bell opened an avenue to experimentally probe the difference between things that were inherently random and things that appear to be random because of our ignorance of internal structure which they might have. Our experiments since that time indicate that Einstein's postulate of local hidden structure in these small particles is not accurate.

The predictive power of quantum mechanics is one of the most amazing accomplishments of modern science. Its predictions have been verified to unrivaled accuracy. Personally, I've measured optical quantum mechanical effects that match predictions to the fifteenth significant figure.

But in this realm of probabilities what are these shadows we are measuring? Surely something that is only probably there or an event that has only probably occurred can't be "real," at least not in the Platonic sense of having an existence that transcends our senses. The "real" Form for me and for many of my colleagues is an abstraction called a quantum mechanical state or sometimes a quantum mechanical wave function.

These quantum mechanical states are sufficiently abstract they are difficult to describe outside the language of mathematics. They are similar to Platonic Forms in the sense that they exist beyond the realm of things we can observe directly. They contain all that we can know about an object. In contrast to things we can measure, or even to the object's existence, the quantum mechanical states evolve in time according to well-developed rules (or equations) that are totally deterministic.

The simplest system I can think of to illustrate this would be a beam of silver atoms that have an intrinsic magnetic field associated with them. The rules of quantum mechanics limit this field to pointing in one of two directions that I'll describe as "up" and "down." I can measure whether an atom is pointing "up" or "down" by passing it through the field of an external magnet.

Similar to the way bar magnets attract or repel each other depending on their orientation, the magnetic field of the silver atom will interact with the field of the external magnet, pushing the atom either up or down. This classic experiment is called the Stern-Gerlach experiment (Figure 6). Atoms with an "up" orientation

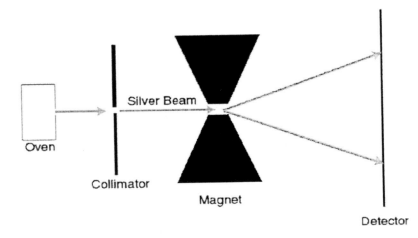

Figure 6. Stern-Gerlach experiment

will be deflected up, and atoms with a "down" orientation will be deflected down. Even though the result of any particular measurement on a single atom can't be predicted until after the measurement is made, each measurement itself has a definite result.

My point of this discussion is that the result of a quantum mechanical measurement is, in general, indeterminate. I can't accurately describe the atom has being in either the "up" state or the "down" state. My inability to make this determination is not a matter of ignorance about the atom; it is that my measurements are essentially just the Platonic shadow of what I'm learning about the atom. Its essence, the equivalent of a Platonic Form is in its quantum mechanical state. I can know this state perfectly by how I prepare the system. In that sense, it is very much like a Platonic Form. However, I can never really measure its Form, only the probabilistic results from various experiments.

This simple example has in interesting side note. In the process of measuring the orientation of the silver atom, I will also change its quantum mechanical state. Once I have measured its orientation as being "up," it can no longer be a combination of "up" and "down." I've altered its state to one that will always be up. In this sense I've now made its state into one where I know with a certainty what the results of an up/down measurement will give.

Other features of the atom are equally rooted in its quantum mechanical state and have only probabilities evident in what I will measure. This would include the atom's position, speed, momentum, and energy, for instance. The larger the atom (in other words, the more it is like macroscopic things with which I have everyday experience), the smaller the uncertainties in many of these quantities.

Another simple example of a quantum mechanical system would be the motion of a single free particle such as an electron. Typically, these objects are produced in states that have an associated pair of quantum mechanical probabilities, one related to the probability of measuring a particular position and the other the probability

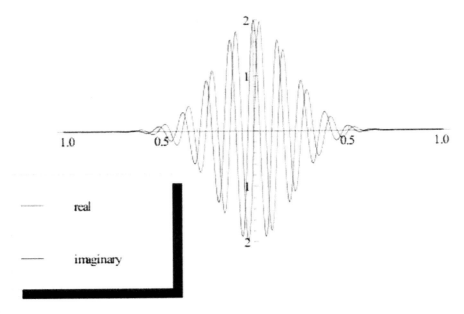

Figure 7. Electron wave function

of having a particular momentum (or speed). The quantum mechanical relationship between these two distributions gives rise to the well-known Heisenberg Uncertainty Principle. The mathematical description of the quantum mechanical state of a free particle is a quantity known as its wave function. It is a complex function that has real and imaginary parts. An example is shown in Figure 7.

The absolute value squared of this wave function gives the probability of finding the particle at various locations (Figure 8). In this case, the probability is maximum at the point $x = 0$ and becomes negligible for x less than -0.5 or greater than 0.

The probability of detecting a particle in a particular region is the area under the probability curve. In Figure 9, I've highlighted the area for detecting the electron at a position between -0.1 and -0.2. It has a numerical value of 23%.

Once this function for the position of a free particle is known, we know everything we can know about the particle's position and momentum for all time. However, we don't know with certainty the results of any particular position or momentum measurement. In this sense, the wave function is a determined ideal object, similar to a Platonic Form. The object itself, with its properties measured in any given experiment, is more like a shadow of its actual form.

BACK TO PLATO

In conclusion, I'd like to return back to Plato's cave. As a physicist, I'm left to acknowledge that indeed my discipline is built on reasoning about the shadows that are accessible to us. We continue to look at those shadows from different angles and

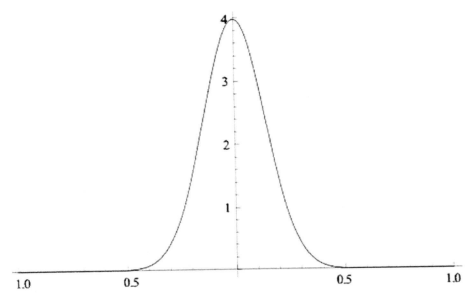

Figure 8. Electron probability curve

in different realms. Historical precedent would indicate that the true Forms we are seeking leave much to be discovered.

   Newton's remarkable accomplishments in outlining the fundamental ideas (or Forms) behind the motion of objects both on and under the Earth and above the Earth stood for centuries, but eventually had to be generalized by the work of Einstein. What's to say that Einstein's ideas might not eventually be found to be some lower dimensional shadow of a more general law (or Form) yet to be discovered?

   There is strong evidence that such a generalization awaits us. Physicists are probably the ultimate reductionists. We are currently able to encapsulate all of the intricacies of the Universe in only four fundamental forces: the electromagnetic force, the strong nuclear force, the weak nuclear force, and the gravitational force. Three of these four forces have been shown to essentially have the same form and actually combine at very high energies.

   The rich tapestry of form and substance we see in the universe with hundreds of elements and an almost unlimited variety of combining these elements into compounds is mostly built on combinations of electrons, protons, and neutrons. However, as we've pushed the limits of what we can see in the microscopic structure of the shadows we call particles, we found that these particles have hundreds of cousins we can see under very energetic circumstances. We've reduced this zoo of particles to collections of again a handful of fundamental particles we call leptons and quarks with another small group of particles to take care of the interactions between these particles.

   With these tremendous successes, most of us will readily acknowledge there are several abysses we've encountered that indicate we still have much to learn about these shadows and forms. To start with, our two strongest theories to explain interac-

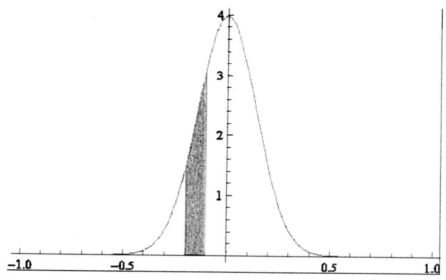

Figure 9. Electron detection probability

tions of the smallest things in the universe (quantum mechanics) and the most massive things in the universe (gravity through General Relativity) are fundamentally inconsistent with each other. How could these ideas both be universal Forms and be inconsistent with each other? String Theory offers hope for a solution, but it is still enough in its infancy and so far removed from experimental verification it is hard to be sure it isn't just the shadow of a reality itself.

These two ideas have to come to play together for us to understand the physics of the earliest times in the beginning of our universe (if a universe it truly is, and not one of several "multiverses"). We actually know very little of the physics needed to understand the earliest moments of the Big Bang.

With our remarkably sophisticated and successful models of matter, we've recently realized that this "normal" matter is not the material out of which most of the universe is made. Astronomical measurements clearly show that most of our universe is made up of what we call "dark matter," which behaves very differently from the matter composed of quarks and leptons that I talked about earlier.

Additionally, we see many situations in modern physics that are intractably complex. Even in regimes governed by the well-understood formalisms of classical mechanics, it's easy to find situations where the outcome depends so sensitively on the initial conditions, that our ability to predict the final outcome of the experiments is limited by the complexity of the inherent chaos.

Finally, we have seen wonderful recent advances in physics by exploring areas where physics intersects with other disciplines. We have defined our discipline in terms of a system capable of unifying our understanding of things we can verify through physical measurements. As a religious man, I readily accept the idea that there are realities beyond the self-imposed limitations of what can be measured in my laboratory. The intricacies and complexities of consciousness may well be a window to truths and forms we can't discover by limiting ourselves to the narrow perspective of sensory measurements. That's why cross-disciplinary forums such as this have the potential to be so powerful. These may give us windows to leave our caves and see with a much broader perspective. I resonate with Paul of Tarsus' reflection that we now "see through a glass darkly" but that someday we may "know even as also [we] are known" (I Corinthians 13:12, KJV).

Liberal Education and Liberal Arts

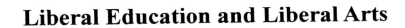

Liberal Education:
Transmitting Knowledge though Texts

Molly Brigid Flynn
Assumption College

The theme of this year's conference invites us to reflect on the use of texts in transmitting knowledge from the past and shaping culture for the future. Liberal education, it seems, aims to do this, and uses texts to do so. This theme runs counter to today's typical explanation of liberal education, which exalts "critical thinking" or "thinking for oneself." Such slogans only tangentially connect to the vocation of the human intellect. An adequate justification for liberal education must honor something to which our thinking should submit, something taboo: truth. But when a teacher aims to communicate truth, he or she seems to undermine the liberalness of education. This appearance results from a misunderstanding.

Thinking for oneself is often falsely imaged as an individualistic and critical move, a stand against authorities, traditions, and community. This implies, absurdly, that education and thinking well are enemies. Education is done by others to perfect our skills; to transmit knowledge; to shape our habits; to unify, continue, and improve our culture. Were intellectual freedom to *consist* in sloughing off tradition and community, "liberal education" would be not merely paradoxical but incoherent. Thus, the mere coherence of the idea of liberal education is important.

The idea claims that education true to our personhood liberates us by freeing the mind and frees the mind by cultivating our ability to submit ourselves to truth. It suggests that the human's freedom to form his or her own judgments well needs nourishment from others. This suggestion, however paradoxical, makes sense with what we know about the person. The human mind is not solitary but social, not silent but conversational; reason is not a native reflex or self-executing program, but requires pruning and watering. Liberal education uses texts and teachers to share knowledge and shape culture, convinced not only that the integrity of the human person can bear it, but that the fulfillment of the person requires it.

The question arises, however, whether texts can *transmit* knowledge at all. We need to remember a point at least as old as the *Meno*. Plato's *Meno* suggests that knowledge is teachable but not transmissible. In any transmission of knowledge, mere opinion is received; I may receive the report, but lack the experience needed to make it knowledge. Turning that opinion into knowledge, Socrates suggests, requires reasoning about causes, which is like tying down a runaway slave. The dialogue's myth of recollection suggests the same thing. Some learning involves no transmission-reception. The knowledge is discovered by the learner, guided by a teacher. Since the unschooled slave boy eventually gets the correct answer to the math problem, the slave-boy experiment is supposed to "prove" that the soul comes into life with knowledge built-in. One flaw in Socrates' experiment, however, is that the boy fishes out lots of falsehood from his soul before happening upon the right answer. A necessary truth that is "recollected," like information that is received, is not yet knowledge. It needs to be reasoned through and understood.

Great texts are something like civilization's memory, but memories cannot be just handed around. Socrates reminds us in the *Meno* that is it not enough to recall something that we have once understood: knowledge requires repeating the insight. The new student encounters a text expressing civilization's knowledge. But reasoning and understanding need always to be performed again, if the "transmission" isn't going to run out of the soul. Civilization's treasures are precarious, and our great texts can teach and civilize only when each generation reappropriates the inheritance.

"Transmission" is a metaphor likely to increase our desire for knowledge packaged as information, and likely to heighten our impatience for the less information-friendly disciplines, like the humanities, philosophy, and theology. The knowledge they offer us has a peculiar depth that eludes our full grasp.

The truths contemplated by the humanities have shells that are easily picked up and passed around without being quite understood. These texts only intimate their humane truths by representing events of life, imbuing these events with a style and form that help us grasp life's structure and that shape our imagination. They help us return to life more insightfully. Formation by these civilizing "transmissions" is nothing like reading a newspaper. Buying the information-transmission paradigm will lead us to neglect these humane truths or reduce them to slogans.

A reflection by Edmund Husserl on philosophical knowledge can help us find a better metaphor than transmission. Though he focuses on philosophy, the moral of the story extends to liberal education generally. In a famous manifesto—the 1910 essay "Philosophy as a Rigorous Science"—Husserl attacks naturalism, psychologism, and historicism in order to defend humans as capable of achieving real truth. These isms use knowledge of their own domains to, implicitly or explicitly, deny that we are capable of universally valid knowledge. Husserl attacks them as countersensical. The essay defends the human striving for knowledge against these sophistic attacks on reason. (If we wish to defend the use of texts as a way of sharing knowledge at all, we should start by insightfully rejecting these isms.)

In the essay, Husserl also offers a description of the "rigorous science" of his philosophical aspirations. First, it deals with essential necessities, not with mere facts of existence. Second, he is looking for a "doctrinal system" worked up by a "community of investigators" whose discoveries become a public possession, a "treasure trove" permanently bequeathed to later generations (287, 283). While there is a need for "worldview philosophy" to address the profound unknowns of human existence (283-86), philosophy properly understood is science, replacing apparent profundity with clarity wherever it can. It also replaces personal teachers with reportable results. He insists, "Science is impersonal" (292). He scoffs at Kant's saying that one cannot learn philosophy but only how to philosophize: "What is that if not an admission of the unscientific character of philosophy?" (250). We get the impression from this essay that philosophy should produce textbooks reporting impersonal results.

Husserl followed up on this article twenty-five years later in a few pages of notes—conversing with his past self, you might say, in the context of the developments in himself and the philosophical community since 1910. Here is the old man's opening lamentation: "Philosophy as science, as serious, rigorous ... science—*the dream is over*" (389).

Attention to Husserl's reflections shows that he is not (as commonly reported) taking back his dedication to the project of philosophy as universally valid knowledge. He is lamenting the continental *Zeitgeist* demanding from philosophy existential profundity and a worldview as "a sort of personal religious faith" (390). Husserl also rejects the adequacy of philosophy practiced as piece-by-piece problem-solving analysis. He urges a return to our philosophical history to reinvigorate philosophy in our times. But he is not advocating historical scholarship. Returning to texts from philosophy's past does not mean doing a history of ideas. We read philosophical history philosophically only when we take it up personally and allow it to motivate our own philosophical searching. (Let's broaden the point: We learn from great texts liberally only when we allow them to motivate our own searching for truth.)

"Philosophy," he says, has always existed only as a *project* on its way toward "philosophy" in the strong sense, a system of universally valid truths (390-91). This is the "problematic *telos* of philosophy," problematic because we must aim for universally valid knowledge, but must be unsatisfied with whatever knowledge there is to be found in the tradition or in our own investigations (394). And so, for every genuine philosopher, philosophy must be an "enigma" (394).

We grasp *our* project of philosophy by immersing ourselves in the tradition, and this requires understanding the tradition as a project—*rather than as static, transmitted doctrine*. The most important part of this tradition, our greatest inheritance, is not the results of past philosophers, but the project itself, and its *telos* or task, which we take on in becoming philosophical. When I read past philosophers philosophically, Husserl says, they are part of my living present; they draw me into conversation, and Plato, Aristotle, Descartes, and Kant become my coworkers.

Has Husserl here abandoned his earlier dedication to philosophy as a science? Earlier, science consisted in knowledge in the form of transmittable impersonal doctrine. He now says, "history is not before us like a warehouse containing its assembled wares, such that everyone can convince himself of the existence of these wares as being not dreamed-up, not illusory" (392-93). There is no simple "transmission" of philosophical insight, but not because there is no success and not because real thought requires an individualistic renunciation of inheritance. The communications we receive from others we receive from our own "standpoint," and so they are only as good as we allow them to be, as motivators for our own philosophizing (393). Real insight, universally valid knowledge, is attained, though it may not be recognized by others and cannot be simply handed over to another. The tradition shares its secrets, its successes, its knowledge only by sharing its project, by drawing us into conversation with our coworkers.

Does this mean that Husserl now agrees with Kant that "one cannot learn philosophy, but only how to philosophize"? Perhaps, though that could not mean that the goal is to just 'think for oneself' or design one's own worldview. Philosophizing must mean attaining to universally valid insight. Rather, perhaps now Husserl sees a circle: one must immerse oneself in philosophy to learn how to philosophize, and one must learn how to philosophize in order to learn from any philosophy philosophically. The later Husserl seems to accept that sharing knowledge in philosophy is not quite as easy as transmitting conclusions in the mathematical and empirical sciences, and that conversation with real texts are essential to this task. Conversation, I suggest, is a better metaphor than transmission for learning from texts in a liberal education.

In an interesting contradiction to the Husserl of 1910, Michael Oakeshott *praises* philosophy *because* "There is no body of philosophical 'knowledge' to become detached from the activity of philosophizing," and this makes philosophy "unusually conversable" (492). I agree with Oakeshott. But this is not, I insist with Husserl, because philosophers achieve no knowledge; it is because the understanding won in philosophical conversations cannot be merely reported. Understanding the discovery requires going through the discovering.

Husserl here is commenting on philosophy, but the point should be broadened to liberal education generally. We certainly must not deny that liberal education is an education: knowledge is to be had and a liberal education communicates it. At the same time, the knowledge to be got in liberal education can be gotten only liberally.

To draw some conclusions, I would like to spell out two distinctions that will help us see how texts might act in a liberal education to share knowledge and shape culture. First, texts suitable to a liberal education are not textbooks or encyclopedias, which report conclusions as basically settled and verified. These conclusions seem to be public domain and are presented impersonally, in an anonymous voice. We often introduce academic disciplines through textbooks, and don't mind a bit of feigned certainty so we can transmit some settled conclusions. The ideal of knowledge suggested by textbooks is one of information. Information is settled and verified, is detachable from its discoverer, and is understandable even by those who have not gone through the process of discovery. FDA-approved and ready for common consumption, digestible information-bits are suitable for presentation in textbooks and encyclopedias. Exactly because it is trusted, flat, and so easily understandable, information does not invite contemplation or reflection, and seems to feed easily into uses beyond understanding. The key texts of a liberal education are not like this. They may provide lots of information, but they are not about providing information.

Second, a liberal education's texts are not merely historical documents, though this is how they first appear to the student raised on information. Why read an out-of-date textbook, except for curiosity about how we have gotten where we are? Our texts appear to the textbook-bred student to be antiquarian curiosities, relics. A relic (whether a text, artifact, or opinion) has its place in a past series of transformations. It emerged from a certain history that shaped it, and then it sank away into a future that it may have shaped, that absconds with its relevance, and that it survives only as a corpse. When we view a relic historically, we place it in the series of transformations, and we allow it to evoke nostalgia, awe, or arrogance for how it was shaped, how it has shaped, and how it has been outgrown. For pedagogical reasons, when teaching about the past we sometimes present relics and not just the conclusions they corroborate. Our knowledge gains a surer footing, the imagination and memory are more aroused, the understanding more concrete when handling evidence rather than receiving reports.

Old texts can serve as historical documents, but that isn't what a text suitable for liberal education is. Insofar as a text expresses out-of-date information or atavistic moral standards taboo to our times, we are likely to dismiss it as a relic. We risk being led astray here about liberal education's texts by two false paradigms: the first is the model that sees all knowledge as information, and the second is its partner paradigm, the model that sees education as information-transfer and training for the skillful acquisition of results. In the artificial light of these assumptions, every old work, every book yellowing and well thumbed by ages past, looks like a dated encyclopedia.

The contrast with textbooks and relics suggests a crucial feature of a liberal education's texts: they draw us into conversation. They must be conversable. Textbooks are not conversable. They give us many claims with which we can start humane conversations, but they do not invite us to converse *with them*. Texts read as relics are also not conversable. When our attitude pigeonholes the text as a relic, we shut up our ears to its voice, psychoanalyzing away anything it has to say as merely an expression of its era.

A text read liberally shares knowledge, but only by shaping us as conversation partners. This image of conversation is the one suggested by Husserl's mature reflections of philosophy as a science. It is also the image expounded by Michael Oakeshott. According to Oakeshott, our greatest inheritance as human beings is not "an accumulating body of information," but a conversation "begun in the primeval forests and extended and made more articulate in the course of centuries" (490). Liberal education's "places of learning" are special reserves of time and space and people where this conversation is allowed to play free of many work-a-day requirements, and universities induct their students into this conversation in a special way using great texts from the great human traditions. To want to reduce the course of this conversation to the information that can be gleaned from it would push out the voices that can't just report results and would reduce our inheritance to an heirloom. This is the context that draws the truth out of the slogans about thinking critically and for oneself. We must endow this heritage to future generations as a project and not as a museum.

Works Cited

Husserl, Edmund. "Philosophy as Rigorous Science." Trans. Marcus Brainard. *The New Yearbook for Phenomenology and Phenomenological Philosophy* 2 (2002), 249-295.

———. "Denial of Scientific Philosophy. Necessity of Reflection. The Reflection [Must Be] Historical. *How* Is History Required?" In *The Crisis of European Sciences and Transcendental Phenomenology*. Trans. David Carr. Evanston, IL: Northwestern UP, 1970: 389-396.

Oakeshott, Michael. "The Voice of Poetry in the Conversation of Mankind." In *Rationalism in Politics and Other Essays*. Indianapolis, IN: Liberty Fund, 1991: 488-541.

Plato. *Meno*. Trans. George Anastaplo. Newburyport, MA: Focus Publishing, 2003.

Why Should Science Majors Waste Their Time on the Great Books?

James J. Donovan
Shimer College

The large majority of science faculty that I have met look askance at a Great Books education. Such a curriculum—the Classics, of course—might be fine for the humanities, they say, but how can it help to train young scientists? Aristotle and Ptolemy were wrong. Euclid is opaque. The other Ancients are irrelevant. Anything older than Newton is not science, and even he is unreadable. Since the corpus of science is progressive, the correct parts of the old writers is preserved, the incorrect is abandoned, and it would waste time for the student to sift through it all again. Besides, the point is to solve the problems, not know the history.

It's tempting to dismiss these colleagues as narrow in their view, but similar criticisms have been offered by some of the twentieth century's great minds. Bertrand Russell wrote,

> The subject on which you write is one about which I feel very strongly. I think the [Great Books] people are utterly absurd on the scientific side.... The broad rule is: historical approach where truth is unattainable, but not in a subject like mathematics or anatomy. (They read Harvey!) (Hook 220)

And no less than Albert Einstein states,

> In my opinion there should be no compulsory reading of classical authors in the field of science. I believe also that the laboratory studies should be selected from a purely pedagogical and not historical point of view.... I believe that [lectures on the history of science] should be treated as a kind of beautiful luxury and the students should not be bothered with examinations concerning historical facts. (Hook 220).

With such arguments against a Great Books approach for scientists, why should science majors waste their time on the Great Books?

A better question is this: is the current, non-Great-Books approach fulfilling the needs of young scientists in training? The answer seems to be no. Without reviewing the body of writing that frets over scientific education, one study (Singh et al.) by the American Physical Society illustrates the problem and shows that the current approach even erodes the science students' core competency of solving problems. This study looked at the ability of graduate physics students to address problems in quantum mechanics. The authors found (Singh et al. 43),

> [The students] were not proficient at these functional skills. They often possess deep-rooted misconceptions about such features as the meaning and significance of stationary states, the meaning of an expectation value, properties of wave functions, and quantum dynamics. Even students who excel at solving technical questions are often unable to answer qualitative versions of the same questions.

In short, when a problem is presented in equation form, as in a textbook or problem set, the students are capable; when given as a word problem, they stumble. But life is a word problem, and Nature is not kind enough to give the equations to a researcher. What to do?

The clue to that answer comes from scientists themselves. The National Academy of Sciences, the cream of American scientists, surveyed its members and their educations. The Academy identified that a disproportionate number of its members received their baccalaureate degrees from liberal arts colleges. One of those liberal arts members of the Academy, Thomas Steitz, offers the reasons for the difference: Small classes; Teachers motivated to teach and rewarded for teaching; Cross-training in the humanities and the sciences. Concerning this last item, every science education teaches students the standard way to solve a well-posed problem. The liberal arts college also teaches the student to look for alternatives and to find new ways to solve a problem.

Such an interpretation seems consistent even with Einstein's view. In addition to his comments above, he went on to say:

> On the other side, I am convinced that lectures concerning the historical development of ideas in different fields are of great value for intelligent students, for such studies are furthering very effectively the independence of judgment and independence from blind belief in temporarily accepted views.

In other words, they aid in critical thinking and interpretation—the strengths of liberal arts and especially Great-Book-based education.

Ironically, the natural sciences have long used an original-source text method in teaching, only they have reserved it for graduate students. Every good program in graduate science has a faculty seminar, a journal club, or similar environment where students and faculty read and discuss papers as a group. In addition, students are constantly reading and critiquing papers with their major professor. A Great Books approach for undergraduate science majors supplies this same education four years earlier. In the sciences, this seminar approach needs supplementation with problem-solving and tutorial sessions as well, as happens in graduate school, while keeping the focus on reading, dissecting, critiquing, understanding, and applying the knowledge in the texts.

Perhaps the reason for scientists' resistance can be found in a careful reading of Einstein's comments. He praises historical teaching for the perspective it gives while criticizing it as a body of knowledge for scientists. Many (most?) Great Books courses in the natural sciences are presented as the history of science. Science, however, includes a skill set and body of knowledge distinct from history. A ballplayer learning the history of baseball, an accountant learning the history of accounting, an artist learning the history of art will all be enriched, but to become skilled in her or his profession, each must pick up the ball, the calculator, or the brush, respectively. Scientists can see more merit in the Great Books when they see them as more than just teaching history. As an example of how they can do this, consider jointly two papers: Newton's *Opticks* and Thomas Young's "Experimental Demonstration of the General Law of the Interference of Light."

In the first book of *Opticks*, Newton makes clear his definitions and axioms with almost Euclidian precision. (Physics students usually are not exposed to this clarity of logic until they encounter the postulates of quantum mechanics in graduate school—assuming the professor doesn't skip that chapter.) Newton then painstakingly describes his experiments to demonstrate that white light consists of a mixture of different colored rays, that these rays are "differently refrangible" (refract at different angles) and that our perception of color comes from the different rays selectively reflecting from objects of different colors. Students study the paper and need to reproduce his setup and repeat experiments on their own. Further, they examine the structure of the argument along with its tight logic; Newton finds that each result may have multiple interpretations, and these are tested and eliminated, one by one. The student must master here not so much the facts relating to the spectrum (he or she learned that in grade school.) Rather, the student learns the skill of applying mathematically precise thought to the physical world.

In the third book of *Opticks*, Newton describes the experiments and observations of fringes of light, including those that later became known as Newton's Rings. He struggles with explaining these phenomena, mixing tentative explanations with clear facts. The treatment lacks the firm logical rigor of the first book. Nonetheless, Newton being Newton, his tentative ideas became dogma for the eighteenth century. Students need to distinguish between the style of argument in the two books of *Opticks* and to discern when one or the other style is appropriate in a scientific communication. (Today, the first book would likely be the review article and the results in the third book would be presented in a poster session or verbally in an unpublished conference talk.) The students are also led to better apply skepticism in approaching science and reject arguments from authority despite the way they almost invariably were taught science in grade and high schools and even some other colleges.

In "Experimental Demonstration of the General Law of the Interference of

Light," Young challenges and overthrows Newton's position that light must be cor-
puscular and not of a wave nature. As before, students need to translate Young's
description of his methods and observations into their own apparatus and replicate
his experiments. The point is not to do this as a historical experiment. Rather, it is to
learn the mental skill of designing and reproducing experiments based only on the
written description in a scientific paper. Further, students realize that Young refutes
Newton using Newton's own data, taken directly from *Opticks*. Discussions on the
political and rhetorical reasons why this was effective for Young help train the student early to deal with the sometimes Byzantine environment of academic disputes.
Further, the students sort out the issues of when and why to accept or reject a scientific hypothesis, an ability currently underutilized by the physics community in
discussions about string theory. Through it all, the primary focus remains the skills,
the "doing" of the science more than the facts. Other texts in the curriculum do, of
course, focus more on facts and scientific content and, of course, solving problems.
This example was selected to show how an original sources/Great Books approach
can give a science student essential skills in science that the traditional textbook and
problem set approach does not offer.

Finally, the argument presented in this paper carries a serious flaw that a good
scientist will spot immediately. There is no supporting data. Other than the suggestive correlation seen in the National Academy of Sciences' study, this author does not
have data backing up his claims. Yet.

A few members of the Shimer staff are in the process of designing a randomized
trial to test the efficacy of an original texts approach to teaching science to science
majors. The scientific community already has consensus and even formal standards
of content that science majors need to learn. Our plan calls for developing introductory science courses (General Chemistry, Biology, and Physics) that primarily use
original sources to present this standard content along with supplemental materials to
add details and problems sets. Yes, there is no escaping the problem sets, and a good
scientist wouldn't want to. As suggested above, the replication of experiments represents a significant component of the pedagogy, which would also teach the standard
lab skills taught in the corresponding general lab course.

The eventual goal is to conduct a randomized trial with one cohort of students
taught with a conventional textbook and the other taught with the new materials.
Student performance on written and lab tests at the end of the school year as well as
12 and 24 months later would serve as a measure of efficacy. The hypothesis is that
the students from the original sources course would match the conventionally-taught
students in the standard tests of knowledge while also showing greater retention one
and two years later. In addition, students would be tested for skills of analyzing and
critiquing arguments presented in current scientific disputes with the hypothesis that
the original sources cohort would excel at this skill. Please be patient; this will take
several years, even if the project is funded. Eventually, though, this scientist hopes to
have the data to justify the ideas in this paper.

Works Cited

Hook, S. *Education for Modern Man.* New York: Dial, 1946.

Newton, I. *Opticks.* 4th ed. New York: Dover, 1952.

Singh, C., et al. "Improving Students' Understanding of Quantum Mechanics." *Physics Today* (Aug. 2006): 43-49.

Young, T. "Experimental Demonstration of the General Law of the Interference of Light." *Philosophical Transactions of the Royal Society of London* 94 (1804). Reprinted in Morris Shamos, ed. "Great Experiments in Physics." New York: Holt Reinhart and Winston, 1959: 96-101.

Medieval Political Philosophy, Christianity, and the Liberal Arts

Benjamin Smith
Aquinas College

In what follows, I shall explain the value of studying medieval Christianity for the liberal arts by briefly exploring one of the themes of medieval political philosophy, viz., the relationship between political society as a whole and its constituent parts. To this end, I shall examine what Thomas Aquinas has to say on the matter, because of the representative value and clarity of his work. In what follows, I shall examine Thomas's teaching about the function and structure of political life, how his doctrine exemplifies the worldview of medieval Christianity, and finally the challenge his thought poses to contemporary students of the liberal arts.

According to Thomas, a good human life is ordered to a hierarchy of ends terminating in God (*Summa Theologiae* I-II.2.8). These ends are recognized as objective goods, because they actualize the human person's natural potential. On the basis of these ends, we can discover the natural law, which is a participation in God's eternal law—the providential order of the universe. It is in relation to this order, that Thomas defines the political community as the perfect community (ST I-II.94.2). By "perfect" Thomas means *complete* with respect to the good life, i.e., it is capable of providing or securing all those things required for living well (*Sententia Libri Politicorum* 1.1.23; *Sententia Libri Ethicorum* 1.1.4). In order to understand the merits of this claim, it is necessary to recognize that this principle is a formal definition and as such, it cannot be demonstrated—strictly speaking—according to the Aristotelian logic employed by medieval scholastics. So we cannot expect a deductive proof of the perfection of the polis. Nevertheless, it is possible to find dialectical grounds for supporting Thomas's definition, if we can discover an essential connection between political community and living well.

The dialectical proof of Thomas's definition begins with the hypothesis that there exists in the human person a natural inclination to political life. This claim

seems to be confirmed by observation: wherever possible we find humans forming societies of various sorts, including political communities. The reason for this
inclination is that the completion of human nature requires participation in a wide
variety of communities. Again this seems to be verified by experience. The formation
of families, participation in the economy of the local community, local cooperation
and mutual assistance, and membership in voluntary associations like businesses are
all examples of participation in community that significantly contribute to the good
life. Nevertheless, it is important to recognize that the family, the local community,
and voluntary associations are limited in scope. The family is sufficient to its proper
ends, but its ability to secure the other elements of the good life is highly attenu-
ated. Similarly, the local community can provide a context for minimal economic
life and insurance, but its limited organization and resources prevents it from doing
much more. Such communities are organized around providing specific goods, and
accordingly, they are limited by their very nature to a narrow range of capacities and
perspectives. What is needed is a comprehensive, organizing structure that will unite
and order the functions of limited communities to the good life of the whole, and
provide whatever elements of the good life are missing. The name for this kind of
structure is the polis (SP 1.1.23, 24; SE 1.4).

The polis is the sort of community with sufficient complexity, resources, stability, and security to ensure the availability of all the conditions necessary for living
well. This kind of community is necessary, because *some* natural ends and activities
are *proper* to a truly comprehensive community: enforcing justice, prohibiting grave
evils, defending against armed aggressors whether internal or external, and guaran-
teeing material aid in cases of necessity. Such activities are proper to the political
order, because only the polis can achieve these goods in a rational and efficient manner. On the other hand, often the task of the polis is simply to protect and support
the capacity of persons and limited communities in carrying out *their* proper function (ST II-II.47.10). For example, it supports business associations by enforcing
contracts, providing security for inventory, building and maintaining infrastructure,
etc. In doing so, it does not absorb the proper functions of limited communities,
but provides the external factors required for these communities to perform well. If
the polis were to absorb limited communities, it would violate the person's natural
capacity to participate in and form these sorts of communities. In doing so the polis
would violate the natural law, impoverish the good achievable by the person, and
distort its own nature (SE 1.1.4-5). The various parts of the community each have a
proper function; to undercut this diversity of functions would contravene the good of
the whole, as well as the distinct goods of the various parts. For example, if the polis
was to abrogate to itself the activity of raising children, it would deprive itself of the
natural—and most efficient—form of childrearing and would deprive parents of the
good of raising their own children.

Does it follow that we can conclude that the polis is the *perfect* community?
Although it is difficult to deny that political community is necessary for living well,
one could still object to the characterization of the polis as *complete*. After all the
family, the village, and associations are just as necessary for the good life as the
polis. To put it another way, defining the polis as "perfect" seems to ignore the contri-

butions of other communities to living well. This is a reasonable objection, because it is not the proper function of the polis to give birth to children, plant gardens, or operate the local pub, and, as I have already indicated, Thomas does not envision the absorption of limited communities by the polis. Nevertheless, there is an important relationship between the polis and limited communities, viz., a relationship of ordered dependence.

For example, the sufficiency of the family for its own proper ends is real, but tenuous. The ability of any family to provide for itself and educate children depends to a great degree on external factors, two of which stand out: peace and justice, and a beneficial relationship to other limited communities, e.g., the economy of the local community. The polis, in its comprehensive role, enables the family to achieve its ends by securing the required external factors. Employing the resources and members of the community, it protects families from internal and external aggressors, and through its legal system and infrastructure provides the conditions in which the family can engage successfully in the economy of the local community. Furthermore, the family requires a minimum of material resources, and the polis—while not replacing the economic activity of the family—serves as its material insurer of last resort. This example confirms that the polis uniquely contributes to the good life in two ways. First, it does so by providing goods that limited communities cannot provide, e.g., peace and justice. Second, it fulfills an essential supporting role insofar as it protects, coordinates, and insures limited communities. To put it simply, the polis makes it possible for limited communities to fulfill their specific functions well. What this reveals is that limited communities are really parts of the polis.

For Thomas, the polis is a whole by its unity of order (SE 1.1.4-5). It is not a substance, like an animal, because it is not a thing in its own right, nor does it absorb its parts. On the other hand, it is not merely a nominal whole, like a pile of bricks, because its unity is based on real relations, viz., relations of dependence ordered to a common end. Limited communities are parts of the polis, because they really depend on its support in order to carry out their own functions well. Thus, each limited community is related to the polis as a dependent part. Furthermore, the function of each limited community is the provision of something required for the good life. Indeed, the political community and all limited communities are oriented towards this end. It is the overarching goal that explains the existence of the polis and its support of the family, village, and associations. Thus, not only are limited communities united to the polis as dependent parts; they are also really united in a common end. The incorporation of really distinct limited communities into the polis as dependent parts means that we can attribute the contributions of limited communities to the comprehensive community of the polis. In this sense, the polis really is the perfect community, for it not only makes its own proper contributions to the good life, but it also makes it possible for its dependent parts to contribute their own specific goods.

What does this reveal about the value of studying medieval political philosophy for the liberal arts? It should be evident that Thomas's proof of the perfection of the polis depends on his ability to explain how really distinct things—like the family and the village—are united in a greater whole and at the same time remain really distinct. Thomas's attempt to bring this off is a prototypical expression of the worldview of medieval Christianity, in which the parts of the universe are harmoniously united under a hierarchy of divinely appointed ends and at the same time really remain distinct entities. It should be evident that Thomas's insistence on a balance between the unity of political community and the integrity of pre-political realities is an expression of the medieval belief of harmony within hierarchy. In fact, he has simply translated the medieval view of the universe into social and political terms. Limited communities are at once united to the polis as parts and maintain their distinction. Like a variety of other Medieval Christian thinkers, Aquinas could explain this balance in two ways. First, both sides of the equation are mutually limited by their subordination to the ends appointed to them by divine providence. Second, the harmony between the political whole and its parts could be explained according to the microcosm motif, according to which the political whole achieves rectitude by imitating the macrocosm of the order of the universe. All of the parts of the universe are unified in common ordination to the divine goodness, and yet remain really distinct substances. Each part, as a distinct instantiation of a particular essence, uniquely contributes to the goodness and beauty of the whole universe. Likewise, the many different parts of the polis, when enabled to carry out their specific functions, uniquely contribute to the good life of the political whole.

Since the Protestant Reformation and the rise of modern science, Western culture has rejected medieval intellectual models, including the model of harmonizing unity and distinction under a shared hierarchy of ends. One symptom of this development is that political discourse is divided between the extremes of egalitarian collectivism and atomistic individualism. Thomas's political philosophy—and the medieval Christianity it represents—is important to the liberal arts, because it challenges students and scholars to reflect carefully on modernity's rejection of harmony within hierarchy and the ways in which it has either succeeded or failed to balance political community and the integrity of pre-political realities. Moreover, engaging this tradition of Christian thought serves as the perfect counter to the modern tendency to compartmentalize different forms of knowledge, experience, and community from our beliefs about value and meaning. Medieval political philosophy challenges the modern student to integrate value and community, without denying the legitimate distinction and particular purposes of the parts of the community.

Works Cited

Aquinas, Thomas. *Summa Theologiae*. 1266-1273. Turin: Editiones Paulinae, 1988.
———. *Sententia Libri Politicorum*. 1269/72. In *Opera Omnia*. Rome: Leonine Edition, 1882-.
———. *Sententia Libri Ethicorum*. 1271/72. In *Opera Omnia*, vol. 47. Rome: Leonine Edition, 1882-.

Thinking about Thinking about Justice: *The Abolition of Man* and Reflections on Education

Storm Bailey
Luther College

Books are instrumental in producing certain kinds of persons. As one of the key concepts in C.S. Lewis's 1943 lectures published as *The Abolition of Man*, that idea alone connects the text to the interests and concerns of the ACTC. The substance of Lewis's argument may be especially relevant to the agenda of this particular conference, since Lewis takes on the question of whether normative concepts (such as justice or the good) are parochial, outmoded, or culturally variable. I propose to outline the argument of this text, and to suggest three ways in which it can serve our core text courses: (1) by helping students to understand just what kind of thing normative claims are, and the significance of contemporary accounts and challenges; (2) by equipping students to assess the impact of our own syllabi and text choices; and (3) by provoking our own reflection about the aims and means of education.

This short book consists of three lectures and carries the subtitle: "Reflections on education with special reference to the teaching of English in the upper forms of schools." Lewis begins lecture one with the observation that we don't pay enough attention to elementary texts, and sets out to demonstrate why that matters with an illustration from an English text he calls *The Green Book*. The authors of *The Green Book* introduce the view that normative judgments are nothing more than expressions of the speakers' feelings, though they take the form of describing objective features of the world. These authors say that "This confusion is continually present in language as we use it.

We appear to be saying something very important about something: and actually we are only saying something about our own feelings" (Lewis 3). Lewis objects that students reading this passage will end up believing two things: first, that judgments of value are statements about the emotions of the speaker, and second, that such statements are unimportant.

Lewis thinks both of these philosophical statements are false, and he spends the remainder of the book arguing against them. But, first, he makes a point that is independent of the outcome of this controversy in value theory: these views are not presented as philosophical claims to be assessed on their merits, but as assumptions. The power of these textbook authors, says Lewis, is that they are dealing with (as he put it) a schoolboy who "thinks he is 'doing' his 'English prep' and has no notion that ethics, theology and politics are all at stake." He warns that "it is not a theory they put into his mind, but an assumption, which ten years hence, its origin forgotten and its presence unconscious, will condition him to take one side in a controversy which he has never recognized as a controversy at all" (5).

The remainder of lecture one is given to further illustrations of this theory of value, and to Lewis's alternative—an account of natural law which he labels, for brevity, the *Tao*, and describes as "the doctrine of objective value, the belief that certain attitudes are really true and others really false, to the kind of thing the universe is and the kind of things we are" (18). No direct proof is offered that such a doctrine is true; Lewis's argument takes the form of showing that claims of objective value are distinct from, and not reducible to, descriptive claims, and of attempting to show the implications of rejecting the *Tao*.

The first implication is spelled out in lecture two ("The Way"), where Lewis suggests that the writers of *The Green Book* are not skeptical about all values. "They write," he says, "in order to produce certain states of mind in the rising generation, if not because they think those states of mind are intrinsically just or good, yet certainly because they think them to be the means to some state of society which they regard as desirable." Lewis is pointing out a very familiar sort of skepticism about values: skepticism about other people's values. This is not the view that other people's values (or our own) may be distorted, misguided or mistaken—that possibility should always be considered. But too often we reject the very notion of value when, and only when, it appears in the reasoning of others. To dismiss the moral judgments of others by *denying the doctrine of objective value* is to remove the foundation for *any* possible judgments of value—including our own. And it is normally the case (Lewis shows it to be the case for the authors of *The Green Book*) that our reasons for resisting the moral claims of others are moral reasons. Values used to attack the *Tao* must be derived from the *Tao* (remember that *Tao* stands for the idea of there being an objective normative order, not any particular claims about the content of that order). In this sense, Lewis says that, "the rebellion of new ideologies against the *Tao* is the rebellion of the branches against the tree" (44).

It is, of course, possible to be consistent in rejecting the doctrine of objective value, and Lewis explores this in his third lecture—from which the book takes its title. The human tendency to look at the world in normative, or imperative, or moral terms can be consistently treated as one of our rich and varied *natural* characteristics—and nothing more. What are the implications of this, in light of our increasing ability to control the natural world (or, at least, to control natural human characteristics)? Values themselves, on this view, are natural phenomena, and this means, says

Lewis, that "judgments of value are to be produced in the pupil as part of...conditioning. Whatever *Tao* there is will be the product, not the motive, of education" (61). But how will those with power as "Conditioners" decide what values (valuings) to produce in others? If we are to be consistent, we must recognize that no conception of good—superior to the conditioning process—can provide guidance.

At this point you will recognize that we are in the center of contemporary research and debate on nature, human nature, and morality. These issues are at a key intersection of science and popular consciousness, as indicated by Stephen Pinker's 2008 essay on "The Moral Instinct" and by a New York Times op-ed piece on the topic just last week by David Brooks. Brooks called his piece "The End of Philosophy." Lewis, much less optimistic, calls it the end of humanity (that is what the *Abolition of Man* means).

The value of this little book as a core text does not depend on whether Lewis is right. Its virtue lies in the care with which he distinguishes questions of value from other sorts of questions, and situates that distinction in the web of science, education, and human experience. This is crucial for our students as they seek to understand the broad range of history and texts to which we expose them. Often this distinction is one of our organizing principles—even if we aren't moral philosophers. (For example, last semester our core program at Luther College—Paideia—had "Power and Justice" as a theme. I *am* a moral philosopher, and I saw no way to adequately analyze our texts in light of that theme without being explicit about the kind of thing power is, and the very different kind of thing justice is. I used *The Abolition of Man* to explore the distinction.) And, as I have indicated, Lewis's treatment lands us squarely in the center of contemporary academic discussions of value and human nature. The book works well in conjunction with some of its cultured despisers; Simon Blackburn's naturalistic account of ethics has been useful for me—as would the Pinker piece mentioned above. I've also used *The Abolition of Man* in syllabi alongside Sartre's *Nausea*.

In addition to opening doors to the analysis of value and theories of value, Lewis's book calls our students to a critical analysis of *our* courses and *our* syllabi. Books are instrumental in producing certain kinds of persons, and nobody knows that better than we do. We have text-based core courses because we seek some good. Often—maybe more often than in other kinds of courses—the good we seek involves a conception of the kind of person we think is valuable, and we pick our texts and organize our syllabi to achieve that. We, and others around us, are seeking to *do something to* students—something that involves transformation, not merely the transmission of data. Our students really should realize that, and they should think about it. And in a very straightforward way, this text pushes them to do that.

This leads to my final point. I think this book pushes *us* to think about it too. I have been arguing that students should read this book, but Lewis's subtitle, "Reflections on Education with special reference to the teaching of English...," indicates that teachers should read it—and I am arguing for that as well. This text poses crucial questions about pedagogy and the aims of education. In the first chapter, Lewis considers the possibility that the authors of *The Green Book* want to instill certain moral sentiments in students—but not because those sentiments are good or reflect the truth (that has been denied by the *Green Book* grammarians). They seek to instill the sentiments because it benefits society for their students to have them. This, says Lewis, indicates the difference between he calls the "old education" and the "new education." He writes that:

> Whereas the old initiated, the new merely 'conditions.' The old dealt with its pupils as grown birds deal with young birds when they teach them to fly; the new deals with them more as the poultry-keeper deals with young birds—making them thus or thus for purposes of which the birds know nothing. (23)

I believe that it is possible for us to find ourselves engaged in the poultry-keeping sort of education, even if we hold that there are universal truths about human good. To the extent that we seek to inculcate moral perspectives—even true and universally obligatory moral perspectives—in our students without them being critically aware of those perspectives or those goals, I believe we indoctrinate rather than educate. Few would, I think, disagree with me, yet in practice many of the normative assumptions of our courses are simply not open to question. They are either unacknowledged, or presumed to be beyond question. We can transmit culture that way, and we can transform culture that way. But we can't liberally educate that way—it looks instead like what Lewis himself called "the magicians bargain," in which we trade our souls for power (72).

Works Cited
Brooks, David. "The End of Philosophy." *New York Times*. April 7, 2009.
Lewis, C.S.. *The Abolition of Man*. 1944. New York: HarperCollins, 2001.
Pinker, Stephen. "The Moral Instinct." *New York Times Magazine*. January 30, 2008.

The Futility of Escaping the Mind:
Invisible Man and a Liberal Education

David Dolence
Dominican University

Ralph Ellison's *Invisible Man* is a core text used in all of Dominican University's Freshmen Seminars. The overarching topic of the freshmen seminar is an exploration of the self and how it is formed. Ellison's central character is a wonderful representation of the challenging, confusing, and sometimes painful search for self and the role that a liberal education plays in that search. While the novel certainly faces the question of race in America, it is also much more. To interpret Ellison's work as *just* a novel about race in America is to diminish its more timeless value. In fact, Ellison writes in his introduction to the thirtieth anniversary edition in 1981: "my task was one of revealing human universals hidden within the plight of one who was both black and American" (xxii). The novel thus speaks not only to race, but to the timeless questions that are at the core of any quality liberal education.

The structure of the work is particularly intriguing with regard to a liberal education. Both the prologue and the epilogue are set at the same point in time and present the unnamed narrator as he reflects on his life up to that point, which is retold in the novel by our invisible narrator. We meet him in the prologue at the narrative end of his story. The end of the story is where one typically finds the "answers" and all confusion is cleared up for the reader. Ellison thus adds additional confusion by creating the structural confusion in the narrative. The end, where one typically expects to be enlightened, only begins the confusion that will carry us to the end, which is the beginning. This confusion is emphasized by two parallel lines found at the opening and closing of the novel. The line in the opening pages states, "the end is in the beginning and lies far ahead" (6) and the final line before the epilogue reads, "The end was in the beginning" (571).

This is a particularly interesting point for our freshmen seminar that deals with the formation of the self. The becoming of oneself is often seen as a progression from birth to death (much like the typical novel moving from beginning to end). In other words, I am more myself today than I was yesterday and will be more myself tomorrow than I am today. Education is also seen as something that always brings me forward. However, Ellison's narrator confuses this point from page one. As the narrator tells his story, is he relaying to us the information as it occurred at the time, or is it influenced by what has happened since? Is he seeing events clearer in hindsight, or are they actually more blurred by the person he has become through his experience? The narrator continually expresses his own confusion at who he is and what he saw then and sees now. Many students and faculty find this admitted confusion disconcerting, but it is the result of a liberally educated mind that has been set free.

The unidentified narrator spends the entire novel "hibernating" in his hole. On the surface he spends this time in telling us his story, but in truth he is for the first time seeing his own story with an open mind. In hibernation the body is at rest, but the mind continues to function; in fact, it MUST continue to function to some degree. There is a thin line between a hibernating mind and death. This is an important lesson the narrator imparts to us. Once the mind is activated, it will not let you escape the world around you, even if that world is unfair and harsh. Attempts to escape it are futile: "I couldn't be still even in hibernation. Because, damn it, there's the mind, the *mind*. It wouldn't let me rest. Gin, jazz and dreams were not enough. Books were not enough" (537). The definition that we are given of hibernation is that it is "a covert preparation for a more overt action" (13). The narrator's experiential education from the famous "royal rumble" scene, his education through the Booker T. Washington-esque college and its president Bledsoe, Mr. Norton, and his Harlem experience with both the Brotherhood and Ras are all preparation (covert to him at the time) for two important overt actions. The first overt action is the serious reflection he engages in while in his hole that leads to his first real attempt at finding his true self. The second is his decision that his hibernation must conclude.

In the end, which returns us to the beginning, our narrator has literally fallen away from society and burns the physical remnants of his manufactured self. It is again an interesting point for university freshmen that the first item to be burned for light is the high school diploma. Despite the narrator's physical and emotional removal from society, he is driven to tell us his story. He writes in the Epilogue: "So why do I write, torturing myself to put it down? Because in spite of myself I've learned some things." It was the act of trying to understand himself through his narrative that draws him "upward again" to society. One senses the philosopher's education from Plato's cave in our narrator's struggle within his hole. The philosopher must be taken from the chains "by force along the rough, steep, upward way," and this causes great confusion (515e). Our narrator's overt act of writing his story is torture, but it brings him closer to the light of understanding. Our narrator will also need to return to society as Plato's philosophers will, but for the moment he is isolated in his hole.

People often search for an escape in isolation, and in many ways it may be achieved there. That was the narrator's original intention when he decided that he would stay in his hole. "They were all up there somewhere, making a mess of the world. Well, let them. I was through... So I would stay here until I was chased out.

Here, at least, I could try to think things out in peace, or, if not in peace, in quiet. I would take up residence underground" (571). However, once the mind has been truly liberated, physical isolation is no longer the appropriate end. Our narrator's physical isolation is replaced by contemplative solitude. Solitude brings the mind to the serious questions of living: "In going underground, I whipped it all except the mind, the *mind*. And the mind that has conceived a plan of living must never lose sight of the chaos against which that pattern was conceived. That goes for societies as well as individuals" (580). One may physically hide from the world, but the liberally educated mind can never completely escape the chaos that rages outside. The mind at its highest state will attempt to see the world as it should be.

It is frequently *only* in solitude that the mind can finally see what has been invisible. This does not just include voluntary solitude, but also imposed solitude. One of the greatest statements of a man who conceived a plan of living and saw the chaos upon which that pattern was formed was written by a liberally educated man sitting alone in a Birmingham jail. An America of racial justice and equality was completely invisible to many when Reverend King wrote, "Injustice anywhere is a threat to justice everywhere. We are caught in an inescapable network of mutuality, tied in a single garment of destiny." Whether Thoreau on a pond, Twain in a "castle," King in a jail, or an unnamed narrator in a hole, one thing remains true, and that is that "withdrawal can be for the sake of return" (George). In fact, all healthy solitude must lead to return, or it will lead to madness. One of the final statements from our narrator echoes this inescapable interconnectedness: "Perhaps that's my greatest social crime, I've overstayed my hibernation, since there's a possibility that even an invisible man has a socially responsible role to play" (581).

For many students the start of a true liberal education begins in spite of themselves. Students often enter the university looking to become successful. This is simply defined as the accumulation of material wealth. This is reinforced by some universities as students are encouraged to hibernate in their single discipline or profession. Students take their major area courses and join their professional clubs, all with the same people. At the same time they wonder why they take all these "other" courses that have nothing to do with the real world of their profession. However, a true liberal education must transmit a greater responsibility. It must guide students to the self-discovery that they have "a socially responsible role to play." This can certainly be *aided* by service learning or other experiential pedagogical techniques, imposed or voluntary. Ellison's narrator gained much, good and bad, by being in the real world. However, that experience could only take productive shape after contemplative solitude. A full resume does not make a full soul.

In a university setting this is centrally accomplished through reading Booker T. Washington, W.E.B. Dubois, Richard Wright, James Baldwin, Toni Morrison, and Ralph Ellison. We must prepare students "to leave [their] hole when the moment for action presents itself" (13). We cannot predict when that moment will come or what shape it will take. Many students and faculty believe that recognizing this moment and education as a whole is about helping the student to clarify their place in the world. But a quality liberal education can have a far greater effect by invoking the opposite. The unnamed narrator was writing his story in order to find himself and remove the confusion created by his grandfather's cryptic words. However, he concludes that "the very act of trying to put it all down has confused me and negated some of the anger and some of the bitterness" (579).

The invisible man's confusion, not clarity, is what brought him to his final conclusion. He was lost, but now is found; he was in a dark hole, but now it is lit. It is partially through accepting the confusion that he comes to the realization that "the hibernation is over. I must shake off the old skin and come up for breath" (580). He has not actually found the answer to his questions but he "must come out," "he must emerge," even though he knows "there's still a conflict within me" (581). He may not have the answers, but he knows that the continued search for them is worth the pain.

It is commencement speech cliché to state that graduation is not an end, but a beginning, and that after the "completion" of your education, it is now time to take the answers learned and go out in the world and make a difference. *Invisible Man* is an immensely important text for the liberally educated precisely because it provides no answers. It asks its reader to begin at the end and forces one to continue on until the beginning is reached again. To the fettered mind this appears to be standing in place. However, contemplative solitude is not standing still and doing nothing. Ellison's narrator learns that the mind, once activated, will not go quietly into that good night or an isolated hole. One can try to escape the world, but escaping the free mind is futile. By exposing students to different voices and grander questions, we draw them out into the sun where some confusion is to be expected. Students receiving a liberal education will never accept their isolation in a modern professional hole lit by 1,369 lights powered by Monopolated Light & Power.

Works Cited

Ellison, Ralph. *Invisible Man*. New York: Vintage International, 1995.

George, William P. "Learning Alone: Solitude and the Undergraduate Education." *America: The National Catholic Weekly*. September 15, 2008.

King, Martin Luther, Jr. *Letter from a Birmingham Jail*. Historic Documents Website. 1963. <http://64.203.107.114/histdocs/BirmJail.html> April 25, 2009.

Plato. *The Republic of Plato*. Trans. Allan Bloom. New York: Basic Books, 1968.

An Exemplary Model of Core Text Education: Kuhn's *Structure of Scientific Revolutions* as a Paradigm Provider

Bryan Johnson
Samford University

I teach in a two-semester great books course called Cultural Perspectives, a fairly traditional Plato to NATO course, taught by faculty across the humanities, though primarily English and history. Though a good bit of our self-published textbook is devoted to the Enlightenment and the Scientific Revolution, Galileo's "Letter to the Grand Duchess" is the only required reading important in scientific history. *Origin of Species* is in the book, but it is not required, and I suspect that few of my colleagues teach it. An English colleague recently mocked me for teaching Darwin, while another frequently has fun at my expense for bringing to class what he calls "scientific charts and graphs" (images of the geocentric and heliocentric models of the solar system). This is not unusual, for I frequently hear colleagues in history complain that they can't teach literature and colleagues in English claim that they can't teach Greek philosophy. I've moved in the other direction over the ten-year-history of the course, teaching less to my strengths as a poet or teacher of literature, and I recently realized I'd been teaching the course as if imaginative literature didn't exist between Copernicus and Jane Austen. I have Thomas Kuhn to thank for that. There's nothing particularly innovative about using Kuhn's *Structure of Scientific Revolutions* to teach core texts in the history of science. I've used it to teach Copernicus, Galileo, Newton, Priestley, Franklin, and Darwin. Asking students to read *Structure* alongside Galileo, for instance, has the multiple benefits of historicizing his work, critiquing his scientific methodologies, demonstrating a specific set of scientific and philosophical assumptions, and arguing his influence in the history of science. For instance, Kuhn's short paragraph on the Aristotelian and Galilean interpretations of swinging pendulums (119) goes quite a long way toward helping students understand the nature of the controversy articulated in "The Letter to the Grand Duchess." There is a substantial history of objection to a humanist use of *Structure* (odd because it's history, not science.) In *What's Liberal About the Liberal Arts?* Michael Bérubé explains that many humanities professors misdirect and misinterpret Kuhn's scientific thinking by insisting that "normal science" is a humanist concept. "It is commonly charged," Bérubé explains, "that humanists embraced Kuhn so enthusiastically because he seemed to have undermined the authority and the objectivity of the sciences" (318). They tend to misread Kuhn when they apply his ideas to non-scientific work "partly because humanists' work does not proceed under the same protocols of falsifiability as those of the natural sciences" (318). But Berube does teach *Structure* as the first work in an American literature course presumably because he understands also that for a humanist, the specificity of Kuhn's scientific examples is beside the point. It is the general structure of Kuhn's history of ideas that is so valuable in the core text course, for it is the very logic of a core text education which insists on cycles of revolution and normality. The structure of any core great books course *can* imply that the history of ideas is a series of punctuation marks followed by long periods of emptiness (I'm sure most of us have experienced some version of the student question, "Are we done with Plato?"). *The Structure of Scientific Revolutions* can teach students why that prevailing description of intellectual history exists, seeming less a work of history and philosophy, than a primer for how to read and contextualize core texts. It is a model of its own ideas, functioning as a paradigm for the core texts education, continuously exposing students to the structure of the course.

It is easy in the course of reading *Structure* to forget that Kuhn is writing a history of developments in the philosophy of science. After all, he describes scientific events in such detail—on X-rays, on evolution—that it is no surprise students complain about its scientific difficulty. I've had to remind them numerous times over the semester precisely what kind of a book they are reading—a history of science, not a scientific textbook. Despite that difficulty, Kuhn reminds us early on that one of his chief concerns is how to interpret history. Reading Kuhn's explanation of the development-by-accumulation model of history early in the semester helps students understand the limitations and assumptions of core text choices while, at the same time, reinforcing their paradigmatic nature. The development-by-accumulation model can be dangerous, Kuhn speculates, because it implies that in the history of science, out-of-date beliefs and methodologies are the equivalent of myths, loaded with error and superstition. "If these out-of-date beliefs are to be called myths," he explains, "then myths can be produced by the same sorts of methods and held for the same sorts of reasons that now lead to scientific knowledge" (2). This is an essential discussion at the beginning of the semester because, isolated as discreet representations of great thinkers, it might seem to students that Galileo, for instance, replaces Aristotle or Ptolemy because he's better, smarter, and less primitive rather than the more complex reality that he operates under a different set of philosophical assumptions and has better technology.

Among philosophers of science, the most common critique of Kuhn (Peter Godfrey-Smith, Samir Okasha) has been simple inconsistency, that he seems to reject the development-by accumulation concept at the beginning of the book only to later claim that "the developmental process described in [his] essay has been a process of evolution *from* primitive beginnings—a process whose successive stages are characterized by an increasingly detailed and refined understanding of nature" (170). But Kuhn isn't Kant, giving us a philosophy of progress or human improvement as though we make a cognitive meta-leap from Ptolemy to Copernicus and Galileo. As a historian, he's much more interested in looking at specific scientific problems as they slip into the philosophical. Was oxygen discovered or invented, for instance? This is important, I tell students, because it reinforces the historical relationship between philosophy and science, a relationship that has always existed even if our disciplinary specializations suggest otherwise. It also teaches students that the Scientific Revolution was not an intellectual transcendence, that scientists didn't suddenly replace philosophers as students of nature. What Kuhn does, in other words, is create for students a conceptual structure of knowledge, one in which the ideas they study in core texts are always connected. Bérubé's complaint that a concept like scientific objectivity "as it pertains to objects like quarks and quasars" can't be understood as a humanist one—what he calls "mind-dependent matters such as justice or anxiety"—matters little in a course that invites consideration of such a question (319). There is no misappropriation of Kuhn in asking students to consider "objectivity" as a literary idea even if that relationship ultimately fails.

There are even specific, non-scientific uses of Kuhn in a great books course, parallels between his historiographical conception of scientific revolution, paradigm, and normal science and literary history. They are never exact parallels, but no one is arguing that Kuhn's thinking extends into a fully realized literary theory. We teach Jane Austen in our Cultural Perspectives course because she is representative of a set of nineteenth-century ideas, but she is also revolutionary and paradigmatic, stabilizing a concept of novelistic normality. The free indirect style Austen masters isn't an experiment in point-of-view. Just as evolution precedes Darwin, free indirect discourse extends at least to Chaucer. But Austen turns the novel into what James Wood calls a "mental chamber," inventing "a new, rapid semaphore for signaling a person's thought as it is happening. It is this innovation, the discovery of how to represent the brokenness of the mind's communication with itself, that constitutes its radicalism" (32). There are dozens of nineteenth-century novels we could teach as core texts, but Kuhn provides a general model for any Jane Austen novel over, say, Elizabeth Gaskell's *Mary Barton*, because, like a revolutionary science, Austen provides an acceptable solution to a problem of narration, how to release her characters from the authority of the third-person narrator while, at the same time, advancing the agency and internal complexity of her characters. She advances our concept of psychological verisimilitude, the norm in literary fiction since. Elizabeth Gaskell is never able to get beyond the representational problem of fully realizing characters beyond their political or religious sensibilities. In *Mary Barton*, the narrator does little more than tell us that a character is "in the midst of ...jealous anguish," that "his conscience smote him" (193). Austen would let the conscience do the smiting, for she demonstrates the revolutionary narrative science of inwardness. The lack of inwardness is moral, not political, creating a new and sustaining set of literary problems for the novelist to solve.

Even Kuhn admits that while there are "vast and essential differences" between political and scientific revolutions, parallels are self-evident: "In both political and scientific development the sense of malfunction that can lead to crisis is prerequisite to revolution" (92). This sense of malfunction is often invisible, the failure of "political recourse" forcing a change in what Kuhn calls "the institutional matrix within which political change is to be achieved and evaluated" (93). In the core course, then, *Structure* works as its own "institutional matrix" for understanding how the humanities function as "modes of community life" that develop out of crisis or malfunction. As the contemporary philosopher of science Peter Godfrey-Smith explains, we tend to see the history of science as a series of "head-to-head" competitions: "Darwin versus nineteenth-century creationism, Galileo versus Aristotelian physics, Skinner's behaviorist theory of language versus the 'cognitivist' approach of Chomsky" (213). Kuhn gives us a structure for a history of ideas that preserves those conflicts while complicating the intellectual relationships that exist between one core text and another.

Works Cited

Bérubé, Michael. *What's Liberal about the Liberal Arts? Classroom Politics and "Bias" in Higher Education.* New York: W.W. Norton, 2006.

Gaskell, Elizabeth. *Mary Barton.* New York: Oxford UP, 1987.

Godfrey-Smith, Peter. *Theory and Reality: An Introduction to the Philosophy of Science.* Chicago: U of Chicago P, 2003.

Kuhn, Thomas S. *The Structure of Scientific Revolutions.* 3rd ed. Chicago: U of Chicago P, 1996.

Wood, James. "Jane Austen's Heroic Consciousness." *The Broken Estate: Essays on Literature and Belief.* New York: Random House, 1999: 32-41.

Memory and the Classical Heritage

Homer and the Duty of Remembrance

Karl Schudt
Benedictine University

Socrates argues in *The Republic* that the poets, and specifically Homer, should not be allowed into the ideal city (and therefore not into the soul of which the city is the model *writ* large) because of their tendency to teach false and dangerous beliefs, as well as their appeal to the passions. Nevertheless, he holds out a possibility of a reprieve. If a defense can be made, not in verse, then he will gladly allow poetry to reenter (Plato 607c). Without such a defense, it is not to be allowed. In modern times, we tend not to sing songs glorifying our ancestors. Rather, we tend to write books excoriating them, usually for the crime of not being modern. We also tend to see our contemporaries in the same way: those who oppose us are not epic, not tragic, but mean, venal, and vicious. I suggest in this paper that both Plato and we moderns get it wrong, and that the Homeric, epic mode of remembrance is better, thus trying my hand at the defense of Homer.

I think that we have a duty to a certain way of remembering, lest we distort our understanding of human nature. Imagine what it would be like in Plato's city, where the bad deeds done by human beings were only to be found in moral tales, as object lessons, but never in the imitative poetic arts. Our knowledge of the ways in which one can fall from the heights, of the dangers of ambition, of how great strength or virtue can turn into its own destruction, would all be academic, subjects to be studied like specimens under glass, but not to be *felt*. Contrast this to the modern case where we so often look to the lowest of motives. What do we know of virtue? We doubt its appearance, and look for some other motivation. What would either the denizens of Plato's city or we know of the greatness of human beings, if we took our own stories too seriously?

The duty of remembrance arising out of our common humanity requires that we think of others as well as the facts will bear. The reason is one that Plato would surely appreciate: How could a culture retain its integrity as a culture when the originators and heroes are remembered as villains? One does not wish to pretend that no mistakes or crimes have been committed, but perhaps they ought to be spoken of in ways that still recognize the greatness. Such a mode of remembrance can be found in epic poetry, in which the terrible mistakes and failures of the heroes are presented in ways that still preserve the characteristics that make them heroic. It's usually the good characteristics, in fact, that lead to the tragedy. My primary example will be that failure of failures: Hector.

The device which serves first of all to ensure that the greatness of the individual be preserved is the *epithet*, the description that is used either in place of the name of the character, or along with the name of the character. This is most likely originally a metrical device to ensure that one can always fit the poetry into dactylic hexameter, as the performer of the poem may choose that epithet that gets one to the end of the line best. Some examples are "Swift- footed Achilles," "Brilliant Hector," "Agamemnon Lord of Men," "Son of Peleus," and so on. This may have been a standard tool of performance for improvisational poets in the bronze age, but just as Mozart elevated the stock phrases and patterns of the music of his time into genius, Homer takes the epithets and uses them brilliantly to advance the meaning of the story. It is always good to pay attention to the epithets.

Heroes are always presented with their epithets; perhaps not in every line, but often. It is like clothing, or perhaps the armor that they take such pride in and fight over. To appear without it would be to appear naked. Even when they are at their worst, they are not so dishonored by Homer. Take, for example, the nadir of Agamemnon, in Book IX. He has just suffered a day of defeat at the hands of the Trojans, to the extent that they are threatening to set fire to the ships. He is ready to give up in defeat and return to Mycenae. Yet, he is still called "Son of Atreus," and even "Lord Marshall Agamemnon" while he is summoning his soldiers to hear his speech commanding retreat. The effect on the reader or the hearer is that, despite the tearful cowardice of Agamemnon, this is no mean person, but a great man humbled. His claim to respect is that he has the most soldiers, which, in a Bronze-Age Achaea full of isolated cities, is not a small feat. To get thousands of men to follow in a military expedition, to obey one's commands, is not a small thing: Achilles' rebellion is an *exception*. Tragic he is, brought down by his over-confidence that greatness lies in numbers and wealth (making "Lord Marshall" to some degree ironic), yet still worthy of respect.

Epics are worth emulating also in that almost all of the characters are sympathetically portrayed, even those fighting on the opposing side. *The Iliad* has no "bad guys," no stock characters for the hearer to hate. The Achaeans fight the Trojans in a story written for the heirs of Achaean civilization, but Priam, Helen, and even Paris are sympathetic characters. Hector himself could be the most loved of all those who fought at Ilium. His relationship with his wife and child and his sense of duty to the city make him seem very admirable, despite the fact that he was the enemy of the Achaeans, whose heirs were the audience of the *Iliad*. One finds Virgil similar: Dido may be the founder of Rome's ancient enemy, driven to suicide by mad love, but she is still the woman who crossed an ocean to find a refuge for her people, a lawgiver in the wilderness.

Hector is Brilliant Hector, of the shining helmet, but is also the reason for the fall of Troy, as his wife and Polydamas point out, overreaching in his desire for honor.

With the retreat of Achilles from the field, Hector has overextended his forces and surrendered his greatest asset, the citadel. Andromache warns him that "this might of yours will be your doom" (Homer 6: 407). She then goes on to recommend that he bring his army back to the weakest part of the walls, "by the wild fig tree" (Homer 6: 433), perhaps comparing her husband's wild spirit to the tree—he should root himself in his city as the tree had. It is the correct advice, as the reader or hearer finds out when the Achilles returns to the fight, devastates the Trojan army, and kills Hector outside the walls. If he had taken his wife's advice, he would have not fallen, and Troy could have endured.

Andromache and Polydamas both criticize Hector's plan (Homer 12:216) and point out the simple truth of warfare: if you have an easily defensible position, defend it. It had worked for ten years, after all. Even after Hector's death, it took a stratagem for the Achaeans to win. Hector knows it, too, at the end. As Achilles races toward the final battle, Hector considers whether he could retreat, but cannot, because of his shame at what others will say: "Hector, trusting in his own might, brought ruin on the army" (Homer 22:107). He can't return, because of the same pride that has ruined him, but it turns out that his wife was right all the time. He stays to fight Achilles, and is killed easily. He dies, his wife is widowed, and shortly thereafter, his city falls, his child is killed. Everything he has worked for ends up in failure, and Hector himself knows it before he dies. At the end, before he is killed by Achilles, he contemplates running away, back into the walls, but decides that he cannot because of the shame it would bring him. He recognizes his failure, but compounds it because of the very characteristic that made him the greatest of the Trojans, his pride.

Hector is a failure, but he is still sympathetic, the favorite character of most readers. How is this done? Homer never presents him as having base motives. His failure is not a result of cowardice, of malice, or of moral weakness. Not even the Achaeans would dare make such accusations. In the construction of the epic, Hector is *tragic*, especially in that the cause of his downfall, pride, is also the cause of his greatness. His is a grand failure because it arises out of a grand characteristic, the constant seeking to be better, to be the best, the same thing that he hoped for his son: "Zeus, all you immortals! Grant this boy, my son, may be like me, first in glory among the Trojans" (Homer 6:476-478). He is still Brilliant Hector, with flashing helmet.

This way of describing a person could perhaps be used in the modern world. We wouldn't have to use a lute, or sing in dactylic hexameter. How would it work? The epithets: those we oppose, or those we consider to have failed or to have done evil, should still be referred to with respect, making frequent mention of the parts of their character that deserve admiration. Even if it is a mere "lord of men," the mention of the glory of the man will be beneficial. If the man or woman has indeed failed, as so many of us have, we should do the courtesy of attributing this failure to the best part of the person, the greatest virtue. In other words, we should make tragic heroes out of them. Perhaps the motives we attribute to them aren't *strictly* true, but the fact is that they should be true, or should be believed to be true, not in contradiction to the facts, but because to allow great men or women to be diminished, laughed at, made fun of, even when things have gone wrong, is to commit a sin against the entire human race. If one person is ridiculous, we all are. Hector was a failure, but not ridiculous. If we mock him, if we do not give him his due, then we mock ourselves, and remove the models for our aspirations. The duty of memory is to remember truthfully, but also to remember with an eye to the future, and to the possibility of greatness in ourselves.

The heroes of the epics are generally tragic, falling by their own weight. Yet, they *had* weight. We now generally minimize the character of those who come before us, but are we wise to do so? It is ultimately a question of human nature, whether it is capable of wrestling with the gods, or whether it is simply an arrogant animal. The nobility of the human race is at stake, I think, and the usual way of remembering the past tends to deny this nobility. By denying it, we can therefore close off the possibility. Socrates argues in *The Republic* that Homer and other poets should not be allowed in the ideal city because the stories, even if true, would be detrimental to the morals of the city. But perhaps the Homeric way of telling stories is better: not whitewashing human failures, but giving those who failed the courtesy of assuming the best motives, and presenting our ancestors and others not as small people failing in small things, but giving them the benefit of the doubt, thus preserving both their claims to greatness and our store of heroes.

Works Cited

Homer. *Iliad*. Trans. A.T. Murray. Cambridge, MA: Harvard UP, 1999.

Plato. *The Republic*. Trans. C. D. C. Reeve. New York: Hackett: 2004.

Justius Lipsius and the Re-Invention of Stoicism

Andrew Terjesen
Rhodes College

NeoStoicism is not something that is regularly taught in core classes focusing on the Renaissance and Early Modern period, nor is it usually included in classes exploring the development of political ideas in the West. This is an unfortunate omission as NeoStoicism had a large role to play in the development of classic liberal thought. The cosmopolitanism of NeoStoicism, coupled with the emphasis on individual liberty, were key elements in the development of the classic liberal conception of the state. The attempt to make Stoicism relevant to sixteenth- and seventeenth-century Christian audiences produced a new kind of Stoicism that departed in important ways from the Stoicism of the ancient world.[1] Like many other aspects of the Renaissance, NeoStoicism is not so much an appropriation of a remembered past as it is an invention representing a past that never was. Consequently, classic liberalism, insofar as it relies upon a NeoStoic foundation, is based upon a fiction; and the modern democracies that grew out of classic liberalism have inherited some of the problems attached to that fiction.

Although Justus Lipsius (Joest Lips) was not the first to try and reconcile Christianity and Stoicism during the Renaissance, his *On Constancy* had the largest impact in spreading what would become known as NeoStoicism. The book was translated into English four times between 1594 and 1670. Given his history, it is not surprising that Lipsius was drawn to Stoicism. *On Constancy* is presented as a dialogue between Lipsius and his friend Langius. In 1572, Lipsius's property was seized by Spanish troops as part of the Eighty Years' War between the Low Countries of the Netherlands and Spain. The character Lipsius complains of his public misfortunes, and Langius (the voice of the author Lipsius in this dialogue) offers him a consolation from the Stoic tradition. The title *On Constancy* is taken from Seneca's *De*

Constantia Sapientis ("On the Constancy of the Wise Person") with which it shares some similarities.

Like any good Stoic, Langius counsels Lipsius that "our minds must be so confirmed and conformed that we may be at rest in troubles" (Lipsius 32). To do this he needs to change his mind so that it is no longer "wrongfully subjected to affections" (Lipsius 36). The Stoic emphasis on focusing on our attitudes towards events—as opposed to the events themselves—is clearly conveyed in these passages. "Constancy" becomes defined as "a right and immovable strength of the mind neither lifted up nor pressed down with external or causal accidents" (Lipsius 37). As presented by Langius, Stoicism offers a program by which we can get our emotional reactions under control by putting things into perspective.

In reintroducing Stoicism as a "live option" for Renaissance thinkers, Lipsius confronts head on what he sees as the main obstacle to Stoicism's acceptance. The Stoics did not have a concept of free choice; instead everything was determined by nature, which was also supremely rational, and God, what he referred to as the two "impieties" of Stoicism. Langius states that Stoicism is compatible both with the idea of free choice and a God free from necessity. His reason for thinking that is that Stoicism is not committed to the idea that God is limited by necessity; instead God is only limited by God because God is equivalent to Fate in Roman Stoicism (Lipsius 65). In dealing with the problem of free choice for every being other than God, Langius appeals to the distinction between Providence and Fate/Destiny (Lipsius 67). Our fates are not necessitated, because while we are destined to choose to do X, we are not necessitated to do X. To accomplish this metaphysical feat, Langius states that "we [presumably NeoStoics] do not make the causes always natural" (Lipsius 69).

As presented in *On Constancy*, this appears to be the only real divergence from Roman Stoicism—Lipsius restores the freedom of God and individuals using the Stoics' own conceptual tools. However, this difference is only the surface expression of a deeper difference between Stoicism and NeoStoicism. The reason why Lipsius must assert the freedom of God and individuals is to make room for moral choices (both by God and human beings) in accordance with the Christian conception of sin and salvation. To do this, Lipsius must also accept the vision of the universe that corresponds with a Christian notion of free choice—that there are goods we can choose or fail to choose. This is actually a very sharp break from ancient Stoicism.

According to ancient Stoicism, as found in writers like Seneca, one must not simply control one's emotions—we must be free of them. As Seneca points out in *De Constantia*, "if you say that he [the Stoic] will bear injury calmly, he has no peculiar advantage; he is fortunate in possessing a common quality" (Seneca 55). Stoicism is about more than realizing that we must put up with hardship or that things are not as bad as they seem. Instead, a true Stoic cannot be injured by those things that the average person considers misfortunes. As Seneca explains, "Injury has as its aim to visit evil upon a person. But wisdom leaves no room for evil, for the only evil it knows is baseness, which cannot enter where virtue and uprightness already abide" (Seneca 61). Seneca is not saying that we need to be unconcerned about the things that are fragile (like wealth and honor—some of the things mentioned by Lipsius as "false goods" (Lipsius 42), but rather he is saying that we should learn to disregard all things other than our virtuous attitude. Every kind of good must be despised, because "if the small things do not move him, neither will the greater ones" (Seneca 92). Although Lipsius does acknowledge that people mistakenly cling to some "goods," he does not embrace the stronger Stoic position. Instead he associates many of the false goods and false evils with the body, while the soul and mind (and God) are the source of true goods and true evils (Lipsius 39).

The extreme nature of the Stoic attitude is exemplified by the example of Stilbo, who is described in Seneca's *De Constantia*. Stilbo has lost his wealth, his position, his family, and everything else to conquest. When the conquerors asked Stilbo if he lost anything, he replied with an unqualified "no": "I have all that is mine with me" (Seneca 63). Such an attitude can seem harsh to the modern reader—his daughters were nothing to him? Lipsius tries to soften that image of Stoicism in *On Constancy*. Langius presents NeoStoicism as more of a therapy for dealing with extreme misfortune. He encourages Lipsius to "weigh all things in the balance of reason" (Lipsius 38) and to be "neither puffed up nor pressed down with either fortune" (Lipsius 41). The wise man is someone who is able to "scatter abroad the thick mist and behold things in clear light" (Lipsius 113). Lipsius' NeoStoics are not people who think that only virtue has value. Instead they think that people have developed a distorted picture of what is and isn't valuable. This interpretation makes sense if you consider that Lipsius' references to problems with "false goods" focus on the idea that we think ourselves more important (puffed up) because of that good. As Langius puts it, we need to "esteem all things according to their worth" (Lipsius 79). But this appears to presume that there is something that has worth apart from virtue. At the end of the dialogue, Langius' final strategy is to tell Lipsius to reflect on how much worse things were in the past. Instead of telling Lipsius to let go of the idea that some things are "good" (apart from virtue) and some things are "bad" (aside from vice), Langius is telling Lipsius that things aren't as bad as they seem.

Lipsius' reluctance to separate us from all external things makes sense in a Christian context. To begin with, if we have choice, we need something to choose, which is what we would normally call "goods." In addition, according to Christian doctrine, God is good, and all things created by God are good. To deny the goodness of things like friends and family would undermine that Christian concept. In the NeoStoic world, God loves us, the world is beautiful, certain things in our lives are good, *etc.* It is not that Lipsius' interpretation of Stoicism is without foundation. Seneca and the other Stoics make it clear that virtue (i.e., reason or God) is the only good, but virtue is also thought of as an understanding of how nature works. Thus, Seneca does talk about preferring certain things over others in order to preserve the universe. Lipsius acts as if there is little difference between that which is to be "preferred" because it preserves the world and that which is "good." Langius tells the character Lipsius, "let us lift up ourselves, and whatsoever damage we sustain privately, let us know that it does good in some part of the whole world" (Lipsius 96). To support his point, he quotes a letter of Seneca's: "A wise man should not take in ill part whatever happens to him. But let him know that those same things which seem to annoy him do belong to the preservation of the whole world" (quoted in Lipsius

97). It appears that Langius (and the author Lipsius) is equating that which preserves the world with something we can call "good." Once again, this makes sense from a Christian perspective, but not from an ancient Stoic perspective. Lipsius makes it work because he invents a Stoic God who never existed, one who is not simply a rational creature that is equivalent to the cosmos, but is also a personified being who has a will to choose what is good for the world. This may seem like a small change, but it has profound implications for the NeoStoic notion of liberty.

Seneca defines "liberty" as "having a mind that rises superior to injury, that makes itself the only source from which its pleasures spring, that separates itself from all external things in order that man may not have to live his life in disquietude" (Seneca 103). In the context of ancient Stoicism, liberty is valuable because it embodies the Stoic refusal to attribute value to anything other than virtue. This is very different from Lipsius' portrayal of freedom as the ability to choose things (not just virtue) with a clear understanding of their real value. This may seem like splitting hairs, especially since Stoics do acknowledge that there is a rational plan to the universe (as described by Seneca in his *De Providentia*). The reason it matters is that the Christian God has a will that cannot be submitted to the necessity of rational principles. Things are good because God wills them so, not because they embody a rational principle. Since NeoStoic freedom involves choosing the right goods (and avoiding certain evils) and since the notions of good and evil are based on God's will, there can be debate over what God has actually willed. God's intentions cannot be studied the way the universe can. An ancient Stoic would have a much easier time trying to determine what preserves and what destroys the universe, than a modern NeoStoic would have trying to figure out what God wants.

Admittedly, classic liberalism is not committed to the Christian worldview of Lipsius. However, the notion of freedom in classic liberalism seems to be derived from this invention of the NeoStoics. Liberty is equated with a freedom (of mind) to choose what one thinks is best (even if it is not understood to be a God-determined best). It is this understanding of freedom that invites a common criticism of classic liberalism: liberty seems to be a good, so it appears wrong to restrict it, and as a result we must tolerate the intolerant. Similarly, it is not clear what the basis is for regarding some things as good and others as bad. The appeal to God will not work in any pluralistic society, including the world of Justus Lipsius, where Catholics and Protestants battled over how to understand God. The classic liberal solution is to give everybody as much freedom as they can (without infringing on others), but this freedom doesn't change the fact that citizens think that certain people in the state have the wrong view. And it doesn't avoid battles over when to limit freedom, since people can disagree over what constitutes a limit on freedom. Is a ban on legal discrimination against homosexuals limiting the freedom of someone who considers homosexuality morally wrong?

The ancient Stoics did not have to wrestle with these problems because freedom meant withdrawing from the idea that there were any goods (other than virtue) in order to engage in a dispassionate study of an impersonal universe. From the ancient Stoic point of view, the person who considers homosexuality morally wrong is mistaken. At best, they could say that homosexuality is "dispreferred" by the order of the universe. But in order to say that, they would have to have a logical proof based on a study of the universe that any rational person would accept. Unlike our modern notion of freedom, where people are free to disagree, the Stoics held that all truly free people would converge on the same judgments concerning what is to be "preferred" and what is to be "dispreferred." After all, Seneca presents constancy as a quality of the wise (and perhaps nothing is more telling about Lipsius' reinvention of Stoicism than how he shortens the title of Seneca's work so that he omits the wise person). It is something that is achieved once one understands the Stoic point about the nature of good and other aspects of the Stoic view of the universe. In NeoStoicism, constancy is a quality that anyone can achieve, because in the Christian worldview everyone has the freedom to choose. Although classic liberals did not necessarily appeal to Christianity in their discussion of freedom, they did endorse the idea that liberty was something that preceded wisdom, which is very different from the Stoic idea that we attain liberty after we achieve wisdom about the true nature of the universe. Moreover, by separating the exercise of liberty from the attainment of wisdom, classic liberals can be challenged concerning the use of liberty in a way that the ancient Stoics could not. Would classic liberalism be better served by adopting a thoroughly Stoic view, as opposed to the NeoStoic reinvention? Perhaps, though it is beyond the scope of this paper to explore the plausibility of a true Stoic view for a modern audience.

Note

1. For a more thorough discussion of the role NeoStoicism, and Justus Lipsius in particular, played in shaping Early Modern political thought, please see Gerhard Oestreich's *Neostoicism and the Early Modern State.*

Works Cited

Lipsius, Justus. *On Constancy.* Trans. Sir John Stradling. Exeter, UK: Bristol Phoenix Press, 2006.

Oesterich, Gerhard. *Neostoicism and the Early Modern State.* Trans. David McLintock. Cambridge: Cambridge UP, 1982.

Seneca. "De Constantia." *Moral Essays, Volume I.* Trans. John W. Basore. Cambridge, MA: Harvard UP, 2003.

"Literaturizing" Life: Reading and Misreading Homer in Petronius' *Satyricon*

Michael Mordine
Trinity College

The *Satyricon* is one of the most literarily self-conscious texts in the classical corpus, a work which insistently reminds the reader through its pervasive intertextuality that he or she is not only reading a text but reading a tradition. This is also true for the characters themselves, who continually interpret and con*text*ualize their experiences through the framework of previous stories, be it epic or history, tragedy or farce. The characters understand and, effectually, create their world and their own reality *through* literature. So, too, the author and we as readers sharing a literary tradition share also in the creation and understanding of this fictive world. The difference between the characters, on the one hand, and Petronius and his readers, on the other, is the degree of success or failure. For the characters, the more they apply literature to their world, the less they seem to succeed in that world. For us, the reverse is true. In this paper I examine the utility of Homeric references in the *Satyricon* as a paradigm for "reading" life through literature: while this has comically disastrous effects for the *characters,* who thus serve as a kind of hermeneutical anti-model for the use of the literary past, nevertheless Petronius' engagement with his literary antecedents provides the *readers* with a rich model for framing our understanding of the present (his present) through our shared past as readers.

A perennial and, I think, universal problem for teachers of literature is the difficulty of getting students to see themselves in the texts they read, to see how these works, often written by people dead for a couple of thousand years, relate to themselves and their lives. How can and does the past inform the present? In the *Satyricon* the issues of reading, reception, and relating the literary past to oneself and one's present time are crucial. This is a text which is consciously and indeed pervasively "aware" of the past, and the literary past in particular, both through explicit discussions and through a rich intertextual engagement with antecedent texts which were, even for Petronius and his readers, classics of literature. The question I want to ask is broadly, then, how the past is used and misused to understand the present: specifically, the failure of the characters and, by contrast, the success of Petronius in using the literary past to frame one's understanding of the present.

The main characters in the *Satyricon*, Encolpius and Ascyltus, are students themselves: the Latin term is *scholastici*. Add to them their fickle slave/"boy toy" named Giton. (Due to the fragmentary nature of the text, it is unclear whether Giton is an actual slave or merely pretending to be one.) However, all three are, as it were, the complete antitheses of our modern students: where today's students fail to relate literature to their own lives, Encolpius, et al. do not seem to be able *not* to do so. Virtually all of their experiences are self-referentially framed as literary events; this is a fundamental source of the *Satyricon*'s humor. So, for example, when Ascyltus takes advantage of Encolpius's absence to "impose himself" upon Giton, and Giton, who is hardly an innocent, puts up a fight, Ascyltus references one of the fundamental, indeed foundational, stories of Roman identity: the tale of the chaste Lucretia who was raped by the brutal Tarquin. The comedy arises from the ridiculousness of the application of this serious historical event, to the sordid, contemporary scenario they are in: Ascyltus says, "Well, if you're going to play Lucretia, I'm happy to play Tarquin" (*Sat.* 9.5).

So the characters in the *Satyricon*, and Petronius himself, frame various events of the novel through reference to their literary past, be it Livy's history or Virgil's *Aeneid*. It is Homer, however, who provides the hermeneutic text *par excellence* for both the characters and the author. Thus, in a later scene where Encolpius tries to hide Giton from Ascyltus, he puts him under the mattress in a seedy hotel just like, he says, Ulysses hiding under the ram (*Sat.* 97.4). Unfortunately, Giton can't stop himself from sneezing and revealing his hiding place: again, a comic disjunction between an elevated literary antecedent and a sordid present reality. This is the recurring leitmotif of the characters' application of the past to their present: it is comically inappropriate and ineffectual, highlighting the disjunction between their perception of the world and the unheroic reality of it. At one point, Encolpius, deprived of his lover Giton, stews at a beachside hotel à la Achilles and finally works himself up to grabbing a sword and taking vengeance, but a soldier stops him when he notices that Encolpius is still wearing his bedroom slippers. As readers, it is precisely in our recognition of this disjunction that we find the humor. The more we know, the more we have read, the funnier the *Satyricon* is.

The characters of the *Satyricon*, on the other hand, are singularly inept in applying the literature they have learned to the contemporary world and their experiences in it. They are, in fact, like the students described in the opening fragment of the novel, a diatribe in which a teacher of rhetoric, named Agamemnon of all things, complains that schools produce idiots since all they teach them are crazy speeches about "pirates standing on beaches" and "tyrants writing orders for sons to cut off their fathers' heads" (*Sat.* 1.3). (The composition of hypothetical speeches was a mainstay of higher education and rhetorical training throughout the classical period.)

While the characters fail at "literaturizing" their own lives, by contrast Petronius himself succeeds quite brilliantly in "literaturizing" his fictive world and its comic representation of contemporary reality, and we readers tag along for the comic ride. The overarching plot of the *Satyricon* has long been posited to be a parody of Odysseus' wanderings driven by the wrath of Poseidon (Courtney 152-57). Encolpius, in contrast, is driven by the wrath of the ithyphallic god Priapus: literature becomes sex farce. Indeed, Encolpius, under the guise of Polyaenus (an epithet of Ulysses) has a frustrating liaison with a woman known only by her nomme d'amour: Circe (*Sat.* 126.1-139.4).

For the rest of this paper I would like to explore what I see as additional Homeric allusions in the Satyricon, in the *Cena* episode in particular, and how those references can deepen our understanding of the text. In striking contrast to the characters' failure at intertextualizing their lives, Petronius' strategy of intertextualizing the world is a great literary and hermeneutic success.

The dinner party of Trimalchio has long been recognized as inspired and informed by a number of literary antecedents (especially Horace's *Satire* 2.8 and Plato's *Symposium*). However, I would like to suggest that the Phaeacian episode of the *Odyssey* and the adventures that Odysseus tells there may be considered another important text through which we may better read and understand specific moments in the *Cena* and the *Cena* generally. The Phaeacian episode is arguably the most famous dinner party in all of classical literature, at least on a par with Plato's *Symposium* and, given the overall use of the *Odyssey* as a framing device, one might be encouraged to find similarities between the two to be especially suggestive. To give one a couple of parallels: Odysseus awakes on Scheria, the Phaeacian island, to find Nausicaa and her friends playing ball; in the prelude to the *Cena* episode, Encolpius et al. have their first exposure to Trimalchio in the baths where he too is playing ball. Like Odysseus following Nausicaa, they follow Trimalchio to his palatial residence. At the entrance, where Odysseus had encountered golden life-like, indeed living, statues of dogs guarding the palace, Encolpius mistakes a painting of a guard dog, the *cave canem* mural, for a real dog. In turn, Odysseus' account of his adventures seem to have echoes in the *Cena*: there are tales of witches and of humans transformed into animals, and the *Cena* itself turns out to be a journey into an underworld; the first dish served has soporific and narcotic ingredients just as the Lotus Eaters are the first of Odysseus' otherworldly adventures; when Encolpius and his friends later try to escape they find themselves trapped between a monstrous dog and a fishpond—a comic deflation of the Scylla and Carybdis episode (in both instances the Latin encourages the linkage).[1]

Now what is the narrative utility of such evocations? In other words, beyond the pleasures of recognition, how does our appreciation of Homer in the text inform our understanding of its content? How does the past provide insight into the present?

Consider the wealthy host Trimalchio, who might seem at first a kind of Alcinous with a remarkably prominent wife (his Fortunata to Alcinous' Arete). However, Trimalchio instead turns into, or is revealed as, a revolting and monstrous creature who keeps his dinner guests trapped in his dining room, a modern-day bourgeois Cyclops. Like Odysseus and his crewmen, Encolpius and his companions are uninvited guests who hope to be entertained with a free meal but are then trapped in their host's dwelling and forced to participate in and watch a nauseating display of eating. As Encolpius experiences the *Cena*, and as we readers view that experience, it becomes apparent that Trimalchio's idea of hospitality turns out to be a sickening display of gastronomic excess. Like the Cyclops, Trimalchio appears in his dwelling after his guests have arrived; he departs at will, leaving the guests in the dining room, and the guests are frustrated in their attempt at escape, only managing it after Trimalchio has sunk into a morass of drunkenness, self-pity, and a simulated death.

The Cyclops and Trimalchio are particularly analogous as "uncivilized" hosts who get drunk and disgust their guests. After Odysseus gets the Cyclops drunk, for example, he falls asleep and "wine and bits of human flesh came forth from his gullet, and he vomited in his heavy drunkenness" (*Od.* 9.374-5). Similarly, Encolpius says that "the affair was reaching the height of nausea when Trimalchio, weighed down by the most foul drunkenness [had a fresh entertainment brought in]" (*Sat.* 78.5). This is the moment when our heroes manage to make their escape.

With Trimalchio aligned first with Alcinous and then with Polyphemus, culinary excess in the *Cena* is thus configured in paradoxically antithetical terms as both the extremes of civility and coarseness—as both "Phaeacian" and "Cyclopean." This is a paradox of modern hospitality, Petronius seems to be saying: food, and eating—features which are designed to demonstrate the cultivated nature of the host by means of the lavish attentions paid to the guests and by the serving of the finest products with haute-cuisine preparation—are in their very excess revealed to be uncultured and uncivilized. Defined by its degree of urbanity, the conception of "culture" in Trimalchio's world, as configured here by Petronius through Homer, is ultimately determined more by the satisfaction of bodily needs and baser pleasures than with intellectual nourishment and conversation.[2] In effect, Petronius conflates the hyper--hospitality of the Phaeacians with the perverted, anti-hospitality of the Cyclops to create a picture of *uncultured culture* in the *Cena*.

Trimalchio, who at least has aspirations for culture, is a cautionary tale of the failure of an incomplete liberal education: he thinks he knows his Homer and fancies himself a literary critic. A little knowledge is a dangerous thing. (At one particularly egregious point Trimalchio refers to the story of Daedalus who shut Niobe up in the Trojan Horse—a farrago of mismatched mythology.) But Trimalchio is funny precisely because *we* have by contrast a lot, or at least a lot more, knowledge of the past as literature. *We* do know our Homer, and so we know the absurdity of Trimalchio.

This "literary" depiction of Trimalchio, the nouveau riche freedman, typical of the sort of social and class upstart who became prominent in the early empire, gives us greater insight into Petronius' view of his contemporary world. And what Petronius does through this use of the literary past is to provide a deeper understanding of, for him, a present-day social and cultural crisis. Reading Trimalchio as both an Alcinous and a Cyclops reveals that for Petronius, the very nature and idea of culture is under contention. If you apply your Homer, Petronius seems to suggest, you will see that we are now in a world where those things which should be indices of cultural achievement are instead the perverse evidence of a sort of systemic anti-cultural decay.

The characters' misuse of Homer shows both an awareness and an acceptance of the centrality of the "classics." In turn, we readers, as part of that classical tradition, recognize that their attempts to, as it were, apply that literary tradition to themselves in a *literal* way is a comic absurdity. But the figurative application of that tradition—Petronius' allusive engagement with it—does inform his present (fictive) world and can deepen our understanding of it precisely by bringing into relief the stark contrasts between the literary past and the oh-so-sordid present.

Notes

1. These allusions will be detailed in a forthcoming article.
2. The disjunction between the sophisticated and the coarse, between mental and bodily functions and urges, is a central thesis in Conte's analysis of Encolpius' frustrated strivings for the "sublime."

Works Cited

Conte, Gian-Baggio. *The Hidden Author: An Interpretation of Petronius' Satyricon.* Trans. Elaine Fantham. Berkeley: U of California P, 1996.

Courtney, Edward. *A Companion to Petronius.* Oxford: Oxford UP, 2001.

Hobbes's Thucydides and Homer: Translation as Political Thought

Laurie M. Johnson Bagby
Kansas State University

Thomas Hobbes spent much time in his *Elements of Law, De Cive,* and *Leviathan,* criticizing the core texts of his culture—the classics of Greece and Rome, and the way those classics were taught at universities. He blamed them for creating a seditious mentality among his country's elite. It is ironic, however, that he chose to translate two of the greatest classical authors: Thucydides at the beginning, and Homer at the end of his very long career. Often, these translations are ignored by scholars interested in Hobbes's politics, but when they are not, their purpose is debated and continues to be questioned. This paper will briefly take a look at both, and explore to what extent it is possible to see Hobbes's political thought in his translations.

Long before the English Civil War, Hobbes learned lessons about the influence of ideology and demagoguery from Thucydides. His translation of Thucydides was his first published work. It is easy to see the influence of the ancient historian in Hobbes's later political thought, in his view of human nature, what constitutes effective government, and in his skepticism toward religion.

Hobbes took from Thucydides the idea of the "three greatest things" that motivate human beings: fear, honor, and interest.[1] But, as we know, he remained more hopeful than Thucydides about the possibility that fear could overcome the destructive longing for power and honor which was so much a part of human nature. Whereas Thucydides treated the destructive power of love of honor, or *hubris,* as a permanent element of human nature, Hobbes developed a program for rooting it out, and therefore permanently changing the trajectory of politics.

Another lesson about government that Hobbes took from Thucydides was the ineffectual nature of direct democracy, and the harm that comes from the selfish leadership in such a government. Frederick Whelan notices this influence when he writes, "the lesson that Hobbes drew from Thucydides...was that reckless and dangerous policies are likely to result from the eloquence of demagogues who compete to flatter the vanity of their popular audiences" (63).

Hobbes also learned from Thucydides a deep skepticism about the danger and ineffectiveness of religious beliefs, which he often equated with superstition. As a result, he took a dim view of those whose religiosity hindered clear-eyed reason. In his "Life and History of Thucydides," which precedes his translation, for instance, Hobbes associated Thucydides with Anaxagoras (and, it would seem, with himself), "whose opinions, being a strain above the vulgar, procured him the estimation of an atheist" (11). He cited Thucydides' treatment of the general Nicias as overtly critical of superstition (12). One scholar even attributes Hobbes's often terse and graceless translation of Homer at the end of his career to what he learned much earlier from Thucydides: "Like Thucydides, whom he admired enough to translate into English, Hobbes minimizes anything to do with gods or women" (Riddehough 59).

In Hobbes's translation of Thucydides' *History*, we see a forthright admiration for Thucydides as the "most politic historiographer that ever writ." In his footnotes to the translation, we can see that Hobbes clearly gleaned ideas that resonated throughout the rest of his political work. For instance, in the fifth note to Book 1, Hobbes remarks on Thucydides' "digression touching the piracies and robberies of old time; with other notes of savageness." In his later political philosophy, Hobbes often mentioned the "rapine" of earlier times in his discussion of how people live outside of civil society. In Book 1, note 60, Hobbes discussed the Greeks' oracles, which he said "were always obscure, that evasion might be found to salve their credit; and whether they were the imposture of the devil, or of men, which is the more likely, they had no presention nor securewise conjecture of the future." His profound skepticism about religious claims in all forms continued throughout his political thought. In Book II, note 2, Hobbes commented on Thucydides' account of Theseus's unification of Greek cities, in which he brought all the cities under one common council: "This caused the City to grow both populous, and potent, because now the whole nation united into one city, made use of the sea, which divided they could not have done" (597). Hobbes took from this episode that if a nation was united under one head, it was much less assailable and much more secure from foreign enemies than if it remained divided.

When translating Cleon's speech condemning the Mytilenaeans in Book 3, he has Cleon say, "You are excellent men for one to deceive with a speech of a new strain, but backward to follow any tried advice; slaves to strange things, contemners of things usual" (197). In his note on this passage, Hobbes simply wrote, "The nature of the multitude in council, lively set forth" (580). This was certainly the view of the multitude that Hobbes held throughout the rest of his career. His note in Book 8, where the government of the Four Hundred fell into turmoil, states, "Ambition of the oligarchicals amongst themselves overthroweth their government" (583). This view of the weakness of oligarchy, manifesting in the Hobbes's translation sometimes revealed his particular way of looking at the world or his idiosyncratic use of the English language, but it does not seem to serve as a vehicle for Hobbes's political thought so much as an inspiration for his political thought. An example of how Hobbes's "voice" comes through in his translation appears in Book 8, a book in which there is heavy emphasis on the follies of democratic leadership. On the oligarchic leader Antiphon, Hobbes translates Thucydides' tendency of oligarchs to compete for popular allegiance, was certainly a view he continued to hold in his later political works.

> But he that contrived the whole business, how to bring it to this pass, and had long thought upon it was Antiphon: a man for virtue not inferior to any Athenian of his time, and the ablest of any man both to devise well, and also to express well what he had devised: and though he came not into the assemblies of the people, nor willingly to any other debatings, because the multitude had him in jealousy for the opinion they had of the power of his eloquence; yet when any man had occasion of suit, either in the courts of justice or in the assembly of the people, came to him for his counsel, this one man was able to help him most. (546)

The Rex Warner translation of the same passage reads:

> But the man who had planned the whole thing so as to bring it to this point, and who had given most thought to it, was Antiphon, one of the ablest Athenians of his times. He had a most powerful intellect and was well able to express his thoughts in words; he never came forward to speak in front of the assembly unless he could help it, or competed in any other form of public life, since the people in general mistrusted him because of his reputation for cleverness; on the other hand, when other people were engaged in lawsuits or had points to make before the assembly, he was the man to give the best and most helpful advice to those who asked him for it. (577)

Especially in the use of the terms "virtue," "multitude," "jealousy," and "eloquence," we can see Hobbes's unique voice coming through, but we can also see that there is no actual insertion or deletion of material that would truly change the meaning of the text. The tone is different, but the meaning is largely the same.

Another shorter example will suffice to demonstrate this point. In his translation of Thucydides' depiction of the Athenian General Nicias in Book 7, we see a stronger term being used by Hobbes to describe Nicias's attachment to superstition (an attachment that caused the fatal delay that led to utter defeat in Syracuse):

> And not only the greatest part of the Athenians called upon the generals to stay, but Nicias also (for he was addicted to superstition and observations of that kind somewhat too much) said that it should come no more into debate whether they should go or not, till the three times nine days were past, which the sooth-sayers appoint in that behalf. (484)

The Warner translation reads thus:

> Most of the Athenians took this event so seriously that they now urged the generals to wait, and Nicias, who was rather over-inclined to divination and such things, said that, until they had waited for the thrice nine days recommended by the sooth-sayers, he would not even join in any further discussion on how the move could be made. (511)

We can see that the translations are fairly similar, but Hobbes uses the term "addiction" and "superstition," words that are arguably stronger in tone than "over-inclined" and "divination." They indicate what Hobbes would like to emphasize about this incident, perhaps, but they do not represent a true departure in meaning from the original text if two translators, so far apart in time, could come this close in their respective versions of this passage.

While Hobbes's translation of Thucydides has been dismissed by some as a part of his pre-scientific phase, and so not necessary for understanding his political thought, clearly his reading and translation of Thucydides instigated themes that Hobbes continued to validate in his later writings. And despite his belief in the scientific approach to political thought, Hobbes returned to the business of translating classical texts at the very end of his life, after decades in the pursuit of hard-hitting "political science." Why did Hobbes bother to return to this humanistic endeavor as an old man?

In conjunction with his annotation of Hobbes's translation of Homer, Political Scientist Eric Nelson raised an old but only sporadically asked question about the possible political nature of Hobbes's translation of Homer. He argued that the translation of Homer could be viewed as an *extension* of Hobbes's political thought. From our vantage point this would mean that, whereas Hobbes *drew from* Thucydides many core lessons that would remain with him throughout his career as a political philosopher, he *applied* the lessons he had learned when doing his translation of Homer. Many commentators have dismissed Hobbes's translation of Homer as a source of amusement in his old age, and nothing more than that, a form of entertainment when he had said all he could about politics. Hobbes himself wrote in an essay accompanying his *Odyssey* that he translated it "Because I had nothing else to do" (Homer *Translations* xv). Nelson gives the following reasons why Hobbes must have considered his translations a more serious enterprise:

1. He spent at least four years doing the translations, and had to deal with physical impediments (palsy) which necessitated the hiring of a secretary (xvi).

2. He had been prohibited from publishing his political, theological and historical thought from mid-1660's on. Fearful of persecution on charges of atheism, one avenue left open to him was through literary endeavors (xix-xxi).

3. Civil War and he saw his translations as an opportunity to cut Homer down to size (xxi).

So Hobbes's task was to make Homer's heroes what they should be, truly admirable and virtuous. As we know, these heroes were a mixture of virtue and vice. And we also know that much of Hobbes's political thought revolves around preventing the criticism of those in power so as to avoid civil conflict. Hobbes's *Leviathan* can be seen as his ultimate expression for the support of absolute sovereignty and the silencing of all arguments about the morality and justice of the sovereign power. In Hobbes's view, any portrayal of great men that elicited criticism of them could inspire disobedience toward contemporary authorities. So, argues Nelson, Hobbes sanitized Homer's characters to make them more mundane (xxxvii). In his translation, he downplayed Homer's highflying style, removed criticism (implicit or explicit) of Agamemnon, and any attempts to diminish the validity of kingly power, and in general employed a less impressive vocabulary in his translation that effectively diminished Homer's grandeur.

One area where Hobbes's intervention into Homer's text is most evident is in Homer's frequent references to the gods and their influence on men. Below is what Hobbes has Achilles say to Calchas, priest of Apollo, to try to get him to speak his mind despite fear of Agamemnon: "Chalchas, replied Achilles, do not fear, But what the god has told you bring to light: By Phoebus, not a man shall hurt you here, As long as I enjoy my life and sight; though Agamemnon be the man you dread, Who is of all the army most obeyed" (Homer *Iliad* 2-3).

Compare Hobbes's translation to George Chapman's, which preceded it (Chapman's translation was published in 1598): "Achilles answered: 'All thou knowest speake, and be confident: For by Apollo, Jove's belov'd (to whom performing vowes, O Calchas, for the state of Greece thy spirit Prophetique shows Skils that direct us) not a man of all these Grecians here (I living and enjoying the light shot through this flowrie sphere) Shall touch thee with offensive hands—though Agamemnon be The man in question, that doth boast the mightiest Emperie Of all our armie'" (26).

There is a marked difference between these two that not only highlights Hobbes's disagreements with Chapman's translation (with which he was familiar) but also with the way of thinking about Homer at Chapman's time, which tended to dwell on the role of the gods or the spiritual in the epic. Hobbes's translation is notably briefer, and leaves out all but the most necessary references to gods. It leaves out entirely any reference to Calchas's value as a prophet, and it changes the characterization of Agamemnon at the end, more or less simply acknowledging Agamemnon's power rather than making it seem overweening as the Chapman translation does. Here is the modern translation of Robert Fagles:

> And the matchless runner reassured him: "Courage! Out with it now, Calchas. Reveal the will of god whatever you may know. And I swear by Apollo dear to Zeus, the power you pray to, Calchas, when you reveal god's will to the Argives—no one, not while I am alive and see the light on earth, no one will lay his heavy hands on you by the hollow ships. None among all the armies. Not even if you mean Agamemnon here who now claims to be, by far, the best of the Acheans. (80)

In Fagles' translation we see the same elements missing in Hobbes's translation—more mention of the gods, and a characterization of Calchas's role as prophet: He prays to Zeus, he reveals god's will. The dubious or boastful nature of Agamemnon's power makes a comeback as well.

Another example illustrates Hobbes's wish, when possible, to downplay Homer's depiction of the great King Agamemnon's folly. In Book 9 of his translation, we find Agamemnon ready to relent in his great rage toward Achilles and not only give him back Briseis but many other gifts to appease his anger. Here is Hobbes's translation of the passage in which Agamemnon admits his fault:

> This said, Atrides penitent replied, O Nestor, all you charge me with is true, And for Achilles' sake, 'tis not denied, Jove does th' Achaean army now subdue. He whom Jove loves worth a whole army is. But since I made Achilles discontent, I'll make amends for what I did amiss, And send a noble present to his tent. (Homer *Iliads* 98-99)

Again, we have Fagles' modern translation:

> And Agamemnon the lord of men consented quickly: "That's no lie, old man—a full account you give of all my acts of madness. Mad, blind I was! Not even *I* would deny it. Why look, that man is worth an entire army, the fighter Zeus holds dear with all his heart—how he exalts him now and mauls Achaea's forces! But since I was blinded, lost in my own inhuman rage, now, at last, I am bent on setting things to rights: I'll give a priceless ransom paid for friendship." (255)

Lastly, here is Chapman's translation of the same passage:

> "O father," answered the King, "my wrongs thou tell'st me right. Mine owne offence, mine owne tongue grants. One man must stand in fight For our whole armie: him I wrongd, him Jove loves from his hart: He shewes it in thus honoring him, who, living thus apart, Proves us but number, for his want makes all our weaknesse seene. Yet after my confest offence, soothing my humorous spleene, I'le sweeten his affects againe with presents infinite." (184)

In both the Fagles and Chapman translations there is a more self-deprecating message coming from Agamemnon. He characterizes himself in a way that speaks to his previous unreasonable disposition: whether his "inhuman rage" or "humorous spleen." There is no such admission in Hobbes's translation of this passage—Agamemnon admits his fault but does not characterize himself. Especially in Fagles' translation, this message comes out—Agamemnon even admits to "madness." Also notice that what Agamemnon is to give Achilles is downplayed in Hobbes's version, even to the point of using the singular "present." Fagles' translation has him giving a "priceless ransom," and for Chapman it is "presents infinite."

These two examples give the reader a taste for the kind of translation Hobbes engaged in with Homer, and it does seem that Hobbes imposed more changes of meaning on the text of Homer than he did much earlier in his life with Thucydides. But why? Despite what seems at least like a strong bias that leads to omissions in his translation, some scholars are dubious about whether or not this was intentional. Quarrels have even emerged over how much to read into these types of discrepancies in translation. For instance, A.P. Martinich takes on Paul Davis for seeing in Hobbes's Homer an anti-clerical agenda,[2] where Martinich sees nothing but an attempt, perhaps a rather poor attempt, at translating poetry. He asks, if Hobbes's agenda was to insert his political views into Homer's text, why is it that no one in his own time picked up on it?[3] Martinich argues that Davis uses "unnecessary, extravagant explanations, explanations that appeal to recondite or overly subtle considerations" (148).

It is easy to see how one could go on a "fishing expedition" into Hobbes's translation of Homer and find just about anything. Yet at the same time, it is hard to believe that any translator refrains completely from injecting himself into the work he is translating. Also, the modern ideal is to keep translations as literal as possible while still rendering them pleasantly readable, but this emphasis on the literal translation was not so much the case in former times when men like Chapman or Hobbes engaged in the enterprise. Chapman's particularly florid translation is even better proof of this difference than Hobbes's. Hobbes was not just any translator, but a very opinionated one, one who had spent his life in the writing of bold, acerbic, and unpopular political proposals. While it might be hard to prove a systematic agenda of atheism in Hobbes's translation, one can certainly see his skepticism about religious matters coming through from time to time.[4] While we may not be able to see an overt agenda of supporting absolute sovereignty in his translation, we can certainly detect his aversion to humbling kings.

If Hobbes could draw ideas from Thucydides and continue defend them in his later political thought, he might have also turned to Homer at the end of his career as a reverse attempt to inject his political thought into a greatly admired classic. It is indeed difficult to imagine a thinker as wily and cantankerous as Hobbes simply deciding to spend the last few years of his life playing with a figurative jig-saw puzzle to while away his time. Perhaps Hobbes did think that he could achieve an objective in line with his lifetime of very consistent political views. It is worth at least considering this possibility and reviving an interest in his translations as conscious attempts at transmitting political thought.

Notes
1. See Ahrensdorf for a great discussion of the similarities and differences between Hobbes and Thucydides.
2. Martinich characterizes Davis's argument in this way: Hobbes was attacking the Cambridge Platonists Homerus-Sophos interpretation by bringing Homer down to earth through the use of plain language and the diminishment of the priestly class in the epic poem. See A.P. Martinich, "Hobbes's Translations of Homer and Anticlericalism," and Paul Davis, "Thomas Hobbes's Translations of Homer: Epic and Anticlericalism in Late Seventeenth-Century England."
3. Closer to Hobbes's time, Alexander Pope, in the preface to his own translation, noted that Hobbes sometimes made clumsy omissions and mistakes and attributed these not to cleverness but to carelessness.
4. To give one brief example that Davis points out, Hobbes has Agamemnon (a bit after the portion of text examined above) accuse the prophet Calchas that he "Inventest prophecies to cross my will." Davis argues that there is no basis in the original Greek for injecting "Inventest" or "cross my will," but Hobbes puts these in to represent his own point of view (235).

Works Cited
Ahrensdorf, Peter. "The Fear of Death and the Longing for Immortality: Hobbes and Thucydides on Human Nature and the Problem of Anarchy." *The American Political Science Review* 94.3 (2000): 579-593.

Davis, Paul. "Thomas Hobbes's Translations of Homer: Epic and Anticlericalism in Late Seventeenth-Century England." *Seventeenth Century* 12.2 (1997): 231-256.

Homer. *Chapman's Homer: The Iliad, The Odyssey, and the Lesser Homerica.* Ed. Allardyce Nicoll. Vol. 1 Bollingen Series XLI. New York: Pantheon Books, 1956.

———. *The Iliad.* Trans. Robert Fagles. New York: Viking Penguin, 1990.

———. *The Iliads and Odysses of Homer.* Trans. Thomas Hobbes. English Works 10. London: Longman, Brown, Green and Longmans. Elibron Classics Series (facsimile reprint), 2006.

————. *Translations of Homer*. Trans. Thomas Hobbes. Ed. Eric Nelson. Oxford University Press, 2008.

Martinich, A.P. "Hobbes's Translations of Homer and Anticlericalism." *Seventeenth Century* 16.1 (2001): 147-157.

Riddehough, G.B. "Hobbes's Translation of Homer." *Phoenix* 12.2 (1958): 58-62.

Thucydides. *Hobbes's Thucydides*. Ed. Richard Schlatter. Piscataway: Rutgers UP, 1975.

————. *History of the Peloponnesian War*. Trans. Rex Warner. New York: Viking Penguin, 1986.

Whelan, Frederick G. "Language and Its Abuses in Hobbes's Political Philosophy." *The American Political Science Review* 75.1 (1981): 59-75.

"But I Did Not Love Only Him": Helping Students Discern Platonic Values in *Sense and Sensibility*"

Steven Epley
Samford University

Samford University requires undergraduates to take a two-semester sequence entitled "Cultural Perspectives" that views the Western intellectual tradition within a global context. The first work on our syllabus is Plato's "Allegory of the Cave," and I approach virtually every subsequent reading in the light of Platonic philosophy. For example, I foreground for students how, throughout Jane Austen's novel *Sense and Sensibility*, Elinor Dashwood models a Platonic form of disinterested love for the good, partly for the benefit of her younger sister Marianne, who for much of the narrative sub-scribes to a selfish form of Romanticism. After her seducer, John Willoughby, spurns the impoverished Marianne in favor of a lucrative match with an heiress, Marianne embarks on a painful progress toward self-knowledge guided by Elinor's example of benevolent love that finally leads Marianne up several rungs of the ladder of love described in the Platonic dialogue *Symposium*. Ultimately, Marianne relinquishes her self-centered complaining and vows to undertake what *Symposium* calls "beautiful pursuits and practices" (105) such as strict self-discipline and a new determination to "live solely for my family," as she phrases it (245). In this essay, I will argue that the two most recent motion picture adaptations of *Sense and Sensibility*—the Columbia Pictures version released in 1995 starring Emma Tompkins and Kate Winslet and the British Broadcasting Corporation's televised "mini-series" of 2008—negatively rein-vent Austen's plot in ways that obscure or remove its Platonic overtones. By encourag-ing students to read the novel against the grain of these two cinematic representations, I hope to help them discern important Platonic values in the novel, especially the ascent towards higher forms of knowledge and love than the superficial forms on display in the otherwise admirable adaptations.

My students remind me that, in a film adaptation of a novel, omissions and tightening of scenes and dialogue from the novel are necessary. However, I remind them that editorial alterations reflect the values of the screenwriter, not necessarily those of the author of the original work. An interview with Andrew Davies available on the *PBS/Masterpiece* website helps students to see this for themselves. In the interview, Davies, who wrote the screenplay for and directed the BBC version, recalls his decision to "butch the men up a little bit" because, for example, Austen's novel did not "convince" him that "Marianne, the very romantic one, could make the change from being passionately in love with Willoughby to being happily in love with Col. Brandon" ("Longing, Betrayal, & Redemption"). However, such a progression in Marianne's attitude toward love can be plausibly understood in Platonic terms, specifically with reference to the following advice that Socrates, in *Symposium*, recalls receiving from Diotima:

> For let me tell you, the right way to approach the things of love, or to be led there by another, is this: beginning from ... beautiful things, to mount for that beauty's sake ever upwards, as by a flight of steps, from one to two, and from two to all beautiful bodies, and from beautiful bodies to beautiful pursuits and practices, and from practices to beautiful learnings. (105)

Marianne starts at the bottom rung of the ladder, where passion reigns, but by novel's end, as we shall see, she has ascended to the level inhabited by Elinor from the beginning. The narrative thus requires no romantic retrofitting of Col. Brandon's person or character to explain why Marianne can end up "happily in love" with him. That Davies felt such manipulation to be necessary only substantiates Deborah Kaplan's assertion that film versions of Austen's culturally and linguistically complex novels tend to lower them to the level of "mass-market romance" (177).

Another example of this phenomenon involves the casting of heartthrob Hugh Grant as Edward Ferrars in the Columbia Pictures version, directed by Ang Lee, although this character is described in the novel as "not handsome" (14). This casting frustrates Austen's design by privileging outer beauty, associated most clearly with the duplicitous Willoughby, over the lasting, transcendent beauty that both Edward and Col. Brandon possess and for which both are ultimately rewarded through marriages with the elder Dashwood sisters. Similarly, both films also invent one grand romantic gesture not found in the novel, when Col. Brandon scoops up the unconscious Marianne and carries her indoors after she collapses during her hopelessly nostalgic nature walks when she is at her most depressed psychologically. Col. Brandon's action recalls Willoughby's first appearance in the novel, when he similarly rescues the wounded Marianne after she has fallen on a hillside during a storm. However, the novel more prosaically records simply that Col. Brandon shows concern over Marianne's ill-advised excursions, and that she walks back into the house on her own power *before* falling deathly ill.

Even more significant than these radical revisions are the ways in which the films omit dialogue and reorder scenes that foreground Elinor's role as her sister's Platonic mentor and Marianne's need of the guidance that she initially spurns. In the novel, after Willoughby ignores Marianne at a London ball and sends her an insulting "Dear Marianne" letter that grieves her deeply, Elinor implores her, "Exert yourself, if you would not kill yourself and all who love you. Think of your mother; think of her misery while *you* suffer; for her sake you must exert yourself," to which the grieving younger sister replies, "I cannot, I cannot, leave me, leave me, if I distress you; leave me, hate me, forget me! but do not torture me so" (131). The 1995 movie omits this exchange, while in the BBC version Elinor says simply, "Exert yourself," without any reference to the family members for whose sake the exertion is being encouraged. Even very subtle differences are sometimes important, as when Austen's Marianne adds, "Happy, happy Elinor, *you* cannot have an idea of what I suffer" (131), as opposed to the BBC Marianne's line "You have no idea of what I suffer." The original Marianne believes wrongly that Elinor feels no sorrow of her own and that it is impossible for those without sorrow to understand the suffering of others. She must be disabused of both notions, especially the latter, before ascending to a higher, nobler form of love.

This disabusing takes place when Elinor informs Marianne that she has known for four months of the secret engagement between Lucy Steele and the man whom Elinor loves, Edward Ferrars, but has kept it a secret for the sake of her family. In the novel, Marianne asks, "How have you been supported?" "By feeling that I was doing my duty" replies Elinor. Still incredulous, Marianne gasps, "Four months! And yet you loved him," to which Elinor replies, in perhaps the most crucial line of dialogue omitted by both films, "But I did not love *only* him," adding that she was "glad to spare" those dear to her from knowing how deeply she grieved (185; emphasis added). The BBC film preserves Elinor's stoicism while excising its Platonic motivation. Says Elinor, "I bore it because I had to. And I was glad to spare you from knowing how much I felt." In the novel, Elinor, describing the "constant and painful exertion" required of her, tells Marianne, "If I had not been bound [by Lucy Steele] to silence, perhaps nothing could have kept me entirely—not even what I owed to my dearest friends—from openly shewing that I was *very* unhappy" (186). The more recent film version, omitting the reference to Elinor's Platonic debt to her family, reduces the speech to angry mean-spiritedness: "Believe me, Marianne, had I not been bound to silence, I could have produced proof enough of a broken heart even for you." Moreover, both movies omit the remaining dialogue in the scene, beginning with a chastened Marianne's reply, "you have made me hate myself for ever. How barbarous have I been to you! You, who have been my only comfort, who have seemed to be only suffering for me! Is this my gratitude? Is this the only return I can make you?" (186). This speech effectively begins Marianne's Platonic rehabilitation, which comes to full fruition after her recovery from her serious illness, and by omitting it, the films sacrifice considerable depth and complexity, not to mention Marianne's development as a character.

It is true that both film versions show Marianne praising Elinor's example, but neither spells out the ways in which she comes to imitate Elinor, and this omission obscures a crucial Platonic feature of the novel. Walking along the beach with Elinor near the end of the novel, Marianne acknowledges that she now compares her past behavior to that of Elinor, whom, it is inferred, she will now set up as a model for her own future behavior. To the extent that Marianne's character changes at all, however, it does so only by learning the difference between affected feeling and authentic feeling. Marianne spends most of the novel trying too hard to display an elevated sensibility and extreme capacity for suffering that are essential elements of the romantic narrative that she seeks to construct for herself. At movie's end, especially in the BBC version, where Marianne calls the older and arthritic Col. Brandon the "true Romantic" on account of his selflessness, she has come to reject the conventional Romantic narrative. But the screenwriters do not show it, as the novel does, being replaced by a more elevated view of love that allows her to overcome her detestation of her past conduct. Both movies omit any reference to Marianne's lengthy acknowledgement of past guilt and promise to "now live solely for my family." The most that the BBC Marianne can summon is a terse confession: "I was a fool to myself and inconsiderate to everyone else. I compare my conduct to yours. I hope I am wiser now." In the novel, Marianne says, "Your example was before me; but to what avail?" She rhetorically asks, "Did I imitate your forbearance, by taking any part in those offices of general complaisance or particular gratitude which you had hitherto been left to discharge alone? No: not less when I knew you to be unhappy, than when I believed you at ease, did I turn away from every exertion of duty or friendship, scarcely allowing sorrow to exist but with me" and insisting on being "miserable for my sake." Inspired by Elinor's Platonic example, Marianne vows that henceforth her "feelings shall be governed" and her "temper improved. They shall no longer worry others, nor torture myself" (245).

Despite this hopeful signal near the end of the novel, neither sister ascends to the heights of the Platonic ladder of love, where the searcher finds "the perfection of beauty" (*Symposium* 106) that is eternal and unchanging in the realm of the Forms or Ideas. "There in life and there alone," Socrates recalls being told by the inspired Diotima, "is life worth living for man, while he contemplates Beauty itself" (106). As Richard Hunter points out, this "harshly intellectual" perspective "ignores basic, universal facts of human experience" and provides scant comfort "to all but a Socrates" (98). Hunter reminds us, though, that the Socrates of *Symposium*, like the hero of an epic or tragedy, embodies ideals to which we may aspire, but that he is not intended to serve as a model, even if it were possible for most humans to copy him. Nonetheless, Hunter insists that the "idea" of Socrates can be put to "more productive" uses, such as the ones that I have tried to sketch based on the relationship between Elinor and Marianne in *Sense and Sensibility*. By comparing the film adaptations with the original novel, I hope to help students understand what they may otherwise never appreciate—the extent to which Austen subscribes to Platonic notions about love and the role that a positive role model like Elinor can play in a character's, and a reader's, ascent out of the cave of intellectual and spiritual darkness and into the light.

Works Cited

Austen, Jane. *Sense and Sensibility*. Ed. Claudia L. Johnson. *Norton Critical Edition*. New York: Norton, 2002. Print.

British Broadcasting Corporation. *Sense and Sensibility*. Dir. and screenplay Andrew Davies, 2008. Film.

Columbia Pictures. *Sense and Sensibility*. Dir. Ang Lee. Screenplay Emma Thompson, 1995. Film.

Hunter, Richard. *Plato's* Symposium. Oxford: Oxford UP, 2004. *NetLibrary*. Web. June 29, 2009.

Kaplan, Deborah. "Mass Marketing Jane Austen: Men, Women, and Courtship in Two Film Adaptations." *Jane Austen in Hollywood*. Eds. Linda Troost and Sayre Greenfield. 2nd ed. Lexington: UP of Kentucky, 2001. 177-87. Print.

Plato. *Symposium (The Banquet)*. In *Great Dialogues of Plato*. Trans. W.H.D. Rouse. Ed. Eric H. Warmington and Philip G. Rouse. New York: Penguin/Mentor, 1984. Print.

Public Broadcasting Service (PBS). *Longing, Betrayal, & Redemption: An Interview with Screenwriter Andrew Davies*. "Clip 11: Impressions of *Sense and Sensibility*." Interview. *PBS/Masterpiece*. Web. June 29, 2009.

Freedom and Happiness from the Renaissance to Modernity

The Originality of Pico's *Oration*

Neil G. Robertson
University of King's College (Halifax)

Pico's *Oration* is often used in core text programs to establish the Renaissance, and particularly the Renaissance sense of the human. In the course in which I teach (The Foundation Year Programme at the University of King's College), it or Petrarch's *Ascent of Mount Ventoux*, is used as the first work from the Renaissance the students encounter. In turn, in such courses, the Renaissance is often portrayed as the beginning of modernity. So the way in which this text is approached can have some far-reaching implications for the whole narrative of history that students are presented with and in particular how the Renaissance is understood within this larger trajectory.

The first issue, and one that our conference's Call for Papers draws our attention to, is the point, often made, that strictly speaking Pico is not a humanist, not a proponent of the *studia humaniora* in the way Petrarch is. Indeed Pico, in a famous letter, defends against the "humanists" the use of "corrupt" medieval Latin in the articulation of philosophical and theological truth (Copenhaver and Schmitt 170-1). The assertion that Pico's "humanism," his exaltation of human dignity, is not identical to Renaissance humanism strictly considered seems to undermine his role as the initiator of the Renaissance. Equally, Pico scholars will point out that the title of the work is simply *Oratio*—it was called *The Oration on the Dignity of Man* only after Pico's death—and that, justified by this revised title, the emphasis made in many core text programs upon its opening passages has led to fundamental distortions of his thought (Copenhaver and Schmitt 166-76). These scholarly accusations lead us to the central question of the paper: is there a fundamental distortion of Pico's thought in reading him as a deeply original thinker, heralding a crucial break from the Middle Ages and the Ancient World and announcing a distinctly "modern" humanity?

In the mid-twentieth century, the dominant account of Pico came from a group of largely "neo-Kantian" scholars, such as Ernst Cassirer or Paul Kristeller, who saw in Pico a beginning of not only the Renaissance, but of modernity.[1] As has been pointed out in the secondary literature, Pico and his *Oration* were both given a prominence that was nowhere mirrored in Pico's own time. While not without some legacy of influence, it was only in the nineteenth century that the Oration came to any kind of prominence, and it was really the school of German neo-Kantians at the end of the nineteenth century that raised the Oration to its current status. So the question naturally arises—were these followers of the definitively modern thinker, Immanuel Kant, in fact reading into Pico's text their own standpoint and so distorting its true position?

In the 1970s, there was a backlash to the then prevalent account of Pico as originating or prefiguring modernity. This scholarly backlash argued that Cassirer, Kristeller, and the great Pico scholar Eugenio Garin had provided an anachronistic and simply inadequately informed account of Pico's argument in the Oration.[2] Pico was in fact presenting something that was, not only not the beginnings of modernity, but in fact, and in spite of his own claims, not notably original.

But before analyzing these readings of Pico, it is worth recalling Pico's own words from the contested beginning of the *Oration* where he gives an account of the creation to explicate what is fundamental to rightly grasp "the dignity of man":

> Everything was filled up: all things had been laid out in the highest, the lowest, and the middle orders.... Finally, the best of workmen decided that that to which nothing of its very own could be given should be, in composite fashion, whatsoever had belonged individually to each and everything. Therefore He took up man, a work of indeterminate form; and placing him at the midpoint of the world, He spoke to him as follows:

> "We have given to thee, Adam, no fixed seat, no form of thy very own, no gift peculiarly thine, that thou mayest feel as thine own, have as thine own, possess as thine own the seat, the form, the gifts which thou thyself shalt desire.... Thou like a judge appointed for being honorable art molder and maker of thyself; thou mayest sculpt thyself into whatever shape thou dost prefer." (Pico 4-5)

For the neo-Kantian scholars, this declaration of the distinction of the human from the created order and its power of self-fashioning was a startling declaration of modern humanity in its autonomy and self-legislating power—that standpoint most fully articulated by Kant. In contrast to a medieval account where the human is placed in and defined by an order, a Great Chain of Being, here man is declared as willing and choosing what he is to become. So there is a radical break from man as the humble medieval pilgrim seeking to fulfill his nature and proper end in God. In this reading, Pico is being seen as a paradigmatic Renaissance figure, where the Renaissance is understood as both a break from the Medieval and the initiation of the Modern.

But, as I have suggested, there is another group of scholars who have strongly resisted this reading of Pico and in the world of Picoan scholarship have really become the dominant account since the 1970s.[3] For these scholars, Pico is not original. Not only are there other and earlier Renaissance figures, such as Ficino or Valla or Manetti, who state something like his position or prefigure him, but in fact, there is a whole array of ancient, early Christian, and medieval philosophers and theologians who appear to fully anticipate Pico's account. While we can look at a number of ancient texts, Hellenic, Hellenistic, Roman, and Near Eastern, as well as the Jewish Kaballa, the most striking parallels are found in the Christian Neoplatonic theologians of the early church, figures such as Origen, Irenaeus, Gregory of Nyssa, Nemesius of Emessa, Augustine, and Boethius. All these authors wrote texts that point to the dignity of man—often as part of accounts of creation—and some that bear striking textual parallels to Pico's own account. So, on the basis of these textual parallels, Pico has been judged as not at all original and that the use he has been put to by the previous generation of scholars deeply distorts his own account. So one could claim that Pico's "originality" consisted really in reviving an early church account of man—but even this has been contested: Henri de Lubac, the great historian of medieval theology, declared Pico's account of the protean character of man to have become "banal" in the Middle Ages (Lubac 201).

The scholarship of the last forty years has then provided a reading of Pico that is the exact opposite to that of the previous generation: Pico is operating within a long and rich tradition and simply recovers and reiterates that position with notable rhetorical effectiveness. Scholars now fight over exactly in what his unoriginality lies—what his sources are—but there has been a basic retraction of the view that in Pico we see the modern age coming to birth and certainly the strongest rejection of efforts to discover a premonition of the thought of Immanuel Kant.

Let me for the sake of simplification outline the areas in Pico's account which the recent scholarship has found precedents:[4]

1. the protean nature of man: the notion that the human can be anywhere from the lowest slug to an angel on the "Great Chain of Beings;"
2. that man has dominion over nature, that he is King of creation;
3. that man is the contemplator of creation, placed in the center to appreciate God's work;
4. that man is a microcosom, having as his nature the whole content of the created order and connecting and unifying it, even functioning as the mediator of creation itself.

So it very much looks as if Pico is at best providing some rhetorical novelty to a very long tradition.[5] Certainly the claims to startling originality propounded by Cassirer and others appear very hard to maintain in the face of this evidence.

My own argument is that both sides are right and both sides are wrong: Pico is both articulating a new position and is operating within a tradition—and the ambiguous forward-backward, push-me-pull-you character of his position is its whole interest. He is both a modern and a pre-modern: he is a fully Renaissance figure sharing in that age's Janus-like character.

Let me quickly explore this ambiguity in Pico—and I would argue it operates at every point in the text. This ambiguity is captured by looking more closely at exactly in what human dignity consists for Pico. On the one side, Pico wants to emphasize that the human is a "not-being": he is other than and outside the whole structure of the determinate created order. That order is full, and man has no place in it with no nature belonging to him. It is my argument that here the modernizers have ahold of a moment not found in the earlier texts their critics cite, but that in isolating this moment, they misread its import. But it is perfectly right to point out that the dignity of man consists in this indeterminate potentiality, if I can put it that way, in the power of the human to choose. To emphasize this moment is to bring out the "modernity" of Pico.

But Pico goes on to say that human dignity also consists in what one does with this freedom, this potentiality: is one in fact an angel or a beast? The weight can be put on what is actual, the actual content of human choosing in defining human dignity. What will the individual actually make of that freedom which attains its meaning and worth only through the "Great Chain of Being?" This is the traditional side of Pico. The content of human dignity is given; human freedom operates only within a received, divinely realized—and indeed traditional—context. There is nothing original or originating here: human freedom finds its meaning within a given hierarchy that structures and gives shape to human dignity. This is precisely what the newer scholars point to: that the human can and will find a place within a given order of beings is precisely at the heart of the older philosophical and theological tradition—especially as informed by Neoplatonism. These scholars complain that the "modern" Pico is really a product of reading only the first few pages of the Oration and not seeing the restraints and content of that freedom brought out in the text as a whole and in Pico's other writings.

So, just as the earlier generation assimilated Pico to the modern, this next generation has largely assimilated Pico to the pre-modern—the medieval and ancient traditions available to him. We have one side that emphasizes the freedom or potentiality of the Picoan human and the other that points to its given and received actual content. But of course for Pico, there are both sides. Indeed, for Pico, there are really three aspects to human dignity: 1) the potentiality of the human apart from the created order the modernizers emphasize; 2) the actual content of a hierarchical Neoplatonic order, the traditionalizers emphasize; 3) but then also the connection of the two—the making of the potential actual, what Pico calls "holy ambition" (Pico 7). My claim is that it is in this third connecting moment that we see both the originality of Pico and his dependence on tradition—that we see the specifically Renaissance ambiguity of his thought.

In the notion of "holy ambition," there is the need to relate both the side of self-fashioning and the side of a given and received hierarchy. Ambition presupposes both moments. Holy ambition is a beautiful, evocative and deeply unstable thought, in which both potentiality and actuality are at work. In ambition one both possesses one's object and does not possess it. The human is both moved by the given structure of ends—that Great Chain of Being—and the human is also moved by his own will and desire: one must will that end for oneself. In this, the human is beyond the whole hierarchical order and yet fully defined by it.

So I want to suggest that in order to let Pico be Pico, to let the Renaissance be the Renaissance, we need to see this ambiguity as inherent to his position. This ambiguous place of the human is neither simply medieval nor properly modern. There is not the definition of the human by its end in the divine, nor is there the self-grounded certainty of the modern subject. Pico's self has stepped out of the order of being into a new indeterminacy, but the whole key is that this new indeterminacy and potentiality is only in relation to an assumed hierarchical order alone in which content can be found for this indeterminacy—but as its work, as chosen by its will. This Picoan image can be found to inform a whole array of Renaissance figures. In Machiavelli's Prince we see the same indeterminacy, now in relation to secular ends of power and glory acting within an assumed political order. This is also the figure of the Renaissance artist, such as da Vinci or Michelangelo, whose artistic indeterminacy allows all of nature to appear as it is. And we again encounter this type in its collapse at the end of the Renaissance in Montaigne's *Essays*—especially his portrayal of the reversal of perfectionist ambition in "On Experience"; or again in the plays of Shakespeare, where we find a similar critique, for instance in the hypocritical and ironically named Angelo of *Measure for Measure*. In all these ways, we see both the power and instability of this Picoan type—where the stepping out from nature into indeterminacy necessarily leads back to that very natural order. So, as Pico figures it, God gives us no place and yet puts us in a place—the middle. Here can be born a being that is capable of unheard of beauty and goodness, but also of a new kind of evil and indeed infinite and insatiable desire, whether holy or unholy. The figure of Marlowe's Dr. Faustus brings out just the problem of a being that is beyond the order that defines him—that would be a demi-god—but is trapped in time and desire and ends life not in glory, but in despair and futility.

If we see Pico as directly modern or fully traditional, we lose sight of this deep ambiguity and, to my mind, lose sight of the subtle development of the western tradition—being blind to both the implication of the medieval in the modern and the distinction of the modern from the medieval. I want to suggest that this isn't merely an academic point about periodization and its many issues, but has also a pedagogical aspect. If we lose sight of the complexity of the Renaissance, the complexity of holy ambition, we will see ourselves either as simply "modern" or simply "traditional"; so equally our reading and teaching of books in our core text programs will be in danger of falling into these opposed moments. What Pico suggests is that we must ask our students to exercise and recognize the context of their holy ambition—to know their inner freedom and yet also the context in which that freedom finds its content and reality.

Notes
1. See Cassirer; Kristeller. *Sources* 173-8; Garin. For a critical account of the neo-Kantian background to these interpreters, see Copenhaver "Magic" and "Secret." For an overview of the scholarly debate, see Dougherty.
2. For Kristeller's assessment of Pico's place in the larger history, see Kristeller, *Arts.* 107-10.
3. See especially Trinkaus, Lubac, and Copenhaver.
4. For actual sources for these positions, see Trinkaus, Lubac, Copenhaver, and Dougherty. This issue was in a way anticipated by Pico when on the opening page of the *Oration* he listed alternative accounts of human dignity that he claimed failed to capture the "outstandingness of man" (Pico 3).
5. For the claim Pico is primarily only rhetorically innovative, see Dulles and Craven. For a more balanced account, see Kraye who writes, after citing Lubac, "Although there

were many discussions of man's protean nature in patristic and medieval literature. Pico gave this traditional idea a striking new formulation." According to Kraye, this novelty consists in that "Pico removed man from the centre of the Neoplatonic hierarchy of being and allotted him instead an indeterminate ontological status" (313).

Works Cited

Cassirer, Ernst. "Giovanni Pico della Mirandola." *Journal of the History of Ideas* 3 (1943): 124-44 and 319-46.

Copenhaver, Brian P. "Magic and the Dignity of Man: De-Kanting Pico's Oration." *The Italian Renaissance in the Twentieth Century.* Ed. Allen Grieco. Florence: Leo S. Olshki, 2002.

———. "The Secret of Pico's Oratio: Cabala and Renaissance Philosophy." *Midwest Studies in Philosophy* 26 (2002): 56-81.

———. and Schmitt, Charles B. *Renaissance Philosophy.* Oxford: Oxford UP, 1993.

Craven, William G. *Giovanni Pico della Mirandola: Symbol of His Age.* Geneva: Droz, 1981.

Dougherty, M.V. "Three Precursors to Pico della Mirandola's *Roman Disputation* and *The Question of Human Nature.*" *Pico della Mirandola: New Essays.* Ed. Dougherty. Cambridge: Cambridge UP, 2008: 114-51.

Dulles, Avery. *Princeps Concordiae: Pico della Mirandola and the Scholastic Tradition.* Cambridge MA: Harvard UP, 1941.

Garin, Eugenio. *Italian Humanism: Philosophy and Civic Life in the Renaissance.* Trans. Peter Munz. New York: Harper and Row, 1965.

Kraye, Jill. *Moral Philosophy: The Cambridge History of Renaissance Philosophy.* Ed. Charles B. Schmitt. Cambridge: Cambridge UP, 1988: 303-86.

Kristeller, Paul Oskar. *Renaissance Thought and the Arts.* Princeton. Princeton UP, 1990.

———. *Renaissance Thoughts and Its Sources.* New York: Columbia UP, 1979.

Lubac, Henri de. *Pico de la Mirandole.* Paris: Aubier Montaigne, 1974.

Pico della Mirandola, Giovanni. *On the Dignity of Man.* Trans. C.G. Wallis, P.J.W. Miller, and D. Carmichael. Indianapolis: Hackett, 1965.

Trinkaus, Charles. *In Our Image and Likeness.* 2 vols. South Bend: U of Notre Dame P, 1970.

Death and Core Tradition in a Polish Renaissance Lament

James Roney
Juniata College

The conference theme asks us to reconsider the role of core texts in human memory and communication, given that any universal core tradition is inherently inadequate to the authentic expression of diverse human experience and that no one can master all the particular core traditions in the world today. One of the core texts of the Polish literary tradition demonstrates not only that such problems are not new (If they are not a part of all human culture, they have certainly been a part of European culture since the Renaissance) but also that core texts derive much of their vitality from such "problems."

Jan Kochanowski's *Laments* (*Treny* in Polish, after the Greek Threnody) confront the contradictions between core traditions and intense personal experience. When his brother and two daughters died in the late 1570s, he wrote a cycle of nineteen poems mourning the death of one daughter and exploring his anguish as poetic talent and rational virtue failed before death's brute reality. Rather than abandoning the stability of core traditions or denying the chaos of individual experience, Kochanowski reconciled them in an ironic vision.

Humanism was both a way of life and a creed of personal responsibility for one's fate. An admirer of Erasmus, Kochanowski believed in a rational God, the master artisan of a world beautiful in the perfect harmony of its parts. Universal reason grounded the order of the world; rational virtue ensured the harmony of the self, by controlling our responses to whatever events fortune brought. Classical art and Renaissance poetics had discovered universal laws governing the harmony of content and form. His daughters' deaths challenged this worldview. If the natural order includes the death of a two-and-a-half-year-old innocent, full of unrealized potential, the world is neither harmonious, nor rational, but brutal and unthinking. If virtue fails

when misfortune strikes, our minds are controlled by the fates, not by us. If the genre
system prohibits serious poems about a personal loss without national significance,
then one must violate it by incorporating elements from personal life, multiple traditions, and various lower genres.

Kochanowski's *Laments* change the rules for the Renaissance lament codified
by Joseph Caesar Scalinger in 1561 (Ziomek 318). An epicedium was a single poem
with a fixed, five-part order: praise for the deceased; demonstration of the extent of
the loss; mourning or expression of grief; consolation of the bereaved; and moral conclusion. The epicedium was written in a high style about people of public importance
whose accomplishments could provide inspirational moral lessons. Kochanowski
violated the genre by writing in a high style about personal loss; the social code of
the time did not even support extensive public grieving over the death of a child,
an event that was common and considered a family matter (Baranczak xvii-xviii).
While maintaining the general progression from expression of loss and praise of
the deceased through grief to consolation and moral conclusion, Kochanowski composed not a single poem, but nineteen laments, tracing the development of parental
grief. He rearranged the characteristic personal roles to provide not the consolation
of rational certainty but the emotional necessity of faith, expressed in a dream vision
that consoles only by accepting the uncertainty revealed by death.

Kochanowski's earlier epicedium "On the Death of Jan Tarnowski" showed the
prescribed roles: 1) an important personage whose deeds were praised in a high-style
narrative; 2) a surviving relative who was consoled and given a moral lesson of
general importance; and 3) the inspired poet who provided the praise, consolation,
and moral instruction. The *Laments* have strong lyrical elements because the praised
individual is a child too young for public deeds and the surviving relative and poet
are the same person (Ziomek 319). The poet focuses on his own loss and desperate
search for a voice responsive to his suffering, directly addressing the Greek muses,
Greek authors of laments, Greek gods, the Christian God, objects, concepts, his lute,
and his dead daughter. The desired response comes in his dead mother's nocturnal
visit and raises a number of questions: Does this voice come from the poet as the
genre assumes? Is it only a psychological necessity, or a real visitation sent by God
in response to his prayers? Is it a rediscovered Christian faith or a restatement of the
challenged humanism?

The cycle form leaves these questions open because, despite the belated praise
of the Slavic Sappho, heir to her father's lyre and singer of an improbably elo-
quent and poised final speech, the cycle is more about the reactions of a parent and
Renaissance humanist to trauma than about her. Calling on Greek authors to help
him mourn his daughter, he explains why he must write: his daughter's unnatural
death has destroyed both his equilibrium and the assumed order of the world. She is
an appropriate subject for a lament not for what she has accomplished but for what
her premature destruction by cruel Persephone reveals about the human condition.

Indeed, the *Laments* explore both the personal and philosophical dimensions
of mortality. Kochanowski strikingly situates laments about the greatness of his
loss in family space describing the details of Urszula's now useless possessions and
the holes she has left in his home. He contrasts the many virtues Urszula displayed

around the house with the sorrow she has left her parents. The grief is concrete and intimate rather than public and elevated. How can a parent survive this? In the universal space of humanism, personal loss becomes the failure of stoicism. Brutus was right: virtue is a trifle that has never helped anyone in the face of real disaster. Human vision is too dull for heavenly forms. The classical models offer precedents for despair but no way out of it. Can Kochanowski's lyre help him follow Orpheus and get Pluto to release Urszula? Can his narrative of Niobe's grief lessen his own? Since even his beloved Cicero, despite claiming to be a self-sufficient citizen of the world, mourned the loss of Rome and daughter, Kochanowski concludes that reason always fails and only time can ease his pain.

Drawing on the imaginative diversity of humanism, Kochanowski implores the dead Urszula, if she still exists, to appear to him in any form as dream, shade, or phantom. Personal pain demands personal consolation, even if it is an illusion. Any tradition will do; humanist philosophy has been shown to be inhuman in its pretensions, demands, and failed consolations. As a parent, Kochanowski presents such a conclusion as unavoidable; as a humanist, he finds it unacceptable, asking whether he is about to lose both his joy and his reason.

Two psalms change the tone, accepting the failure of reason and entreating the Christian God to have mercy on human failings. The first echoes the book of Job. God's hand can reach us no matter how secluded and innocent a life we live; the second resembles a prayer asking God to punish us in our arrogant success, but only within the limits of our endurance and with the mercy for which he is famous. Kochanowski's prayer is seemingly answered as his dead mother brings him his daughter dressed as if she were on her way to morning prayers. Has the Christian tradition provided the necessary consolation?

Yes, but the dream may not be real, and his mother's consoling lessons are those of Renaissance humanism and classical stoicism. Your daughter avoided the dangers of life in this uncertain world and is at peace with the eternal. Do not ruin your health through pointless worrying. You spent years acquiring knowledge; now use it to accept your grief. Time overcomes sorrow by giving us more layers of experience; wise men should do the same by preparing themselves in advance for the unavoidable sorrows of the human condition. The final "Dream" has not so much replaced the earlier poems as joined them in a more complicated understanding of life. We have no choice but to bear humanly the human lot, but this does not mean that we always can. The Christian and classical views are reconciled in a rational world order, but the lives of individuals within that order are governed by fortune whose random brutalities can crush the individual. Fate and our guilt before an angry God can be accepted but not endured without the image of a responsive, maternal face.

Kochanowski's *Laments* prove that his daughter was an appropriate subject for a poem. Her death and his grief allowed him to combine the personal, philosophical, poetic, and religious in a work that first challenges and then reasserts the traditions of Renaissance humanism. By creating a more complex view of the world's order, by demonstrating the ability to reassert reason and virtue in the face of extreme grief, and by creating a new genre, he created a work that feels constantly new because it has achieved a new balance among its own contradictory elements. By combining diverse traditions with personal experience to turn blunt trauma into memory and death into communication with self and others, Kochanowski showed how a vital core tradition lives and enables life.

Works Cited

Baranczak, Stanislaw. "Introduction." Treny/*Laments*. Trans. Stanislaw Baranczak and Seamus Heaney. New York: Farrar, Straus, and Giroux, 1995. V-XX.

Kochanowski, Jan. "O smierci Jana Tarnowskiego." *Treny*. Ed. Janusz Pelc. Wroclaw: Zaklad Narodowy Imienia Ossolinskich, 1978. 53-64.

———. Treny/*Laments*. Trans. Stanislaw Baranczak and Seamus Heaney. New York: Farrar, Straus, and Giroux, 1995.

Ziomek, Jerzy. *Renesans*. Warsaw: PWN, 1976.

Freedom and Its Limits:
Molière's Don Juan as Freethinker

Diane Fourny
The University of Kansas

"Nothing matters in this life but getting what one wants." (*Don Juan*, I: 2)

As citizens living in a western democracy who enjoy enormous freedom and economic privilege, many of our students do not find the question of freedom particularly worrisome or challenging. This is perhaps due to the way we transmit knowledge of that notion when it is taught primarily as a question of political freedom, the path of which seems to follow a steady and progressive trajectory of enlightenment, from Plato's *Apology* and Aristotle's *Politics* through Luther's *Christian Liberty*, Locke's *Second Treatise* or *Declaration of Independence*, and J. S. Mill's *On Liberty*. Content with the "givens" of these texts, and accustomed to an extraordinary access to and enjoyment of freedom, students often ignore the complexity of the issue as it pertains to individual freedom, particularly when it is a question of restricting that freedom. Add to this the fact that our "consumer-driven" society equates freedom with unlimited access to lifestyles emphasizing material gain and hedonistic pleasure-seeking at all costs, and the notion of freedom becomes a fuzzy concept at best, better left unquestioned to the Bill of Rights. When asked to reflect about the limits of freedom, we shouldn't be surprised if students even toss out Mill's golden rule of "no harm to others" in favor of some absolutist notion of "my rights" understood in everyday parlance as "every man for himself" and "not in my back yard."

This paper will argue that lost within the transmission of our understanding of political rights has been the distinction between individualism and social or political freedom, that one's personal freedom to pursue whatever path desired or toward self-realization does not necessarily lead to freedom in any social or political sense. A student today often conflates individualism with notions of freedom when what is at the heart of individualism is freedom metaphysically understood: the possibility of limitlessness or absolute freedom of the human will. To illustrate the problematic relationship between metaphysical and social or political freedom, it is useful then to turn to a work that offers an extreme example of individualism, especially when that text offers a tantalizing portrait of the iconic hedonist as "freethinker" whose destructive egotism wreaks moral havoc in a world of unclear boundaries (moral, social, political, etc.).

Moliere's seventeenth-century dark comedy, *Don Juan*, offers students just such an example of individualism, positing a hero possessing an unrestricted access to unlimited freedom. More importantly, it provokes students to question their assumptions about unlimited freedom when they find themselves in front of a hero who is really an anti-hero, and have to deal with their own ambivalent feelings toward the main protagonist who is both dastardly villain and audacious virtuoso of seduction and wit. True, Don Juan's world of "law and order" pursues him with a vengeance in its attempt to punish his debauchery, impiety, criminality, and hypocrisy. Yet he ends by making dupes of everyone he abuses: the women he seduces and then abandons; the nobleman he affronts; a father, sovereign, and caste he dishonors; the manservant he cheats out of wages; his tailor he never pays—no one "collects" his or her debt. We spectators or readers are perhaps the Don's biggest dupes since we are literally seduced by his brilliance and bravado. Even the final scene seems deflated compared to the deliberate speed and courage with which Don Juan grasps the Commander's hand, pulling him to his hellish demise. As one critic concludes, "the transcendental stature of [Don Juan as] Victor suggests the true measure of a freedom and a power which, as the play as a whole seems designed to suggest, had made a mockery of all human and terrestrial constraints" (Brody 567). I will argue in this paper that Don Juan's seductive appeal and repellent nature are related, precisely, to his practice of freedom at all costs. He symbolizes an act of freedom that indeed scandalizes; he points to freedom's complicated dimension at the level of individual agency.

As other critics have argued, Molière's protagonist embodies the "assertion of absolute freedom for the self" (Ball and Ellis 147). As difficult as Don Juan's world makes the practice of that absolute freedom, the protagonist nevertheless succeeds with impunity to impose himself and his desire upon the rest of the world (Brody 559). He becomes the reified Subject embodying absolute freedom and autonomy whose myriad victories are not so much the consequence of his physical prowess as they are of his mental force.[1] Don Juan even asks at one point, "And have I a right, do you think, to behave that way?" rhetorically rationalizing on political grounds that his individual freedom is the political "right" ensuring access to his desire. His trusty valet, Sganarelle, is quick to inform us in the opening scenes that his master is part of that dangerous group of "free-thinkers" who also "play at *unbelievers*" (they are *impie*, i.e., "impious," a code word in Molière's time for the skeptical humanist thinker or writer). Molière knew his audience would connect these references to the seventeenth-century cultural phenomenon of what critics have since termed "erudite libertines" (*les libertins érudits*): the philosophical, scientific, and literary group of writers and thinkers who challenged orthodoxy, authoritarianism, and imposture in all forms during this troubled period of intolerance, civil strife, and massive economic and political turmoil. This was a loose agglomeration of intellectuals spanning an era from Montaigne, Galileo, Descartes, and Gassendi to poets and writers such as Theophile de Viau, Cyrano de Bergerac, Molière, and Fontenelle, to mention only the well-known.[2] Following the cabal of French religious bigots who condemned his masterful comedy against religious hypocrisy, *Tartuffe*, Molière rewarded his audience with this more outrageously defiant comedy, *Don Juan*, in a gesture, as one critic has suggested, of absolute artistic freedom (Ball and Ellis 153).

Molière illustrates the early modern "free-thinking" phenomenon by way of staging numerous, seemingly gratuitous dialogues between master and servant, Don Juan and Sganarelle. Each encounter serves as a perfect soapbox for comically pitting Faith against Reason, Ignorance against Knowledge, or Convention against Skepticism.[3] Credit goes to the intellectual pummeling the Don metes out against his servant. The hero wins every argument by use of impeccable reason, leading poor Sganarelle through the twists and turns of the valet's simplistic "credences." Don Juan scorns and laughs at Sganarelle's superstitious warnings, moral platitudes, and irrational fears while the servant cautiously criticizes his master's lack of piety, and mockery of moral and social duty. His lust for women, Don Juan argues, is not to be taken as mere brutish sexual desire, but instead as an ultimate act of reverence before the ideals of Beauty and Love (Molière 15). In another instance, Don Juan rationally explains physical desire as nothing more than heeding the call of Nature or the physiological "stirrings" of the body (15). While Sganarelle trembles with fright upon witnessing the Commander's statue nod its head "yes" at them, Don Juan calmly offers a material explanation of what has most likely occurred: an optical illusion of some sort, that is, their senses are playing with their minds (99). Compared to Sganarelle's superstitious fear of trespassing on the dead when visiting the Commander's ornate tomb in the woods, Don Juan admires the architectural beauty of its marbled columns and statues, as if gazing at an edifice built by Palladio (91-92). He freely divorces his observations and thoughts from the moral portent of the moment and place, standing as he does in front of the tomb of the man he murdered. His tastes in women, lodgings, artwork, food—all point to the "Epicurean" in him: a man of impeccable manners and vast education who seeks out the pleasurable wherever it exists (Pensom 99). In another scene, Don Juan's filial contrition before his father's tongue lashing turns out to be a "prudent strategy of deception," placing hypocrisy at the service of his desire; he'd rather freely and consciously falsify his intentions to "reform his ways" than lose a father's protection against the tide of "vexations" waiting to befall the son (Molière 134). Don Juan's virtuosity depends not on his aristocratic upbringing and caste privilege, but rather on the role he plays as "free-thinker."

Don Juan and Sganarelle form this Janus-like figure standing in for all of us who, on the one hand, jealously guard our intellectual authority and absolute freedom to advance our personal desires and needs, and on the other, so often abdicate that very freedom to act on our will and desires out of fear, loathing, and ignorance. We cheer on the dazzling virtuosity of this freethinker who outsmarts his upright and pious opponents every time. Fearless at the hour of his ultimate undoing, Don Juan meets the Specter of Death with the daring of a rational materialist. He cries: "Hah! Nothing on earth can terrify me, and I mean to find out, with my sword, whether this thing is body or spirit" (144). We almost forget that the Don is a pursued murderer and adulterer (if not rapist), a blasphemer, a cheat, and a stubborn and cruel Master, if it weren't for Sganarelle's utterly farcical, yet deadly ironic pantomimes of the intellectually gifted free-thinker: Sganarelle's disquisition on the qualities of "snuff" to "purge and stimulate the brain" (7); Sganarelle as the Moralist (13-18); and Sganarelle as the Doctor ("This costume has sharpened my wits, and I feel in the mood to debate" [70]). Don Juan's absolute freedom monopolizes the action and dialogue, but it is the groveling servant who obeys the authority of his masters, his religion, and his God who gets the last laugh—or we think he does.[4] It is Sganarelle who helps assuage our guilt for admiring Don Juan's enormous freedom knowing full well he uses it immoderately and without a care for the tragic consequences to surely follow.

Perhaps the most puzzling illustrations of freedom in the play take place in Act III, which portrays the hero at his best and at his worst. In scenes 3 and 4 we witness Don Juan's startling transformation into an honorable hero who now saves lives, rescuing a fellow nobleman under attack by brigands. The latter turns out to be none other than Don Carlos (the wronged woman Donna Elvira's avenging brother). Has Don Juan finally met his well-deserved destiny—a duel to the death with Don Carlos—and why would Molière turn his protagonist into a morally good hero? Molière gives us no such satisfaction here; rather he utterly confounds us when the two gentlemen acknowledge their allegiance to a mutually recognized code of aristocratic honor. The code prohibits, on the one hand, Don Carlos from immediately killing his sister's seducer because Don Juan has just saved his life; on the other, it forces Don Juan to pledge to Don Carlos his future assistance in rendering to his fellow nobleman the very knave Don Carlos seeks, that is, Don Juan himself, at a place and time of the former's choosing. In our twenty-first-century casteless society, it is difficult to consider an aristocratic code of honor being other than an outdated version of "honor among thieves." However, within its seventeenth-century aristocratic context, it well relates to the Aristotelian notion of virtue or the pursuit of excellence at all levels of existence: physical, social, moral, and political. Virtue is to be found in the self-achieving individual who acquires knowledge, courage, self-mastery, temperance, and virtue. It becomes quite plausible then to consider Don Juan's perfect practice of aristocratic virtue as one that could only have been nurtured in a world in which a privileged few who, enjoying an almost perfect freedom to exercise their mind and body, attain the highest levels of self-achievement. This is not to say that we should now declare Don Juan a moral hero in any normal sense of the word, but his act of "generosity" in these scenes points to the limits—or lack thereof—of that pursuit of individual freedom in the name of perfect self-realization. As twisted as it may appear, Don Juan's magnanimity in these scenes oddly confirms his social and even moral virtue as a seventeenth-century nobleman. Outraged, Don Carlos' brother, Don Alonso, looks on unbelieving at his brother's "debt of honor" owed to this seducer while the two gentlemen carry on a discourse in utmost seriousness on the moral burden of their caste and function regarding the "laws of honor." If we embrace in principle the idea of one's right to absolute freedom, then where do we draw the line with an individual whose use of that freedom, while adhering to a particular virtue, remains abhorrent (Don Juan) or absurd (Don Carlos)?

In the preceding scene 2 of Act III, Don Juan's encounter with an obstinate Poor Man is even more perplexing. At its center the two protagonists could not be further apart: the privileged aristocrat with his purse and the starving pauper who promises to pray for his benefactor's prosperity and good if Don Juan would obligingly offer a coin. As is to be expected, Don Juan ridicules the gullible and stupidly pious pauper whose faith dictates he pray for the benefit of the rich. Ever the rational thinker, Don Juan counsels the Poor Man to pray for his own prosperity rather than for the prosperity of others who already have it. Faith meets Reason in a scene between these two men of obviously unequal status and qualities but who nevertheless share a not-so-obvious equal freedom. The Don offers the gold coin but only on condition that the Poor Man "blaspheme[s] a little" his god (Molière 77-78). He insists three times, and three times the Poor Man refuses, saying finally, "No, Sir, I'd rather starve to death" (78). There is nothing rational or grand in the Poor Man's gesture; his obstinacy is anchored in an ignorant faith and/or irrational fear of God's retribution against blasphemers. The secular rationalist on the other hand, having made his point, will nevertheless act upon his first impulse—to reward the Poor Man for his assistance—and give him his gold piece, with one condition. Don Juan gives not out of Christian charity but out of a most secular reason: "I'll give it to you for the love of humanity" (78).

While we have seen that Don Juan indeed embodies one of the greatest "assertions of absolute freedom for the self" to ever visit the stage, we can't help but condemn that freedom when it destroys the lives and happiness of others. And yet, an approving nod is given to a hero whose actions rise above ignorance, convention, imposture, and superstition; to a hero in hot pursuit of desire gained by intelligence, virtuosity, curiosity, and courage. In Moliere's world of Counter-Reformation France—a period of bloody religious and civil strife, of the intolerant Inquisition persecuting science and new scholarship, of garrulous displays of pomp and crushing authority by Church and State, of inordinate social inequity stemming largely from the existence of a rotting social model based on feudal privilege, and of desired conformity to new standards of taste, comportment, and invention—Don Juan is not such a strange duck. Neither justified nor admired, his actions are at least comprehensible. Albert Camus even went so far as to offer an understanding of Don Juan, judging his world as "absurd"—a society in which religion, law, medicine, and authority had little or no meaning when they arbitrarily enriched or bettered the lives only of a privileged few (Pensom 102).

Reading about past worlds and eras of social, economic, political and moral decay that share an affinity with our own world in certain respects, students can profit from Moliere's ambiguous lesson about freedom. Many stand in awe of the new-money multi-millionaires (the younger and more audacious, the better); of bellowing talk show hosts and cynical television pundits; of the NFL superstar quarterback whose celebrity protects him from arrest for spousal abuse, drugs, or illegal dog fighting; of the talentless socialite and the hypocritical evangelical pastor in his mega-church. All of these modern-day Don Juans assert an uncompromising freedom to greedily pilfer, outrage, assault, scandalize, and bamboozle their admiring fans for whom they have become cultural role models as "self-

made" individuals. Or are they not at all Don Juan but instead the modern-day
versions of Molière's Nobleman, Doctor, Moralist, Father, Preacher, or Eternal
Woman? For today's Don Juans, is there a line to be drawn when it comes to
personal freedom? If so, where do we draw these limits? Or do we instead assert
a right to absolute freedom? Molière's comedy serves as a good springboard for
examining the various dimensions of freedom—metaphysical, social, and political—in an attempt to better understand its nature, practice, and limits.

Notes

1. While we learn through dialogue that Don Juan has murdered a man (Donna Elvira's father), Molière "stages" his hero's use of violence in only one scene (Act
   III: 3), and this, solely in a figurative way: Don Juan sheathes his sword after
   having, ironically, defended the life of Elvira's brothers who are being attacked
   by bandits (and his own honor). The idea of Don Juan's physically violent nature
   probably stems from a confusion with Mozart's interpretation of the nobleman
   in his opera, *Don Giovanni,* which makes Don Juan's violent nature explicit in
   the first act.
2. Though recognizing that Molière deemed his hero a "free-thinker," Jacques
   Prévot suggests that Don Juan is a false "libertin" because he is incapable of
   "being conscious of his own contradictions," for example, limiting the freedom
   of others to ensure his own, being enslaved to his lascivious desires for women,
   and so forth (xliii).
3. "Sganarelle's ventures into intellectual rivalry with his master illuminate but one
   aspect of the more generalized contest in this play between conventional views
   of the world and Don Juan's iconoclasm, between order and freedom, obligation
   and independence, society and the individual" (Brody 562).
4. The play famously concludes with Sganarelle's final words: "My wages! Who'll
   pay me my wages?" (146).

Works Cited

Ball, David, and Frank H. Ellis. "*Dom Juan*: Form, Meaning, Audience." *Modern Philology* 81. 2 (1983): 146-158.

Brody, Jules. "*Don Juan* and *Le Misanthrope,* or the Esthetics of Individualism in Molière." *PMLA* 84.3 (1969): 559-576.

Molière, Jean Baptiste Poquelin de. *Don Juan.* Trans. Richard P. Wilbur. San Diego: Harcourt, 2001.

Pensom, Roger. "*Don Juan* ou faire de la philosophie." *Poétique* 89 (1992): 93-104.

Prévot, Jacques, ed. *Libertins du XVIIe siècle.* Vol. I. Paris: Gallimard, Editions de la Pléiade, 1998.

Freedom and Coercion in Locke's Treatment of Religion and Politics

Thomas Powers
Carthage College

That Locke's *A Letter Concerning Toleration* is a fitting topic for thinking about the question of cultural memory and transmission and core texts is easy to defend in the United States because his teaching shapes the American understanding of religion and politics so profoundly. Because the United States Supreme Court begins its understanding of the First Amendment by way of an unapologetic reliance upon the work of Madison and Jefferson and because Locke's influence on Madison and Jefferson was direct and overwhelming, the American connection to Locke is more powerful here than perhaps in any other area of life (see Malbin 29; Sandler).

But if then understanding the *Letter* would be useful from the point of view of understanding ourselves—our memory and our likely future—the complexity of the *Letter* raises some obstacles that need to be addressed. Locke employs a wide variety of different kinds of arguments (at least six) to set forth the ideal of religious toleration in *A Letter Concerning Toleration*. Often Locke advances theological arguments from the perspective of a certain interpretation of Christianity (emphasizing charity and freely chosen inward belief and rejecting theocracy). He also advances a distinctively liberal ecclesiology, providing an account of the nature of the church and the role of the clergy, and Locke's theological arguments are accompanied by (and may at points depend upon) what seem strictly philosophical or epistemological arguments about the nature of belief as such. Sometimes Locke argues from a very practical point of view, speculating on the basis of general claims about social and political life (maintaining that religious diversity and religious tolerance will lead to peace among religious groups). At other points, Locke argues from the point of view of "natural rights" theory and the logic of the social contract. Finally and perhaps most generally, Locke frames his entire discussion by providing an outline of the division of civil and religious realms.

The simple problem of the complexity of the *Letter* is compounded by a basic tension in the character of these different arguments. Some of them would seem to be religious (theology, ecclesiology), and others are secular (epistemology, natural rights theory, practical political speculation). Which of these two perspectives is most authoritative for Locke, and which of the two provides the ultimate basis for his account of the division of religion and politics?

I believe that the best way to sort out the status of the different approaches taken by Locke in the *Letter* is by way of a direct examination of his account of the division of religious and political life itself. Locke himself "esteem[s] it above all things necessary to distinguish exactly the business of civil government from that of religion," the two being "in their original, end, business, and in every thing, perfectly distinct, and infinitely different from each other" (Locke 393, 403).[1] This division frames the structure of the *Letter* in a general way. After beginning with a general statement of the central importance of separating out the religious and political domains, Locke discusses in about twenty paragraphs first the civil side of that divide then the religious (paragraphs 5-13, 14-24). But the same divide continues also to frame Locke's account of the "duty of toleration" which comes in the next 35 paragraphs or so, considered first from the point of view of the private sphere (churches, private persons, and clergy) and then the public (paragraphs 26-34, 35-71).[2]

But the more fundamental reason to follow out this dimension of the argument is that it most clearly reveals Locke's view of the place of religion. Locke in fact draws the line between religion and politics two different ways. One suggests in a way the primacy of religion, the other the primacy of politics. If we could sort out in a non-arbitrary way which of these two lines of division is paramount for Locke, this might provide us with a key to understanding the rest of the *Letter*.

Initially, the division is one between the spiritual and earthly concerns of human beings. The domain of churches is "the salvation of souls," while the domain of the civil authority extends only to "civil interests." "Civil interests I call life, liberty, health, and indolency of body; and the possession of outward things, such as money, lands, houses, furniture, and the like" (393). But Locke also draws the line by reference to the modes of persuasion, inducement, or enforcement permitted to the two spheres. While churches may employ the "arms" of "exhortations, admonitions, and advice" to keep members "within their duty," "force belongs wholly to the civil magistrate, and the possession of all outward goods is subject to his jurisdiction" (399).

It is the latter division, it seems to me, that we must privilege, since the question here is ultimately one of the priority or ranking of the two realms. The question is made more pointed by Locke's discussion of the possibility of *conflicts* between the religious and political and by his account of the resolution of those conflicts. Though Locke does not address the issue until relatively late in the *Letter*, his treatment suggests fairly clearly the predominance of politics over religion. Locke asks the question first from the point of view of the religious person: "What if the magistrate should enjoin anything by his authority that appears unlawful to the conscience of a private person?" (423). Locke also asks the question from the point of view of the civil authority: "But what if the magistrate believe that he has a right to make such laws and that they are for the public good, and his subjects believe the contrary? Who shall be judge between them?" (424).

Locke's answer is not simple and seems crafted to soften the blow for those sympathetic to the cause of religion. The answer to the latter question above—who shall judge between the magistrate and his subjects—is to begin with "God alone" (424). Similarly, Locke holds that such conflicts will "seldom happen...if government be faithfully administered, and the counsels of the magistrate be indeed directed to the public good" (423).

But ultimately Locke's answer is decisive and clear and all on the side of the magistrate. As for the subject facing what he or she deems to be a law contradicting the duties of religion, "such a private person is to abstain from the action that he judges unlawful, and he is to undergo the punishment which it is not unlawful for him to bear. For the private judgment of any person concerning a law enacted in political matters, for the public good, does not take away the obligation of that law, nor deserve a dispensation" (423). Locke goes on to draw the conclusion about the magistrate's authority that necessarily corresponds to what he has already indicated about the religious citizen's duty to obey. "There are two sorts of contests amongst men, the one managed by law, the other by force; and these are of that nature that where the one ends, the other always begins.... You will say, then, the magistrate being the stronger will have his will and carry his point. Without doubt; but the question is not here concerning the doubtfulness of the event, but the rule of right" (424).

It is crucial to see that this predominance of the civil authority extends not only to matters of "action" (to borrow from American First Amendment jurisprudence) but to those of religious "belief" or opinion as well. This is suggested already by the involvement of "the conscience of a private person" in the conflict mentioned above. But it is also made an explicit theme by Locke when he takes up the question of the vitally important area *shared* by both the religious and political domains, that of morality. Locke first presents this as a problem or danger from the point of view of religious liberty. "Moral actions belong therefore to the jurisdiction both of the outward and inward court; both of the civil and domestic governor; I mean both of the magistrate and the conscience. Here therefore is great danger, lest one of these jurisdictions intrench upon the other, and discord arise between the keeper of the public peace and the overseer of souls" (421). But Locke's resolution of this problem is one consistent with what we have already seen: "no opinions contrary to human society, or to those *moral rules* which are necessary to the preservation of civil society, are to be *tolerated* by the magistrate" (424, emphasis supplied).

Paying attention to the hierarchical relationship between church and state that emerges here also helps to make sense of a passage earlier in the work that seems strange coming from Locke the defender of religious freedom. In something of an aside, Locke seems to go so far as to say that religious opinion is actually *derived from* political life.

> But, to speak the truth, we must acknowledge that the church...is for the most part more apt to be influenced by the court, than the court by the church. How the church

was under the vicissitude of orthodox and Arian emperors is very well known. Or if those things be too remote, our modern English history affords us fresh examples, in the reigns of Henry VIII, Edward VI, Mary, and Elizabeth, how easily and smoothly the clergy changed their decrees, their articles of faith, their form of worship, every thing, according to the inclinations of those kings and queens. (409)

If this interpretation of Locke's division of religion and politics is correct, then it would seem necessary to read Locke's *Letter* as a work designed to limit religion's power under the guise of creating a framework ostensibly to protect it. This would suggest a way to begin to read the other arguments—from theology, ecclesiology, epistemology, natural right, and political practice—in the work as well.

Notes

1. All references indicate page numbers in Wootton's 1993 edition, unless otherwise indicated.
2. Note: there are 78 paragraphs in the letter, not including the short postscript. The paragraph divisions are not uniform among different editions of the *Letter*. The Wootton edition (which I am using for citation purposes) adds four more paragraphs to the above list. The Wootton numbers would be: after beginning with a general statement of the central importance of separating out the religious and political domains Locke discusses first the civil side of that divide (paragraphs 6-14), then the religious (paragraphs 15-25). But the same divide continues to frame Locke's account of the "duty of toleration," considered first from the point of view of the private sphere (churches, private persons, and clergy (paragraphs 27-37) and then the public sphere (paragraphs 38-75).

Works Cited

Locke, John. "A Letter Concerning Toleration." *Political Writings of John Locke.* Ed. David Wootton. New York: Mentor, 1993.

Malbin, Michael J. *Religion and Politics: The Intentions of the Authors of the First Amendment.* Washington, D.C.: American Enterprise Institute for Public Policy Research, 1978.

Sandler, S. Gerald. "Lockean Ideas in Thomas Jefferson's 'Bill for Establishing Religious Freedom.'" *Journal of the History of Ideas* 21.1 (1960): 110-116.

Ambition, Happiness, and Adam Smith's *The Theory of Moral Sentiments*

Edward J. Harphame
University of Texas at Dallas

Why should modern social scientists read the core texts? What do these texts have to offer disciplines such as economics, political science, and sociology, fields of study that are seeking to provide empirically verifiable explanations of human behavior in modern complex commercial societies? Aren't the core texts out of date in a world dominated by social scientists who sing the praises of the rational actor model?

I imagine that the people attending this conference all have fairly definitive answers to these questions. Many would agree with the growing criticism that the rational actor model of human behavior that underlies much of modern economic and political thought is too simplistic. Students need to be exposed to a broader understanding of social life that includes more than a discussion of the unintended consequences of self-interested behavior in the marketplace. Students of economic behavior need to recognize the complexity of human nature and human decision-making, as well as to be able to reflect upon the often-tragic nature of human interaction in commercial societies. The value of the core texts lies in their ability to bring contemporary social science in contact with the concerns that have shaped western thought since the time of the ancient Greeks.

I would like to argue today that core texts like Adam Smith's *The Theory of Moral Sentiments* (1982) can provide social scientists with a richer insight into human nature than is found in much of modern economic and political theory. While Smith is often considered to be the founder of the modern science of economics, he is also an important moral philosopher in his own right. *The Theory of Moral Sentiments* went through six editions in his lifetime and played a major role in shaping moral discourse throughout the 18th Century. Obviously, in the limited space available to me here I cannot talk about all the complex interpretive issues surrounding either *The Theory of Moral Sentiments* or the *Wealth of Nations* (1981). So to make my point I will focus my attention on a brief story— the tale of the poor man's son, as told by Smith— to explain the psychological foundations of economic behavior and their relationship to Smith's understanding of happiness.

The tale of the poor man's son found in Chapter 1 of Part IV in *The Theory of Moral Sentiments* is the story of an ambitious individual who is dissatisfied with his place in the world and imagines that he will be better off in other circumstances. By observing those around him, the poor man's son naturally comes to admire the condition of the rich. He "finds" that his father's cottage is too small and "fancies" that he would be better off in a palace. He "feels" himself to be naturally indolent and he "judges" that a large number of servants will save him a great deal of trouble (*TMS:* 181).

The poor man's son "thinks" that if he could just attain all these things he would be content to enjoy himself "in the thought of the happiness and tranquility of his situation" (*TMS:* 181). He then becomes enchanted with this idea of happiness and tranquility, and devotes himself to the pursuit of wealth and greatness. Ironically, to obtain all the conveniences made possible by wealth and greatness, he suffers "more fatigue of body and more uneasiness of mind" in the first month of his endeavors than he would have experienced without these conveniences. In pursuit of an idea of "artificial and elegant repose which he may never arrive at," he suffers the tragedy of sacrificing the real tranquility of mind that, all along, has been in his power to attain (*TMS:* 181).

For those less familiar with Smith's moral theory than his economic theory, the tale of the poor man's son comes as something of a shock. Smith is offering us a psychological account of human motivation that flies in the face of much rational choice theory. Simply put, individuals are not necessarily the best judges of what will make them happy in this life. Yes, people have preferences as to what they believe will make them happy. And yes, they make choices based on these preferences, seeking to better their condition in life. People pursue happiness as best they see it. But in the end, Smith believes they often do not see happiness appropriately, nor do they act in ways that might achieve it. Such failings inevitably lead to personal tragedy.

Commentators on Adam Smith have spent much time trying to understand the full significance of the tale of the poor man's son to Smith's other works. They consider the idea of "bettering one's condition" found in the *Wealth of Nations* synonymous with the psychological analysis underlying the tale of the poor man's son in *The Theory of Moral Sentiments*. This is a serious mistake. To be sure, the two are related: the tale of the poor man's son builds on the idea that humans have an inborn desire or hope to better their condition in the world. But motives that drive the poor man's son should not be equated with the idea of calmly bettering one's condition, as set out in the *Wealth of Nations*. The latter refers to "a desire which, though generally calm and dispassionate, comes with us from the womb, and never leaves us till we go into the grave. In the whole interval which separates these two moments, there is scarce perhaps a single instant in which any man is so perfectly and completely satisfied with his situation, as to be without any wish of alteration or improvement, of any kind" (*WN*: 341). The former is the story of an individual whose capacity for "calm dispassionate" judgment has been displaced by an unquenchable ambition. The psychological motives that drive the poor man's son may rest upon the "calm and dispassionate desire" to better one's condition, but they have been transformed by the imagination into something quite different.

On the face of it, the tale of the poor man's son appears to offer a relatively straightforward theory of human happiness that echoes some of the concerns of the ancient Stoics. Neither wealth nor greatness can bring us real or lasting happiness. Seriously ill individuals quickly discover what is important in life. If only we could escape the useless desires that are impressed upon us by our imaginations, we could discover authentic happiness. Appearances, however, are deceiving. Smith's actual argument is much more complex, and his teaching is more subtle.

According to Smith, happiness is not an objective statement about our condition in the world but rather something subjective that resides in the mind. It depends more upon "the healthful or unhealthful, the mutilated or entire state of the mind, than upon that of the body" (*WN*: 787). Happiness consists of tranquility and enjoyment. "Without tranquility there can be no enjoyment; and where there is perfect tranquility there is scarce any thing which is not capable of amusing" (*TMS:* 149). Like the Stoics, Smith believes that passions such as anger and hatred are poisons to the happiness of a good mind. Such passions can destroy the tranquility and composure of mind that is necessary to happiness (*TMS:* 37).

A natural state of tranquility resides in the mind of every man exerting himself when freed of violent passion or emotion. All humans can find "true happiness" in life if they can find a position of tranquility for their mind from which they might enjoy the various pleasures that life has to offer them. Failing that, of course, means that they may be doomed to misery.

One key to happiness lies in reconciling oneself to one's position in life and in not allowing either excessive joy or excessive sorrow to overwhelm one's basic acceptance of the way that the world is. Smith thus agrees with the Stoics who argued that there is little difference between one permanent situation an individual faces and another from the perspective of "real happiness" (TMS: 149). However, his position on happiness moves beyond the Stoics in a number of important ways. First, Smith accepts the idea that certain minimal levels of physical and material well-being must exist for an individual to be considered happy. A healthy Aristotelianism balances the stricter demands of Stoicism. It is unreasonable to think that the mind's happiness is ever completely freed from either the body or the material conditions under which the body lives. In the final, sixth edition of *The Theory of Moral Sentiments*, Smith appears to add another precondition to happiness: a sphere of personal liberty (see *TMS:* 150). Such a condition is hardly surprising in light of the fact that slaves would seem to lack the security in body, the tranquility of mind, or the cultivated conscience that happiness demands.[1]

Second, Smith argues that the chief part of human happiness arises from "a consciousness of being beloved" (*TMS:* 41). There is an inter-subjectivity to Smith's notion of happiness that is largely missing from the Stoics. Stoics sought happiness by freeing an individual from the evaluations of others. Smith, on the other hand, believes our happiness is tied to our perception of the happiness of others and to our understanding of how others perceive us. The consciousness that others not only love us but also believe that we deserve to be loved is an essential element of Smith's teaching about "real happiness" (*TMS*: 149) or "true satisfaction." (*TMS*: 183). Indeed, the consciousness of being beloved is the bedrock upon which Smith's vision of real happiness rests. Coupled with our own impartial evaluation of ourselves deserving to be loved, it is for Smith one of the most pleasurable feelings that humans can experience.

Third, Smith declares that we rarely view happiness in such an "abstract and philosophical light" as that offered by Stoicism. The "splenetic philosophy" of the Stoics may be adopted in times of sickness or low spirits, when our imagination is "confined and cooped up within our own persons" (*TMS*: 183). But our imagination naturally expands outward during times of ease and prosperity, cultivating a more complex view of what comprises happiness. The mind naturally reconciles itself to its situation in the world once it recognizes the unlikelihood of change, as during illness or after a life-altering injury. But in good times it naturally strikes out for more and comes to view the pleasures of wealth and greatness as something "grand and beautiful and noble" (*TMS*: 183). In other words, in normal conditions of life we are motivated by more than a vision of happiness as tranquility. We seek out challenges stimulated by the imagination and our passions. We seek the life of action and all the pains that are encompassed by that life.

The conclusions a Stoic might have drawn from the tale of the poor man's son are not hard to imagine. Limit the reach of your desires; do not allow yourself to become dependent on others or upon their judgments about you; simplify your life. But these are not Smith's conclusions. On the contrary, he accepts the inevitability of people being driven by their imaginations away from a life of simplicity and happiness and argues that ambition and misplaced understandings about what will make people happy unintentionally serve a larger interest in society. It is good that we are deceived by nature about what will make us happy. It is good that we chase after that which we believe is beautiful. It is this "deception which rouses and keeps in continual motion the industry of mankind. It is this which first prompted them to cultivate the ground, to build houses, to found cities and commonwealths, and to invent and improve all the sciences and the arts, which ennoble and embellish humans" (*TMS*: 183).

As a core text, *The Theory of Moral Sentiments* offers us two important lessons. First, more than just enlightened self-interest motivates individuals in a modern commercial society. Other motivating factors, such as ambition, can underlie social interaction in economics and politics. Just like rational self-interest, these other factors can have unintended consequences for the individual and society far different than one might expect. Second, we must look at economic and political behavior with a wider lens than that offered by much of contemporary theory. As the ancients knew so well and Adam Smith reminds us so powerfully, there is more to life than economic progress. We are compelled to act in this world by the many passions that percolate through our bodies and minds. The calm passion to improve one's lot in life is but one passion among many that drives us to action. The ultimate lesson derived from Smith's tale of the poor man's son for students of economics and politics is profound and troubling: a tragic life, rather than a happy one, may be the destiny that awaits us in a commercial society, whatever our rational intentions.

Students who read Adam Smith's *The Moral Sentiments* alongside the work of John Maynard Keynes and Milton Friedman will enjoy the fruits of a perspective that sees modern social science as part of an ongoing conversation stretching back over 2000 years. With an economic education that is richer and more useful, they can continue the conversation today and tomorrow.

Note

1. I am arguing for a softer Stoic side to Smith's *Theory of Moral Sentiments* than other commentators, such as Martha Nussbaum or Samuel Fleishchacker. They argue that Smith appears to claim that happiness is available to anyone whatever their lot in life. They support their position by citing a passage in Part IV of *The Theory of Moral Sentiments* where Smith writes, "In what constitutes the real happiness of human life, they are in no respect inferior to those who would seem so much above them. In ease of body and peace of mind, all the different ranks are nearly upon a level, and the beggar who suns himself by the side of the highway, possesses that security which kings are fighting for" *(TMS* 185). I read this passage differently. I do not believe that Smith is claiming here that everyone, in all circumstances has equal access to happiness. He is claiming that what constitutes human happiness for the rich is that same as that which constitutes human happiness for the poor. Smith's is an egalitarian argument. Happiness is the same for the rich as for the poor. It is another question entirely as to whether or not a poor man or a rich man is more likely to find this happiness, or if certain minimal levels of physical and material well-being are needed to achieve it. Smith's point is not that a beggar is necessarily as happy as a king, only that he can potentially have, on his own terms, an ease of body and peace of mind. A king who is sick in body may be as far removed from happiness as a beggar who is in debt. One advantage of a softer Stoic reading of Smith is that it allows us to identify continuity in Smith's thought between all editions of *The Theory of Moral Sentiments* and *The Wealth of Nations*. An alternative resolution to the happiness paradox in Smith can be found in Dennis Rasmussen, who focuses on the role that the rise of commercial society plays in promoting happiness by alleviating misery. I believe that Rasmussen largely ignores the tragic dimensions to Smith's analysis.

Works Cited

Fleischacker, Samuel. *On Adam Smith's* Wealth of Nations: *A Philosophical Companion*. Princeton: Princeton UP, 2004

Nussbaum, Martha. "Duties of Justice, Duties of Material Aid: Cicero's Problematic Legacy." *Journal of Political Philosophy* 8.2 (2000): 176-2006.

Rasmussen, Dennis C. "Does 'Bettering Our Condition' Really Make Us Better Off? Adam Smith on Progress and Happiness. *American Political Science Review* 100.3 (August 2006): 309-18.

Smith, Adam. *An Inquiry into the Nature and Causes of the Wealth of Nations*. 2 vols. Eds. R. H. Campbell and A.S. Skinner. Indianapolis: Liberty Classics, 1981.

—————. *The Theory of Moral Sentiments.* Eds. D.D. Raphael and A.L. Macfie. Indianapolis: Liberty Classics, 1982.

Camus's *The Fall*: Remembering the "Great Books" in Light of Modernity's Fall

Christopher E. Baldwin
Rhodes College

Modern political philosophy, from its inception, has been hopeful and lived in hopefulness. Thinkers like Machiavelli and Hobbes, as well as the more liberal heirs of modern political thought like Locke, have sought to control (if not conquer) the problems posed to us by political life—from war and conflict to political instability, inefficient government, and economic scarcity. Thanks to the ideas of these thinkers and their heirs, the modern, liberal West today enjoys a world of unprecedented peace, stability, and prosperity. We are, of course, pleased by and grateful for the blessings of such a world, and we are often pleased with ourselves for creating such a world. Yet, somehow strangely, we are not simply pleased. Some of the twentieth century's greatest thinkers and writers have expressed (to varying degrees) discontent with the modern world and modern man, our world and ourselves. But why? What do these thinkers and writers sense is wrong with our world and with us? To begin to explore this question, I look to Camus's *The Fall*, a particularly compelling and thoughtful exploration of modern man's discontent with himself and the world he has created. *The Fall*, I will argue, helps us understand both what is timeless and what is unique (and uniquely troubling) about modern man's fallen-ness. I will further suggest that, perhaps despite Camus's intention, *The Fall* can help us see the importance of remembering and studying what we might, for lack of a better term, call the "Great Books."

In *The Fall*, we are made privy to the intriguing and engrossing story of the life of (the self-styled) Jean-Baptiste Clamence, both his current life in Amsterdam after the Second World War and his life in Paris before the war. Perhaps the most noteworthy aspect of Clamence's world is the fact that, as Nietzsche's madman observed, God is dead and nobody (or almost nobody) seems to care. The proprietor of Clamence's home away from home, a dingy bar called the *Mexico City*, is a "worthy ape" (Camus 3), the product of (limited) evolution rather than divine creation, whose uncommunicative nature in no way prevents him from understanding and satisfying (when he so chooses) his customers' less than saintly wants and needs. Clamence's fellow Parisians are, to be sure, more civilized than the proprietor and patrons of the *Mexico City*. They are not, however, any more saintly. Their human-all-too-human desires extend no further than "fornicat[ing] and read[ing] the papers," and most are utterly unfamiliar with and uninterested in the claims and teachings of the Bible (6-7 and 9). The belief in God plays no role in their lives, individually or collectively, and they are altogether untroubled by this fact. In fact, if anything troubles them, it is when somebody is so gauche or backward as to mention God in polite and enlightened society (93). Such, it could be argued, is precisely the world that modern political thought hoped to bring into being.

Modern political philosophers like Machiavelli and Hobbes observed with dismay that religion was but one more source of faction and conflict in political life. Motivated by humane intentions, they sought to lessen (if not eliminate) the role of religion in politics and to reconstitute political life (if not all of human life) on more strictly rational grounds. Although admittedly often cold and harsh, the political rationalism of Machiavelli and Hobbes was ultimately meant to create a more human—even if less saintly and morally pure—world. They sought to create a world in which man would no longer be plagued by senseless religious or holy wars and would be free to enjoy the "natural and ordinary" desires of this world—*e.g.,* security, prosperity, and the pleasures of love and family—rather than tempted to sacrifice these perhaps imperfect but real goods for the sake of more splendid but perhaps illusory goods in another world (Machiavelli 14). Later and more liberal thinkers, such as Locke and his heirs, certainly deviated from Machiavelli and Hobbes's cold political rationalism in important respects, but they maintained their perhaps most fundamental hope and goal—a world where man is free of religious war and persecution and feels wholly at home in this world and satisfied with its pleasures. These thinkers and their ideas played a decisive role in shaping the modern world that Clamence's contemporaries are so pleased by and proud of. And why should they not be? They first fought and overcame the forces of pre-modern darkness and inhumanity and then, in the Second World War, the forces of modern darkness and inhumanity in order to establish and secure an enlightened and humane world of peace, stability, and prosperity. Modern enlightenment and humanity had prevailed. What was there not to be pleased by and proud of?

Clamence was initially as satisfied with himself and the modern world as his contemporaries. He was the very model of a modern, enlightened and humane human being. He was completely at home in this world, "altogether in harmony with life, fitting into it from top to bottom." Successful in his career, in society, in love, and able to enjoy all the pleasures and delights of this world from sports to the arts, he was "fundamentally pleased with himself" and his "successful life" (Camus 28). Moreover, as a successful lawyer, he benefitted not only himself but the cause of law and justice, as well as generously and humanely helping those most in need of help—specializing in "noble cases" involving "widows and orphans" and such (17). Yet this ideal modern man began to doubt himself and the world he and his contemporaries created. Clamence regains his memory.

With his memory restored and more complete self-knowledge, Clamence begins to sense that he and his contemporaries are ridiculous, even contemptible. He falls out of the easy harmony he has so far enjoyed with the world and his conscience. In a chance traffic incident, when a stalled motorcyclist refuses to get out of the way so that Clamence and others behind him may pass, despite Clamence's polite request that he do so, we see that the world is not so harmonious (51-54). There are those who would follow their will—in this case the will to be at the head of a line of traffic—even at the expense of others. More important, we see that Clamence is no different. He too wants to be at the head of the line and was willing to come to blows with the motorcyclist for this position. Thwarted in his attempt to do so by a bystander who strikes him to prevent him from striking the motorcyclist, Clamence entertains violent revenge fantasies regarding both men for several days. Although perhaps a trivial incident in itself, from it Clamence begins to learn something about his fellow man and himself. We are not fundamentally in harmony with one another or our ideal image of ourselves as enlightened and humane modern men.

After the incident with the motorcyclist, Clamence comes to see or to remember his preference for the satisfaction of his animal lusts over his desire for enlightenment and to recognize that he is guided not by a cosmopolitan humanitarianism, but a selfish (even brutish) desire for superiority and preeminence, preferably at the expense of others (59-60 and 55). Even his good deeds are performed out of a desire to appear superior and better than others in the eyes of others, without which motive he learns he is willing to let other human beings die because saving them is too much trouble if nobody is present to witness his nobility (23-25, 69-70). He comes to see his enlightenment and humanity as but a ridiculously boastful pose covering over his contemptibly lustful and brutish nature. He is nothing more than a "salacious monkey" or "Cro-Magnon man lodged in the Tower of Babel," a brute with a mere veneer of sophistication and humanity (102, 4).

What is true of himself personally is also, Clamence suggests, true of us all, as is attested to by Clamence's passing references to and remembrances of (if we allow ourselves to remember) the atrocities of the twentieth century—such as, to name but a few: the Second World War, the Holocaust, and various devices of torture and destruction we have used our powers of mind to invent. If we allow ourselves to remember *all* of what we are and capable of, we realize how hard (maybe impossible) it is to live harmoniously and contentedly with each other and our ideal image of ourselves or conscience. We come to be out of joint with the world and ourselves, filled with a sense of our guilt or fallen nature, like Clamence.

As the personal confession of its narrator's fallen condition—a confession meant to remind us of our own similarly fallen condition—Camus's *The Fall* cannot help but remind us Augustine's *Confessions*. So too does Clamence's longing for redemption and some form of participation in what is immortal and eternal. Unlike Augustine, however, Clamence cannot bring himself to believe in the redemption offered by Augustine's God. He is too enlightened, too modern to accept such a belief. God is dead in Clamence's modern world. Yet Clamence still seems unable to let go or forget about such belief. He regularly refers to the Bible and Dante and keeps a stolen painting, "The Just Judges"—all works inspiring or inspired by belief such as

Augustine's. Clamence—modern man—is sick. He is plagued by the problems that troubled pre-modern men and, like Augustine, longs for a cure, but he finds himself unable to benefit from the medicine that cured his predecessors. He is therefore seemingly doomed to linger in his sickly state, just as Clamence seems likely to linger in the sickly state we find him in at the end of *The Fall*.

The Fall, then, suggests that the hopefulness that has characterized modern political thought and life from its inception is misplaced. All is not well with modern man and the modern world. Modernity, for all its blessings, fails to remedy our gravest problems and to satisfy our deepest needs. The modern world and modern man are plagued by the same problems that have always plagued humanity. Yet modern man's condition, Camus seems to suggest, is not only the same as but actually worse than that of pre-modern man. The success of modernity—of the world imagined by the likes of Machiavelli, Hobbes, Locke and their heirs—has closed off the overwhelming majority of mankind—like most of Clamence's contemporaries—from an awareness of those central questions and problems that have so long plagued humanity, thus closing them off from a central aspect of our humanity and diminishing them. Moreover, those few who, like Clamence, do remember and are troubled by those fundamental human questions find themselves too enlightened and skeptical— too modern—to take seriously the answers offered by past (or perhaps any) thinkers to those questions—questions about how we might best live together politically, realize our deepest moral hopes, and satisfy our longing for the eternal and divine. Their modern skepticism and irony prevent them from confronting fully and adequately those fundamental questions and problems of humanity and thus also prevent them from answering those questions and curing those problems, at least to that extent humanly possible.

Camus's *The Fall* clearly paints a bleak picture of the modern world and of the prospects for the future. But I wonder if it cannot also be thought to point, perhaps despite Camus's intention, to a ray of hope for those of us who teach, for lack of a better term, the "Great Books." *The Fall* points to the timelessness of humanity's great questions, the needfulness of their remembrance and study, and the irresistible attraction of the ideas of those "Great Books" of the past that Clamence (and we) simply cannot forget for all our reservations about them. And while Camus helpfully and rightfully reminds us of the great difficulties and questions that can and should stand in the way of our giving ourselves over to the answers offered in those (or any) books, we might still wish to draw some comfort in the thought that what is very difficult, even what is almost impossible, is still not *simply* impossible.

Works Cited

Camus, Albert. *The Fall*. Trans. Justin O'Brien. New York: Vintage Books, 1956.
Machiavelli, Niccolo. *The Prince*. Trans. Harvey C. Mansfield. Chicago: U of
    Chicago P, 1985.

Work, Leisure and the *Vita Contemplativa*– Pieper's *Leisure: The Basis of Culture*

Terry Hall
University of St. Thomas

The connection between the notions of leisure and of culture is the central theme of Josef Pieper's classic study, *Leisure: The Basis of Culture.*[1] As his title intimates, Pieper's book presents an argument the two-fold conclusion of which is that (a) culture is founded on leisure and (b) leisure is yoked to the contemplative life. That is to say, Pieper contends that leisure is a necessary condition for culture: absent leisure, there is no culture. At first glance, this claim might seem to be somewhat pedestrian. For who would deny that a society in which no one has the leisure, say, to paint or to compose symphonies or to write poems and novels will by this very deficiency lack culture? Although this way of understanding the matter captures an important aspect of Pieper's view, it does not disclose the heart of his claim about leisure and culture. It is not just the *outcome*, the cultural products or artifacts, to which he wants to direct our attention; he wants also to emphasize a certain habit of mind, a horizon of understanding, which not only can give rise to the notable achievements of culture but also enrich those whose lives are lived out on a more prosaic level. Only when we get clear on the role of work, leisure and contemplation are we able to discern what culture means for a flourishing human life for all. The central contention that prepares the way for grasping this trio of notions is that the power of reasoning and the power of intellectual understanding are related to each other in an integral way. Pieper refers to these two powers as *ratio* and *intellectus*.

FROM RATIO TO INTELLECTUS

The distinction between the power of understanding considered as *ratio* and the understanding considered as *intellectus* is the point from which Pieper's argument unfolds. Accordingly, one must begin with this distinction. Moreover, it is crucial to appreciate that this pivotal distinction is rooted in common experience. For Pieper, everyone who possesses an unimpaired understanding of ordinary things has had many experiences of what he terms *ratio* and *intellectus*. As I interpret Pieper, the sort of contemplation to which he draws our attention—the term for which is not *ratio* but *intellectus*—need not be confined to mystical or even metaphysical contemplation; it is not necessarily focused on the highest objects of knowledge, although of course sometimes it is so focused. *Intellectus* in its more prosaic and mundane instances include less elevated objects. Even so, the implications of such intellectual engagements are profound.

Ratio prepares the ground for the contemplative engagement of *intellectus*. *Ratio* is the activity of discursive reasoning; it is the step-by-step motion of the mind when it is involved with "searching and examination," when we are working with "definition[s] and drawing conclusions" (9). It is what we do when we are launched on the attempt to understand a broad range of things: a problem, say, in mathematics; or the essential point of Pericles' funeral oration; or Marx's dialectical logic of history; or an oxidation-reduction equation; or Ike McCaslin's discovery of the terrible secret of his family in *Go Down Moses*; or Augustine's discourse on the Trinity. Initially, we do not grasp these things. We therefore must reason about them, think our way through them, bring their meanings and significance to light. *Ratio* typically requires persistent mental effort. It requires persistence over time as we go from one aspect of the problem to another to a third component, and so on.

To be sure, we might fail in this effort of reasoning. Our persistent efforts might not pay off. For example, we might just not understand that math problem. It remains opaque to us, so that we fail to see the solution. We might remain confounded by Augustine's account of the trinity, so that the triune nature of God remains entirely beyond our understanding. Even so, unless we put forth the effort, we are virtually guaranteed not to understand what we are aiming at. As Pieper says, *ratio* is the condition for, though not the cause of, our finally grasping the essence of the matter we are attempting to understand (16). *Ratio* is a kind of understanding, even when it fails, but not one which in that case reaches its end.

When, however, we do reach the understanding at which are reasoning has been directed, we arrive at an understanding in the most pregnant sense. This is an achievement of the understanding in the mode of *intellectus*. Pieper says that *intellectus* is "the name for the understanding in so far as it is the capacity of *simplex intuitus*, of that simple vision to which truth offers itself like a landscape to the eye" (9). When we understand a mathematical proof, for example, we suddenly just see it. When we solve an oxidation-reduction equation, we suddenly see the answer fall into place. In the "flash of an eye" we understand precisely why Ike McCaslin in Faulkner's novel is horrified at the actions of his grandfather vis-à-vis the two slave women. After extensive ratiocination we finally get it—when to our *intellectus*, our understanding, the terrible secret of Ike's family is laid before us like a landscape. These sudden moments of clarity we may call the "aha! moment." Archimedes had an "aha! moment" when he suddenly understood why the level of water in his bath rose whenever he stepped into the tub. He cried out, not "aha!" but "eureka!" The meaning of the exclamation is, of course, the same. Both attest to the flash of insight, which is indeed, finally, a "seeing into" what has hitherto perplexed us. When this occurs, reasoning achieves its sought-for end and terminates in an act of intellectual contemplation.

Let us bring out another distinguishing feature of *intellectus*, or contemplation. When *ratio* is operating, we are engaged in a kind of motion. Our mind reasons from one aspect of the problem to another aspect. We move through all the parts of the problem or topic, seeking that break-through insight. The understanding is "on the way towards," which is to say it is in motion. If and when we arrive at the moment of insight itself, the mind comes to rest. It rests in the enjoyment of the understanding that is like having the thing spread out before us. The movement of the mind inherent in the operations of *ratio* has been brought to a kind of closure. This stillness can be—perhaps we should say that it typically is—of short duration. The point is that it is stillness, effortless, a cessation of our powers of reasoning. We are at leisure, Pieper says. Whereas *ratio* is active and restless, *intellectus*/contemplation is passive—or more precisely, Pieper is quick to emphasize, it is receptive (9). The mind receives the illuminating vision. In this mode of understanding, the mind is not limp, not "on hold," not awaiting illumination. It is at one and the same time active and relaxed.

What we have said to this point might give the impression that *ratio* and *intellectus*—the activity of reasoning and the act of contemplation—are always related sequentially, such that first we engage in *ratio* and then, later, we achieve understanding. This is too static and abstract, however. Pieper points out that in fact "[t]he mode of discursive thought [*ratio*] is *accompanied* and *impregnated* by an effortless awareness, the contemplative vision of *intellectus*....(9, emphasis mine). That is to say, we already bring to our efforts of reasoning prior achievements of understanding. Were this not the case, we could not even begin to reason. We build on prior understandings in order to reason further to new understandings. Prior understandings, achievements of *intellectus*, are embedded in our present reasonings. The two modes of understanding can be distinguished in thought, and they do sometimes come at two different times, but they tend to intertwine as we move toward a new episode of contemplation.

THE IMPEDIMENT OF THE WORKADAY WORLD

The impediment to achieving the fruits of intellectual contemplation is our immersion in the workaday world. This immersion, Pieper argues, tends to conscript us into what he calls the world of "total work" (33-44). If left unchecked, the world of work, of utilitarian pursuits directs us away from the space of leisure that is required for the episodes of *intellectus*, of contemplating the things that *are*. To be sure, we not infrequently have moments of intellectual understanding—Pieper says that they frequently impregnate our reasoning activities—but typically we are too busy to pause to rest in, to stop and take notice of, the "aha!" moments. We don't thematize them, and so we tend to be unmindful of their significance. We have work to do that directs us to more useful pursuits. We must perform at our jobs, pay our mortgage, feed our families and ourselves, deal with the problems of our children. Above all, we find it easy to simply pursue and enjoy what Hobbes terms "comfortable and commodious living."[2] That Pieper's book originated as a series of lectures given in the summer of 1947 in Bonn—that is, very shortly after the close of World War II, when many

German cities had been reduced to rubble—is significant. When it surely seemed that years of long, hard work of rebuilding was the most pressing need facing his fellow citizens, Pieper's spirited defense of contemplation and leisure was most likely arresting indeed, as he intended it to be. Men required a focused effort to be able to "pierce the dome" of the workaday world, to raise their sights to a higher source of nourishment (67). The body is nourished and satisfied by the products of work, while the soul is nourished and satisfied by understanding what is the case. As the phenomenologist Robert Sokolowski puts it, human beings are agents of truth and not just laborers.[3] The contemplation of truth both requires and is an instance of leisure.

From Leisure to Culture

This last phase of Pieper's argument in *Leisure: The Basis of Culture* stresses the need for release from our immersion in the world of work. We need, he says, to take a holiday from our utilitarian concerns. Commensurate with the immense importance of *intellectus*, from the engagement of contemplation, this holiday cannot be like any mundane holiday—a day at the beach, for instance. We should recall Pieper's contention that the occasions when we are able to "rest" in the enjoyment of intellectual comprehension come upon us as from a source that transcends human achievement. *Ratio*, we remember, is a necessary but not sufficient condition for such understanding. In his view, recognition of this fact moves us into the realm of theology. The inspiration he would have us recognize occurs under the rule of divine agency. The holidays we seek are consequently better thought of as holy days. Holy days typically involve a festival—a feast of thanksgiving. From ancient times, men have ceased working, toiling, laboring in order to feast and give thanks for the gifts of the gods. To this end, they produced imposing and enduring works of art: music, dance, liturgical forms and ceremonies, poetry, architecture, philosophical reflections.

All of this puts us in touch with several of the most ancient senses of "culture," namely the sense of "cultus" or cult and also the sense of cultivation (as in agriculture).[4] The first, of course, brings out the religious dimensions of culture. The second, with its intimations of cultivation of the soil, lends itself to an analogy with the cultivation of the mind, of the highest powers of the human soul. The two are joined when we appreciate that both require the active leisure that stands aside from the workaday world. Without leisure there is no culture worthy of the name. (To speak of the "culture of the workplace" is no more than an ersatz sense of the term.) The servile (or practical) arts build bridges and bake bread and consequently sustain us in our physical well-being. Liberal learning bakes no bread and builds no bridges, but it frees us for the engagement of leisure that alone sustains culture.

Notes

1. All references to *Leisure: The Basis of Culture* are to the translation by Alexander Dru, originally published in 1952 by Pantheon Books and reprinted by Liberty Press. Citation is by page number in the Liberty Press edition.
2. See Thomas Hobbes, *Leviathan*, Part 1, chap. 13 (90).

3. See Robert Sokolowski, *Introduction to Phenomenology* and *Phenomenology of the Human Person*. Also pertinent in this connection is Hannah Arendt's distinction between labor, work and action in *The Human Condition*, chapter 1.
4. For some helpful articulations of the term "culture," see the *Oxford English Dictionary* s.v. "culture."

Works Cited

Arendt, Hannah. *The Human Condition*. Chicago: U Chicago P, 1958.

Hobbes, Thomas. *Leviathan*. Ed. Richard Tuck. Cambridge: Cambridge UP, 1991.

Pieper, Josef. *Leisure: The Basis of Culture*. Trans. Alexander Dru. Indianapolis: Liberty Press, 1999.

Sokolowski, Robert. *Introduction to Phenomenology*. Cambridge: Cambridge UP, 2000.

———. *Phenomenology of the Human Person*. Cambridge: Cambridge UP, 2008.

Transmitting and Transforming through Core Texts

Teaching the Reformation Through Luther's Galatians

Jarrett A. Carty
Concordia University, Montreal

The tumultuous period of Western church schism known as the Reformation presents to the core texts professor a common curriculum challenge: how to bring to life an otherwise alien world to inexperienced students through the narrow lens of a period text. However, the Reformation presents its own particular challenge; since the period is best distinguished by acute theological disputes within Western Christendom, professors are likely to find their students unable to relate or understand the weight and significance that Christian theology could have upon church, politics, and society. Not the least of many reasons for this challenge is the force of secularism in the current student body. Secularism forces the general separation of religion from reasoned inquiry and political debate, relegating it to the realm of personal belief. Without suspending this force and its assumptions and judgments, an understanding of the Reformation period will not be fostered. Another pedagogical challenge to teaching the Reformation is historical ignorance. In the face of this challenge, the teacher must open the students to the myriad of conditions and complexities of the Reformation that will allay the students' facile reductions based on contemporary prejudices. Finally, the teacher of the Reformation must also confront a widespread Biblical illiteracy in the student body. The effects of this problem are pernicious: not only are students missing a basic knowledge of the single most important referent of the Reformation, but they are also thereby further inhibited from approaching the primary texts—particularly theological ones—that are representative of the age.

In the face of these problems, Martin Luther's *Lectures on Galatians*[1] (1535) is an excellent core text for introducing students to the Reformation era. First, through Luther's often hyperbolic and polemical writing, it presents the theological controversies of the early sixteenth century that had led to schism and political upheaval. Second, the *Lectures on Galatians* more subtly brings to light the intellectual currents, religious movements, and political developments concomitant with the church crisis of the sixteenth century. Third, the *Lectures on Galatians* abundantly shows the enormous importance of the Bible, and the complexity involved in its interpretation and appropriation. Finally, Luther's lectures provide the core text curriculum with a foil to contemporary secularism and fundamentalism that would otherwise reduce the importance of theological controversies—including those of the Reformation—to the simplest denominators.

Due to Luther's unyielding insistence upon the theological orthodoxy of the "Gospel" and the "Law," his *Lectures on Galatians* abundantly reveals the primary theological issues over the "evangelical" revolt in sixteenth-century Germany. From the introduction onward, Luther's theological purpose is clear: his lectures were to bring forth the "true doctrine of faith," or *sola fides* (by grace alone) soundly grounded in Pauline teaching but under attack from the "doctrine of works and of human traditions" (LW 26:3; Dillenberger, 100). Luther begins his lectures by summing up the argument of the epistle, in a jewel of Reformation thought and writing. The argument, as Luther saw it, was thus: "Paul wants to establish the doctrine of faith, grace, the forgiveness of sins or Christian righteousness, so that we may have a perfect knowledge and know the difference between Christian righteousness and all other kinds of righteousness" (LW 26:3; Dillenberger,100). This distinction, so crucial for Paul, was also vital for Luther; for him divine justification was nothing short of the central teaching of the Christian faith. The reader soon discovers that Luther's doctrine of grace was not only central to his own thinking, but at the heart of the sixteenth-century schism and the high stakes war for the salvation of souls. For Luther, the failure to distinguish Christian righteousness from all human-centered righteousness (such as "political," "ceremonial" or "legal") jeopardized the eternal salvation of souls. Thus the reader discovers that this *sola fides* theology had, in Luther's view, cosmic significance; "if it is lost and perishes, the whole knowledge of truth, life and salvation perishes at the same time lost and gone," wrote Luther, but "if it flourishes, everything good flourishes, religion, the true service of God, the glory of God, the right knowledge of all things and of all social conditions" (LW 26:3; Dillenberger,100).

Just as Luther uses his rediscovery of *sola fides* to come to the "right knowledge of all things and states of life," the reader comes to see that these lectures has much to say about political thought, intellectual currents, and religious movements of the age. For example, Luther emphatically believed that political office (and many other vocations) would be misunderstood and denigrated without a distinction between the "Law" and the "Gospel." Echoing his seminal 1520 treatise *Christian Liberty*,[2] Luther argued in the *Lectures on Galatians* that the righteousness of the law "should have its dominion only over the flesh" but touch not the "conscience," leaving human beings to live their baptismal calling by serving the world not for the sake of the righteousness it brings but for the sake of the righteousness Christ has already won for all (LW 26:11; Dillenberger, 108-109). For Luther, this law and Gospel distinction also demanded a radical reconsideration of the political powers of princes, emperors, and popes, in the midst of a pan-European shift to increasingly centralized monarchies and a politically weakened papacy. Consider Luther's insistence in these lectures that the law had a double use: first, to punish sin and transgressions, and second, to reveal unto humankind its sin and thus push him to the righteousness by faith alone (LW 26: 308; Dillenberger, 139). At once this limited the role of the civil authority to the sins of the flesh, but justified its independence from ecclesial authority; Luther gave it divinely ordained freedom over law, but limited its domain from faith and conscience.

Intellectual and philosophic movements are also introduced in the lectures. Luther's piecemeal appropriations of, for example, northern humanism and nominalism—as well as his divergences from them—are widely detectable throughout the work. In the *Lectures on Galatians*, Luther adopts the humanist stance against scholasticism, but at the same time undermines all human efficacy (including reason) in the reception of grace, giving way to a mysterious God who freely imputes this grace to humanity. For example, commenting on Galatians 3:6, Luther accuses the papal "sophists" of promoting salvation by works and aggrandizing reason. Yet his response to these "schoolmen" is not typical humanism: "but we exclude all works and come to grips with the heads of the beast called reason, which is the fountainhead of all evils" (LW 26: 230; Dillenberger, 128).

Introductions to the other religious movements of the age are also imparted by way of the opposition Luther excoriates. His rejection of the See of Rome and the papalist church are obvious enough; however, there is also considerable justification in the lectures why Luther opposed it on theological grounds. Moreover, the lectures amply show that Luther also vociferously attacked the radical flank (such as the "Anabaptists") of the church schism every bit as much as he attacked Rome. These "neo Arians" as he called them, "are all as ignorant … as the Papists are," for they (in his view) inverted Roman works righteousness for yet another Anabaptist works righteousness (LW 26: 312; Dillenberger, 143).

The *Lectures on Galatians* also reveals the deep and complicated relationship between Luther's thought and the Bible. Luther is no mere literalist, nor a proponent of a simple *sola scriptura*. It shows him to be an interpreter of the Bible through a Pauline Christological interpretation; Luther privileged Paul's epistle to the Galatians precisely because it provided an interpretative key, through Paul's Christology, to the whole of scripture. Therefore, as he argued in the lectures, Luther had to oppose the radical reformers' attempts to revive Mosaic law, for example, because it took the ancient code as presently applicable and thus destroyed the distinction of Law and Gospel and ultimately the core truth of salvation by grace alone. Hence Luther comments on Paul's claim that the works of the "flesh" are obvious (Galatians 5:19) by arguing that true saints are made by the Word of God—the revelation of Jesus' redemption for all—and not by law or human machinations.[3] Like most thinkers of his age, friend and foe alike, Luther considered the Bible a revelation of immense complexity and difficult nuances; the *Lectures on Galatians* shows this not only with Paul's epistle itself, but in the centrality of the *sola fides* theology as an interpretative key to both the Old and New Testaments.

Luther's *Lectures on Galatians* is classic work of both the German Reformation and the sixteenth century in general. As a core text in a liberal arts curriculum, it greatly aids in introducing students to the Reformation period. More than this, it also appropriately challenges contemporary students out of the assumptions of secularism and fundamentalism, assumptions that greatly inhibit them from understanding a key period in the Western heritage that gave rise to, amongst other things, the modern state. Such a crucial period, therefore, ought not to be neglected in a core text curriculum, and Luther's *Lectures on Galatians* remains an excellent introductory text.

Notes

1. There are several useful English editions of the text. While the complete translation is available through the Fortress Press series *Luther's Works*, it is very long. The much abridged translation in the anthology *Martin Luther: Selections From His Writings*, edited by John Dillenberger, is still quite serviceable despite the use of antiquated language. However, references and quotations are from the "Lectures on Galatians, 1535 Chapters 1-4" in *Luther's Works, Volume 26* edited by Jaroslav Pelikan, and "Lectures on Galatians, 1535 Chapters 5-6" in *Luther's Works, Volume 27* also edited by Pelikan, henceforth abbreviated (following the convention amongst Luther scholarship) as "LW 26" or "LW 27." All references correspond to the abridged version in the Dillenberger volume (as noted).
2. Known also as *The Freedom of a Christian*.
3. See LW 27: 87; Dillenberger, 164.

Works Cited

Luther, Martin. *Commentary on Galatians* in *Martin Luther: Selections From His Writings*. Ed. John Dillenberger. New York: Random House, 1962.
———. *Lectures on Galatians* in *Luther's Works, Volume 26*. Ed. and trans. Jaroslav Pelikan. St. Louis, MO: Concordia Publishing House, 1963.
———. *Luther's Works, Volume 27*. Ed. and trans. Jaroslav Pelikan. St. Louis, MO: Concordia Publishing House, 1963.

Galileo's "Two New Sciences" and the Quantification of Motion

Brian P. Schwartz
Carthage College

Dialogues Concerning the Two New Sciences presents us with numerous insights into the study of statics and mechanics, but, perhaps more important, introduces us to a new and fruitful approach to scientific inquiry. Galileo shows us that science itself is a sort of dialogue between the *episteme* held by learned scholars and the *techne* of skilled craftsmen and artisans. A true understanding of motion or mechanics can only come after these two have engaged each other on equal footing. When properly used, the deductive reasoning of Euclid and Aristotle can aid those who work with their hands, while the experience and precision of the engineer can guide those who ponder geometrical or logical abstractions. As a result, there is hope for genuine progress in better understanding the world we inhabit.

Our interlocutors, Salviati, Sagredo, and Simplicio meet at the Arsenal of Venice, the shipyard that helped build one of the most powerful naval and merchant fleets in the Mediterranean. The "constant activity" of the dockyards and the industry displayed by her shipwrights and laborers is about as far as one can imagine from the staid lecture hall, but these provide both a setting and a context for what will be four days of learning and discussion. Salviati opens the dialogue with his observation that the scene, "suggests to the studious mind a large field for investigation" (131). The wise Sagredo agrees, admitting that, "Being curious by nature [I] frequently visit this place for the pleasure of the work of those who, on account of their superiority over other artisans, we call 'first rate men'" (131).

These "first rate men" represent centuries of accumulated wisdom and experience—the *techne* of shipbuilding and manufacture. It is by their skill and craft that Venice has risen to prominence in both war and commerce, not unlike the Athens of Classical Greece. These men, according to Salviati, "have become highly expert and

clever in explanation" on account of their "inherited experience" and "their own observations" (131). Sagredo, too, acknowledges his intellectual debt to these workers,
saying, "Conference with them has often helped me in the investigation of certain
effects" (131). In their own way, these unnamed individuals represent the ideals of
Baconian science—the acquisition of knowledge in the service of mankind, or at
least of the city and its Doge. In particular, their knowledge is gained through a process of imitation, induction, and experimentation, all expressed in the form of *techne*.

Nevertheless, it is clear that *techne* does not contain a complete understanding of
the essence of shipbuilding. While experience is a valuable guide towards a useful
result—the construction of the ship—it does not answer the question *Why?* The artisan may be able to describe how best to build a ship, but he cannot explain why one
method or design is better than another, nor can any improvement be discovered or
developed except by accident or fortune. There is not a problem if one wishes to do
exactly what has been done before, but in a competitive environment, with real win-
ners and losers, any slight advantage can be exploited. Thus we find ourselves at the
conversation that begins the *Dialogues*. Our interlocutors are pondering the remarks
of "the old man" in response to their query about the great quantity of scaffolding
and bracing used to launch a large seagoing vessel compared to what is necessary for
a smaller one. This is the point of departure for Galileo's discourse on problems of
scaling, geometry, statics, and civil engineering, but it is, in fact, a pressing question
in light of the need for the larger and sturdier ships necessary to maintain Venice's
dominance in the Mediterranean.

The discussion that follows shows that *episteme*, too, has its place in gaining an
understanding of mechanics. The old man's answer—that an un-braced ship might
collapse under its own weight, failed to satisfy Sagredo, who argues that, "[S]ince
mechanics has its foundation in geometry, where mere size cuts no figure ... if the
smaller is sufficiently strong for the purpose for which it was designed, I do not
see why the larger also should not be able to withstand any severe and destructive
tests" (131). In other words, a ship or any other machine built on an arbitrarily large
scale should be proportionally as much stronger and more effective than a smaller
one. Sagredo is convinced that a ship or twice the normal size should require twice
as much scaffolding wile under construction. He questions the "common opinion
... [that] devices which succeed on a small scale do not work on a large scale."
Sagredo's skepticism arises from his correct understanding of the *episteme* gained
from Euclid and the geometers. The conventional wisdom, however, suggests that
there is an upper limit in size beyond which a device will not work as intended, and
this is borne out by experience. For example, one could improve upon the cannon in
order to launch more massive missiles greater and greater distances, but eventually,
the quantity of powder required is enough to destroy the gun itself. Similarly, there
are practical limits to the height of towers, the length of bridges, and even the sizes
of animals (132).

Salviati's response to the question and the old man's reply is, at first, a bit puzzling.
He seems to agree with Sagredo, saying, "The common opinion is here absolutely
wrong. Indeed ... precisely the opposite is true" (131). But then he defends the old
man's statements and expounds upon them for most of the next two days. Salviati

points out that a large clock will be more accurate than a small one, and yet, inasmuch as it is a structure, by, "the mere fact that it is matter" it will be weaker—in his words, less "resistant against violent treatment." This is true regardless of "imperfections in the material" and can be demonstrable by geometry (131). So, on the one hand, the larger clock, ship, tower, or gun will perform better as a clock, ship, tower, or gun, but for the fact that it will have a propensity to collapse under its own weight. Thus we see that the artisans—the possessors of *techne*—are correct in their conventional wisdom by saying that a machine can be built so large and no larger, but their lack of *episteme* leads them into error as to the cause of this problem and thus limits the application of their skills and creativity—with perhaps fatal consequences for the Republic. Meanwhile, the disciples of Euclid who rely exclusively on the closed system that makes up the axioms and theorems of geometry are correct inasmuch as they discuss the properties of circles, triangles, and other figures, but can themselves fall into error by misapplying these principles to the physical world. In our three-dimensional universe, a column twice the size of another is four times as strong but eight times more massive. While this may be difficult to illustrate on a two-dimensional plane, it is obvious to the builder who must gather eight times as much stone for the construction of the larger tower. A complete understanding of the strength of material structures requires the weaving together of both *episteme* and *techne*—in other words, through discourse of the one with the other.

The old man referred to in this dialogue is the same Academician of whom Salviati is such a devoted and loyal pupil, as well as the Author of the text on Motion that occupies the third and fourth days of this discussion. He represents Galileo himself, who once again employs a literary device that fooled no one in his *Two World Systems*. Having shown us how *episteme* can be of service to those engaged in *techne*, we are later provided with examples of how *techne* can be a guide to furthering *episteme*.

According to Aristotelian physics, an object may be either at rest or in a state of motion. The motion of an object through space may be classified as a result of "natural" or "violent" causes. The natural motion of a heavy object, whether a stone or the entire Earth itself, is to "fall" to the center of the universe, the "natural place" of earthy matter. Aristotle's mechanics is of limited use to the architect or engineer, but rather serves as a path towards comprehending the structure of the entire universe. For example, his refutation of the void rests in part on the fact that the existence of empty space is incompatible with his description of natural motion (215a). Galileo's project on the third and fourth days of his *Dialogues* is to present his readers with a description of motion as it is observed in our world, rather than as it ought to be observed according to the laws of deductive reasoning and based on the apparent characteristics of our universe. Galileo's carefully crafted apparatus and meticulous observations provide some of the first evidence that the physics of Aristotle may be deeply flawed.

Galileo's use of artificially arranged experiments and inductive reasoning does not preclude his appreciation of the accumulated knowledge of those who came before him. His mechanics is not invented out of whole cloth, but builds on the terminology of Aristotle as well as the geometrical reasoning of Euclid and Apollonius. For example, Galileo divides natural motions into those that are uniform and those that are naturally accelerated. He insists, however, that he will describe "acceleration as it actually occurs in nature" (200). What Galileo observes is that objects undergoing naturally accelerated motions and beginning at rest traverse distances proportional to the square of their time in motion, and that this is true whether the object falls from some height or simply rolls down a plane. The conclusion he draws is that natural acceleration is equivalent to uniform acceleration, which may be defined as a motion that "acquires during equal time intervals equal increments of speed" (200).

This definition marks an important transition in the analysis of motion. Galileo's definition of uniform motion expresses speed as a ratio between the distance traversed and the time-interval that has elapsed. Taking speed to be a ratio allows one to compare greater and lesser speeds, but we encounter difficulties when comparing an object in motion to one at rest, or in considering the transition from rest to motion, or describing a change in the direction of motion, such as when a stone thrown up in the air falls back to the ground. Galileo sidesteps these problems by conceiving of speed as a quantity—one that can be added to or subtracted from—and not simply a ratio. By considering motion as an additive quantity Galileo simplifies the transition from a body being at rest to being in motion. The distinction between rest and motion is one of the difficulties that confounds Simplicio and even gives Sagredo pause (201). But Galileo shows us that an object at rest simply has a speed the quantity of which is equal to zero. An increase in speed from zero to ten is no more interesting or surprising than an increase from ten to twenty, or from a speed of five in one direction to five in the opposite direction. While this insight might seem trivial to anyone who has sat through an introductory physics course, it opens up for the analysis a wide range of new problems. For example, if one neglects air resistance, an object thrown up will spend equal amounts of time on its ascent as it will returning to the original location. As Galileo demonstrates, the object experiences constant acceleration for the entire duration of its flight, even as it is momentarily at rest at the top of its arc. By extension, the analysis of projectile motion, as shown in the fourth day of the *Dialogue*, requires the separation of motion in the horizontal plane from that of the vertical—an acknowledgement of the relativity of motion as a whole. These concepts are not expressible as ratios—they require thinking of speed as a number that can be added to or subtracted from, just as any other quantity, such as the amount of material required for a building project. It is in this way that we see the further influence of *techne* on the *episteme* that guides our study of motion. A builder does not build an abstract house or an abstract ship out of abstract matter; rather he builds a particular house or a particular ship out of a particular amount of several types of matter—wood, pitch, nails, and so on.

Thus we see how requirements of *techne* can inspire those who work in *episteme*, just as a better grasp of fundamental *episteme* can aid those who operate with *techne*. Once Galileo realizes that a quantity of motion can be measured, changed, and controlled, a new era in science can be developed.

Works Cited

Aristotle. *Physics*. Trans. R. P. Hardie and R.K. Gaye. In *The Basic Works of Aristotle*. Ed. Richard McKeon. New York: Random House, 1941: 218-397.

Galilei, G. *Dialogues Concerning the Two New Sciences*. Trans. Henry Crew and Alfonso de Salvio. In *Great Books of the Western World*. Vol. 26, 2nd ed. Ed. Mortimer Adler. Chicago: Encyclopaedia Britannica: 129-266.

Satire as a Means of Transmitting and Transforming Knowledge and Culture

Lyndall Nairn
Lynchburg College

Most Americans today are familiar with satire in political cartoons and in TV programs like *The Colbert Report*. However, the humor in satire makes it inappropriate for academic writing, which is not ironic because in academic writing, we usually mean exactly what we say, and we try not to stoop to the level of making fun of other people. Despite these negative assumptions about satire, it can serve several useful purposes in a Freshman Composition course, particularly one that functions as part of a core texts program. At Lynchburg College, the core texts program is called Lynchburg College Symposium Readings (LCSR); the syllabus of a professor who teaches in this program will be approved by the LCSR committee provided that at least twenty percent of the assigned readings are core texts and that the related assignments facilitate the development of writing, speaking, and critical thinking skills. Because these requirements of LCSR courses fit well with the goals of a liberal arts education, general education courses, such as Freshman Composition, are easily adapted to the LCSR program. One core text that is well suited to the teaching of satire is Jonathan Swift's "A Modest Proposal." This text works nicely as a model for first-year students who are composing their own satirical pieces because it can help them develop their writing ability in at least three ways. First, modeling their own satirical essays after Swift's "A Modest Proposal," enhances freshmen's argumentation skills; second, learning to express irony heightens their awareness of the writer's relationship with the reader, and third, the opportunity to ridicule people or ideas that they do not like encourages more creativity than conventional academic writing assignments do.

Analyzing the structure of Swift's "A Modest Proposal" provides students with an organizational model for their own essays. In the first eight paragraphs, Swift's description of the serious levels of poverty and overpopulation in eighteenth-century

Ireland makes it clear that he is addressing a significant problem. Then in the ninth paragraph, he offers his outrageous solution to the problem: "a young healthy child well nursed, is, at a year old, a most delicious nourishing and wholesome food" (Swift 395). Even if the reader has missed the ironic hints that precede this proposal of cannibalism, this shocking claim makes it obvious that a persona is talking and not Swift, who was a respected leader in the Dublin community and the Dean of St. Patrick's Cathedral. The persona then explains the steps that would be required to implement his proposal: he has calculated the cost of supporting a baby for twelve months, the number of "breeders" (women of child-bearing age) needed, the proportions of male and female babies that would need to be kept alive to reproduce, and the profits that his scheme would generate (Swift 395-396). Next, Swift's persona outlines the economic, cultural, and moral advantages of his proposal; for example, this religious bigot is delighted that his proposal "would lessen the number of Papists" (398); he explains that his plan would improve the standard of living of the poor; it would increase the gross national product, especially through the prosperous restaurant trade, and it would prevent domestic abuse because husbands would not want to beat their pregnant wives for fear of jeopardizing the family's income, and mothers would not want to smack their children because bruised flesh would mean reduced profits (398-399). Swift also includes some counterargument when he discusses an alternative proposal of waiting until the children are fourteen or fifteen years old before slaughtering them. Swift's persona dismisses this alternative because it incurs unnecessary expenses and because the meat of teenagers would be too tough (397). Furthermore, Swift answers objections to his plan, such as the consequence of reducing the Irish population; he logically explains that having fewer mouths to feed will help solve the problem of poverty in Ireland (399). The conclusion reveals the persona to be completely disingenuous. He claims to "have not the least personal interest in endeavouring to promote this necessary work, having no other motive than the publick good of [his] country" because he says that he has "no children, by which [he] can propose to get a single penny; the youngest being nine years old, and [his] wife past child-bearing" (Swift 401). Overall, the clear organizational pattern of Swift's essay is easy for students to follow as a model as they build their own satirical arguments in their essays.

Nevertheless, the point of Swift's satire is to expose a serious problem and to criticize the people responsible for that problem. All through his essay, Swift suggests that at least four groups of people are to blame. First, he is criticizing the English government, who was draining Ireland of all its economic and agricultural resources, meanwhile doing nothing for the welfare of the Irish people (400). Second, he is criticizing the "projectors," politicians who come up with crazy proposals, which, instead of improving people's lives, reduce them to statistics (394). Third, he blames the absentee Irish landlords, who charged their tenants exorbitant rents and evicted them as soon as they fell behind in their payments, while the landlords themselves lived comfortable lives abroad, where the money they spent could not benefit the Irish economy (396, 398). Fourth, and most powerfully, Swift is attacking the Irish people themselves for not doing what they could to address their own problems. Towards the end of this essay, Swift's persona says, "Let no man talk to me of other

expedients" (399). Then he lists many realistic solutions that Swift himself had pre-
viously suggested in public forums. For example, taxes could be imposed on the
rental incomes of absentee landlords; domestic industries could be promoted over
foreign luxury imports; gambling and drinking could be curtailed, and storekeepers
could be prohibited from cheating customers and adulterating food (Swift 399-400).
Swift made these logical suggestions over a number of years, but he was continually
ignored, so by 1729 when he wrote "A Modest Proposal," he was so disgusted by the
Irish people's lack of initiative that he was telling them that they virtually deserved to
eat their own children. As students learn to identify the people whom Swift considers
to be responsible for Ireland's problems, they can begin to focus the purpose of their
own satirical essays.

In addition to developing a clear structure and purpose, to write effective satirical essays, students need to master the techniques of irony, where the reader understands that the writer's true meaning is the opposite of what the words state. Swift
sets up his irony by creating a persona, who at first seems rational, and then by
undermining the persona's credibility. On the one hand, Swift's persona initially appears to be sympathetic to the serious problem. Then he rationally elaborates on the
problem with statistical evidence and logical analysis of the causes. As he develops
his proposal, the persona uses terminology from various fields, such as animal hus-
bandry, economics, and the law. He mentions anecdotes from a number of foreign
countries, making himself look worldly-wise. On the other hand, Swift is constantly
undermining his persona's credibility, most noticeably with his outrageous proposal
of eating babies, an idea that no rational person would ever consider. The persona
uses judgmentally loaded words when discussing the poor who dress their children
in "rags" (Swift 393) and who treat their children as "salable commodities" (Swift
395), but when referring to himself, the persona's word choices become positively
loaded: everyone will appreciate his proposal so much that they will want to "have
his statue set up for a preserver of the nation" (Swift 394). Swift also makes us
doubt his persona's credibility with his questionable statistics; for example, when
counting the children who follow the female beggars, he mentions, "three, four, or
six children" (Swift 393). What happened to five? Why can't he count properly? He
also claims that a newborn would weigh twelve pounds, but in eighteenth-century
Ireland, where many women were malnourished, that is very unlikely (Swift 396).
Swift further undermines his persona's credibility by demonstrating his lack of morality, his blindness to the suffering of others, and his false humility. Students writing
their own satirical essays can make use of all these techniques to create irony, but
the undermining technique that is the most relevant for the development of their
academic writing skills is the citing of questionable authorities. As evidence that
cannibalism has been practiced before in other countries, Swift's persona mentions
Psalmanazar's anecdote about eating the "prime dainty ... carcasses" of young con-
victed criminals in his native Formosa (today's Taiwan) (397). However, any reader
of "A Modest Proposal" in 1729 would have known that Psalmanazar had been exposed as a hoax twenty years earlier; he was really a Frenchman who had never even
travelled to Asia (Barnet and Bedau 182). Similarly, student writers can undermine
their personas' credibility by abusing their sources in a variety of ways: blatant pla-

giarism of not citing well-known sources, obviously misrepresenting and distorting the sources' ideas, making up fictitious sources, or citing inappropriate sources. For instance, Bernie Madoff becomes an expert on the ethical practices of financiers, and Paris Hilton becomes a role model for teenagers' social behavior. By exploring the abuse of sources as a way to undermine the credibility of the persona, students realize the corollary: in other academic writing assignments that do not employ irony and satire, the writer needs to treat the sources seriously so that the reader will not doubt the veracity of the writer's claims.

From my students' point of view, the most appealing aspect of writing satire is the creative opportunity it affords them. They enjoy coming up with outrageous solutions to social problems. For example, the problem of car accidents caused by drunk drivers can be solved by raising the drinking age to seventy; by that age drivers should be able to make mature decisions (Alvarez 1). The problem of young children having accidents while playing on playground equipment can be solved by turning basements into dungeons and by locking up all children between the ages of three and twelve for twenty-four hours a day (Edgefield 1). The problem of illegal immigrants from Mexico can be solved by catching them in the Arizona desert with traps disguised as rocks so that the border patrol can send them back immediately (Batterson 1). The problem of insufficient funding for public schools can be solved by doing away with school buildings and holding classes outdoors; who needs desks, paper, and pencils when students can write in the dirt and count stones (Bull 45-46)?

If Jonathan Swift were alive today, he would have two reasons to feel heartened. Not only would he see that the economy of Ireland has been thriving in the late twentieth and early twenty-first centuries, mainly due to the I.T. boom, but he would also be encouraged to see our American undergraduates in core texts courses using his "Modest Proposal" to develop their writing and critical thinking abilities so that they can easily see through any hair-brained schemes proposed by "projectors" and charlatans. Swift would be pleased to see that once our students have identified such schemes, they have also mastered the writing techniques needed to expose them. In this way, our students can use their liberal arts education as a means of transmitting and transforming knowledge and culture to become the opposite of Swift's "American acquaintance," whose supposed experiences with cannibalism in the colonies gave Swift the idea for his "Modest Proposal" in the first place (395, 397).

Works Cited

Alvarez, Ashley. "Change the Age." Unpublished essay. Lynchburg College, 2009. TS.

Barnet, Sylvan and Hugo Bedau. *Critical Thinking, Reading, and Writing: A Brief Guide to Argument.* 4th ed. Boston: Bedford/St. Martin's, 2002. Print.

Batterson, Jeremy. "What Can America Do?" Unpublished essay. Lynchburg College, 2007. TS.

Bull, Lindsey. "Who Needs a Classroom?" *Agora* 11 (2002): 45-46. Print.

Edgefield, Debbie. "Keeping Children Safe." Unpublished essay. Lynchburg College, 2007. TS.

Swift, Jonathan. "A Modest Proposal." *50 Essays: A Portable Anthology*. Ed. Samuel Cohen. Boston: Bedford/St. Martin's, 2004. 393-401. Print.

Memory, Invention, and Delivery in *Middlemarch*

Mark E. Thomas
James Madison University

How does *Middlemarch* portray writing, and how does it use memory, invention, and delivery—three canons of rhetoric—while showing a humanistic, relativistic realism that informs and compels moral action? What do memory, invention, and delivery mean in *Middlemarch*? This essay discusses how *Middlemarch* deploys and depicts writing and these canons of rhetoric and relates them to what George Eliot called "the moral function" of art. Along the way, it contrasts the novel's moral scheme with what is often derided as moral relativism. Finally, a close reading of a passage about writing shows why reading this novel need not morally improve each reader.

Let's begin with the novel's funniest representation of rhetoric. Chapter 17 presents the scene in which Reverend Farebrother brings his new friend Tertius Lydgate, home to meet the three women he supports: his aunt, his sister, and his aged mother. His mother's warnings about the slippery slope of arguments anticipate some of to-day's conservative cultural critics' arguments about moral relativism. At the same time, the punch-line Eliot bestows upon her recalls the conclusion of Socrates' dialogue with Gorgias. She lambastes argumentation itself as an example of empty relativism:

> "My mother is like old George the Third," said the Vicar, "she objects to meta-physics."
>
> "I object to what is wrong, Camden. I say, keep hold of few plain truths, and make everything square with them. When I was young, Mr. Lydgate, there never was any question about right and wrong. We knew our catechism, and that was enough; we learned our creed and our duty. Every respectable Church person had the same opinions. But now, if you speak out of the Prayer-book itself, you are liable to be contradicted."

"That makes rather a pleasant time of it for those who like to maintain their own point," said Lydgate.

"But my mother always gives way," said the Vicar, slyly.

"No, no, Camden, you must not lead Mr. Lydgate into a mistake about *me*. I shall never show that disrespect to my parents, to give up what they taught me. Any one may see what comes of turning. If you change once, why not twenty times?"

"A man might see good arguments for changing once, and not see them for changing again," said Lydgate, amused with the decisive old lady.

"Excuse me there. If you go upon arguments, they are never wanting, when a man has no constancy of mind. My father never changed, and he preached plain moral sermons without arguments, and was a good man—few better. *When you get me a good man made out of arguments, I will get you a good dinner with reading you the cookery-book*. That's my opinion, and I think anybody's stomach will bear me out." (Eliot 108-109, emphasis added)

Madame Farebrother shares the widely held view that what counts is actions, not words. Her meaning of "arguments" is basically the same as our contemporary culture's definition of "rhetoric," meaning empty verbiage, the view that mere words are worth little or nothing, almost garbage in themselves.

This vacant view of rhetoric also applies to the novel's single example of delivery, the practice of oratory: Mr. Brooke's political speech, which the townspeople parody on the spot, demonstrating that his empty-headed politics have no more substance than his effigy. The novel's private and more important instances of delivery involve the way that fellow-feeling is shared and shown between characters, with the critical, climactic example occurring between Dorothea and Rosamond in chapter 81.

Memory plays a critical role in the novel by enabling Lydgate to contrast his real wife and his ideal wife. Once he brings himself to ask for his wife's help, Rosamond's "What can *I* do, Tertius?" contrasts sharply with his recalling Dorothea's earlier plea, "Advise me—think what I can do" (Eliot 366-367; Ch. 180) when her husband is stricken. Memory also enables us readers to stitch together the several instances that this same phrase is repeated, to different effects, by different characters: What shall I do?—the most fundamental moral question. In chapter 80, for instance, Dorothea answers that question by first interrogating her memory: "Was she alone in that scene? Was it her event only? She forced herself to think. ... 'What should I do—how should I act now, this very day, if I could clutch my own pain, and compel it to silence, and think of those three?'" (Eliot 485-486).

Dorothea is the character most consistently seeking an answer to that question. Her search is like searching for an argument, which also describes the canon of rhetorical invention. Dorothea expresses vaguely at different times her goal to be useful to others, but she doesn't know how to reach it. She begins by hoping that knowledge, an argument from authority, will help her discover what she should do, initially misperceiving masculine knowledge as the means to achieve her goal (Uglow 207). She later reveals she doesn't pray as often as she used to, but she continues searching. The process of

Dorothea's decision-making in chapter 80 displays human values of fairness, reciprocity, and logic, not divine or doctrinal imperatives. In this case, morality depends on the capacity for empathically understanding another. Dorothea relates to Lydgate and then Rosamond through their common marital disappointments.

Fifteen years prior to *Middlematch*, in her *Westminster Review* essay "On the Natural History of German Life," Eliot describes what she already saw as the moral effect of art: by engaging our moral sympathies in an artist's work, we extend ourselves beyond the limited realm of our immediate, personal experience. Here Eliot gives a sort of mission statement on realism in literature, relating it to a moral effect:

> The greatest benefit we owe to the artist, whether painter, poet, or novelist, is the extension of our sympathies. Appeals founded on generalizations and statistics require a sympathy ready-made, a moral sentiment already in activity; but a picture of human life such as a great artist can give, surprises even the trivial and the selfish into that attention to what is apart from themselves, which may be called the raw material of moral sentiment.... Art is the nearest thing to life; it is a mode of amplifying experience and extending our contact with our fellowmen beyond the bounds of our personal lot.... Falsification here is far more pernicious than in the more artificial aspects of life.... We want to be taught to feel, not for the heroic artisan or the sentimental peasant, but for the peasant in all his coarse apathy, and the artisan in all his suspicious selfishness. (qtd. in Pinion 13-14)

Hers will always be "realism" with air quotes around the word, but for Eliot, realism is more than a style or design choice. Furthermore, because of its artistic inclusiveness, Eliot's realism encourages and requires moral tolerance.

On the issue of tolerance, however, Eliot's moral humanism differs from our contemporary atheists' view as publicized by Richard Dawkins, Sam Harris, and Christopher Hitchens, whose books and staged public debates emphasize the evils of religion. Because she had seen people perform acts of kindness and love out of religious impulse, Eliot does not insist that believers are necessarily wrong to hold a belief she does not share. *Middlemarch*, then, presents an alternative to moral relativism that requires us to consider situations from multiple perspectives. The novel also dramatizes the development and practice of core moral and ethical principles, derived not from divine revelation but from human observation and the employment of logic and memory. Eliot's human morality is more stringent and didactic than anything the conservative cultural and academic critic David Horowitz might recognize as secular humanism, and at the same time her realism shows greater tolerance for humankind's variety, inconsistency, and frailty. *Middlemarch*'s humanistic morality is a secular value system different from moral relativism as characterized by conservative cultural commentators, because while it recognizes multiple perspectives, it does not mindlessly equate them. Far from the paralysis incurred by so-called moral relativism, Eliot's moral humanism shows principal characters such as Dorothea Casaubon, Caleb Garth, and Fred Vincy spurred to action by the question, "What should I do?"

Eliot's moral humanism conforms to her realistic method, but the assumptions underlying realistic representation are complicated and problematic, as shown in this passage from the beginning of chapter 41, about the importance of writing:

Who shall tell what may be the effect of writing? If it happens to have been cut in stone, though it lie face down-most for ages on a forsaken beach, or "rest quietly under the drums and tramplings of many conquests," it may end by letting us into the secret of usurpations and other scandals gossiped about long empires ago:—this world being apparently a huge whispering-gallery. Such conditions are often minutely represented in our petty lifetimes. As the stone which has been kicked by generations of clowns may come by curious little links of effect under the eyes of a scholar, through whose labors it may at last fix the date of invasions and unlock religions, so a bit of ink and paper which has long been an innocent wrapping or stop-gap may at last be laid open under the one pair of eyes which have knowledge enough to turn it into the opening of a catastrophe. To Uriel watching the progress of planetary history from the sun, the one result would be just as much of a coincidence as the other. (Eliot 256)

Part of what happens in this remarkable passage is that Eliot admits that rhetorical effects on readers may outstrip authorial intentions. Her quoted passage actually paraphrases chapter five of Thomas Browne's *Urn Burial*, a meditation on the discovery of some Crusaders' bones. Eliot appropriates Browne's Christian message that the souls of those passed warriors matter more than their material remains, applying it to writing. The later effect of writing may far exceed what the writer originally intended.

Eliot's allusion to Thomas De Quincey's writing about the whispering gallery in St. Paul's Cathedral in his *Confessions of an English Opium-Eater* also develops her theme that words' effects may outlive their authors. In his memoir, De Quincey writes that the whispering gallery echoed and amplified whatever was spoken there. The resounding, never-ending echoes of a single utterance are nightmarish, with obvious implications for an addict such as De Quincey, but his description is fantastic hyperbole. St. Paul's Cathedral's whispering gallery carries whispers across the smooth walls of its space; the acoustical effect does not, however, amplify sound.

Finally, this passage evokes the poignant irony from *Paradise Lost* that Uriel, "the sharpest-sighted Spirit of all in Heav'n" (Milton *PL* 3.691), fails to detect Satan's approach to Heaven. From that celestial perspective, one earthly event appears as coincidental or insignificant as another. For Eliot and us on earth, however, the difference between scholarly discovery and a social scandal will be obvious and meaningful, with discrete, unique effects on the people involved. In this passage and throughout this novel, Eliot would like to teach her readers to value and evaluate different perspectives, but she already knows that the consequences even of her own writing are unforeseeable. Eliot's moral purpose is an argument central to this novel, but not all readers will be persuaded by its logic or moved by its pathos.

Works Cited

Browne, Thomas. *Urn Burial*. In *Norton Anthology of English Literature*. 4th ed. Eds. M. H. Abrams et al. New York: Norton, 1979.

De Quincey, Thomas. *Confessions of an English Opium-Eater*. 1821, rev. 1856. Ed. Alethea Hayter. Harmondsworth: Penguin, 1971.

Eliot, George. *Middlemarch*. 2nd ed. Ed. Bert G. Hornback. New York: Norton, 2000.

Milton, John. *Paradise Lost*. Ed. Merritt Y. Hughes. New York: Odyssey, 1962.

Pinion, F. B. *A George Eliot Miscellany: A Supplement to her Novels*. Totowa, NJ: Barnes & Noble Books, 1982.

Uglow, Jennifer. *George Eliot*. New York: Pantheon, 1987.

"Recalling now the obscure shapes, the echoes, the sounds and sights after their sorts": Whitman's Poetics of Memory in "Out of the Cradle Endlessly Rocking"

Brian Nowlin
University of Dallas

As readers and critics have long intuited, Walt Whitman fancies himself *the* poet of the future. Eerily yet matter-of-factly, entreatingly yet confidently, Whitman's multivalent, polymorphically perverse poetic "I" often looks forward by employing a poetic fiction of looking backward. In other words, Whitman's poetic voice has a tendency to speak from out of a liminal, immemorial "space" that is always already anticipating the reader. Among all of his real and imagined orientations, then, Whitman is generally future oriented—the later Whitman even exaggeratedly so.[1] Perhaps because of this undeniable forward thrust of Whitman's poetry, few critics have noted the richness with which some of Whitman's poems—the *Sea-Drift* poems in particular—explore the complex workings of human memory. In "Out of the Cradle Endlessly Rocking," the human act of re-membering, of putting back together the "thousand warbling echoes" (392) of the lived-in past, merges with the self-reflective poetic act. Whitman's poem thus offers readers a poetics of memory, one that remembers the act of remembering, as it were, and in so doing reveals memory itself to be an inherently poetic activity: memory as *poiesis*. If the late Whitman views the future as an abstract locus of poetic and democratic revolutions, the earlier Whitman sees the past as an imaginative *topos* where loss and desire come together to form the poetic impulse. To sing the poet's memorial engagement with the past, Whitman's poem implies, is to confront the "pains and joys" (388) of Love and Death, those two ultimately inseparable primal realities at the heart of the human condition.

Edward Hirsch insightfully claims that "Out of the Cradle Endlessly

Rocking" formally creates the "very rhythm of a singular reminiscence emerging out of the depths of mind. ... Whitman creates through the rhetorical rhythm of these lines the very urgency of fundamental memory triggered and issuing forth" (22). Hirsch does not specifically name the prosodic techniques in Whitman's poem that "loosen the intellect for reverie" (Hirsch 22), that rhythmically rock the reader back and forth into a kind of active dream state that is the sine qua non of memory as *poiesis*, but some of these techniques can indeed be made explicit. Rhythm in free verse, though subtle and seemingly immune to formal analysis, nevertheless results from precise poetic effects. The anaphora of the first three lines ("Out of") combines with internal metrical echoes to create a sense of regularity within difference that immediately evokes the calm movement, the dreamy activity that the poem as a whole describes—note the dactyl plus trochee pattern that splits the ten-syllable first line into two echoing, mirroring halves, thus creating in effect the ghost of a caesura in the medial position ("Out of the cradle endlessly rocking"); the dactyl-trochee pattern recurs at the end of the second line in the phrase "musical shuttle." Additionally, the rapid flights of human memory, which proceed not logically but "[a]s a flock, twittering, rising, or overhead passing" (388), are imitated by an incredible prepositional energy released by the first word of consecutive lines: Out, Over, Down, Up, and From variously flitter about as the opening words of the first fifteen lines. As James Hillman claims in his psycho-linguistic analysis of the poetic imagination, prepositions both precisely position the reader in an imaginative scene and make propositions about the relational matrices at work within (or alongside, or underneath) that scene. Hillman writes: "So, we never seem to catch imagination operating on its own and we never can circumscribe its place because it works through, behind, within, upon, below our faculties. An overtone and undersense: is imagination prepositional?" (175). The prepositions in Whitman's poem indirectly suggest through the poem's manner of proceeding that memory is fundamentally imaginative movement, imagination rhythmically rocking back and forth so that it can prepositionally dart where its memorial whims take it.

If the formal aspects of "Out of the Cradle" imitate the ebb and flow of memory's imaginative flights in general, the content of the poem directly recounts a specific act of memory that is complexly doubled back upon itself. The poetic voice revisits a childhood scene in which "the child / leaving his bed wander'd alone" (388) down to the sea, where he heard the mockingbird's mournful song. The poetic voice thus conjures up his reminiscence

> From the memories of the bird that chanted to me,
> From your memories sad brother, from the fitful risings and fallings I heard,
> From under that yellow half-moon late-risen and swollen as if with tears,
> From those beginning notes of yearning and love there in the mist. (388)

In the line "From the memories of the bird that chanted to me," "memories" functions in an ambiguous, double sense: on the one hand, it refers to the poetic voice's memories of the bird that he heard as a child down by the sea; on the other hand, though, the "memories of the bird" must be taken as the bird's own memories of his vanished loved one, the content of the bird's song. The poet is therefore remembering the bird's memories, turning memory upon itself so that its imaginal ground can be recovered and re-membered. In the last four lines of the first stanza, memory's double movement is so successful that the poetic voice becomes indistinguishable from his childhood past. In the hands of the poet, memory unites dream and action so as to bring the past directly into the present of the poem:

A man, yet by these tears a little boy again.
Throwing myself on the sand, confronting the waves,
I, chanter of pains and joys, uniter of here and hereafter,
Taking all hints to use them, but swiftly leaping beyond them,
A reminiscence sing. (388)

Note that the past and present are united by the poet "by these tears," as if memory remembered itself only by recollecting the timeless ache in its heart. The above final lines of the first stanza also initiate a process in which the poet's own song merges with the song of the bird. From the "beginning notes of yearning and love" sung by the bird in memorial longing for his mate, the poet sings the "pains and joys" of memory writ large. For the rest of the poem, the poet and the bird, the rememberer and the memory, remain virtually indistinguishable.

As absorbed and translated by the poet, the song of the bird expresses yearning for the bird's mate, now vanished. Because of the present absence of the beloved, the past becomes the "object" of the bird's loss and desire, the place simultaneously out of which and to which his mournful memory sings. In an apostrophe that contains one of the most stunning uses of *epizeuxis* ever utilized by a bird (much less a poet), Whitman's bird addresses the past directly:

O past! O happy life! O song of joy!
In the air, in the woods, over fields,
Loved! loved! loved! loved! loved!
But my mate no more, no more with me!
We two together no more. (392)

The haunting past participle *"Loved!"* reveals the interrelationship between loss and desire as the fundamental ground of memory. The bird desires a lost object, and the loss of the object issues in the bird's desire—from this irresolvable tension memory attempts to recreate the past in the present. Strikingly, while the bird's song directly embodies this movement of memory through the circuits of loss-and-desire, the poet's attempt to remember the bird's song and re-create it in the present of the poem *indirectly* communicates such a movement of memory—in this regard, the poet's skillful use of onomatopoeia and of repetition serves not only as a poetic technique but also as a metaphor for an act of memory that seeks in essence to imitate the past and thereby re-call it in the present. Readers thus experience the act of memory in both the content and the process of the poem.

The act of remembering appears successful *for the poet*, who again becomes exultingly inseparable from the boyhood self who directly witnessed the bird's memorial "aria":

> The boy ecstatic, with his bare feet the waves, with his hair the atmosphere dallying,
> The love in the heart long pent, now loose, now at last tumultuously bursting,
> The aria's meaning, the ears, the soul, swiftly depositing,
> The strange tears down the cheeks coursing,
> The colloquy there, the trio, each uttering,
> The undertone, the savage old mother incessantly crying,
> To the boy's soul's questions sullenly timing, some drown'd secret hissing,
> To the outsetting bard.

In his ability in and through language to articulate the stirring of memory, or, better put, in his ability to *sing* memory, the poet discovers a sense of poetic vocation: "Now in a moment I know what I am for, I awake... A thousand warbling echoes have started to life within me, never to die" (392). The ancient connection between poetry, particularly oral poetry, and memory—Mnemosyne is, after all, the mother of the Muses—is remembered by the poetic voice in "Out of the Cradle Endlessly Rocking."

In the latter stages of the poem, the sea, implicit throughout the poem as its guiding image, as indeed the "cradle endlessly rocking," emerges explicitly as a complex trope that manages to locate within the same poetic image both the workings of memory and the work of poetic craft. The sea is both memory poeticized and poetry remembered. Mimetic of the mockingbird's direct address to the past as the locus of loss and desire, the poet addresses the sea as the ineffable reality in which the interrelated mysteries of both poetry and memory resound:

> O give me the clew! (it lurks in the night here somewhere,)
> O if I am to have so much, let me have more!
> ... Are you whispering it, and have been all the time, you sea-waves?
> Is that it from your liquid rims and wet sands? (393)

The sea responds with the "delicious word death," expressing it using *epizeuxis*—which inevitably ties the sea's "Death" to the bird's "*Loved!*":

> Death, death, death, death, death. (393)

The poet directly connects—or fuses, as he puts it—the bird's song with the sea's delicious utterance, as well as with his "own songs awaked from that hour" (393). Love and death, loss and desire are the *prima materia* of both memory and poetry, and the sea is their imagistic "place"—a paradoxical place out of which memory and language attempt to satisfy a never-to-be-satisfied desire, whose hidden face is loss. Yet only the poet can fuse all of these realities into one delicious word, Death, a word whispered by the sea. The poetic voice in "Out of the Cradle" finally exults in the ability of poetry to name, to absorb and to translate both the workings of human memory and indeed its *own* workings. Where memory ends and poetry begins, however, remains an open question. Hints and indirections are no doubt whispered, now and then, by that Whitmanian trope of tropes: the sea.

To take all of Whitman's memorial hints so as to use them, but swiftly to leap beyond them (to paraphrase Whitman's poem), I shall now briefly pursue what accepting the Whitmanian notion of memory as an inherently poetic process—memory as *poiesis*—might mean both for the way we teach the liberal arts in our core classes and indeed for how we conceive of the very idea of a core curriculum. As stated above, Whitman's poetics of memory is grounded in a complex circuit of loss and desire: memory is animated by a desire for a lost object that is presently desired precisely because it is lost. Whitman's poem enacts the way in which this process of loss and desire, which might well be called an erotics of memory, is inseparable from the deepest urgings that constitute the poetic act. What I would here claim is that a similar memorial erotics/poetics characterizes the desire to form, to defend, and to teach a core curriculum, for at its heart the idea of an established "core" collection of texts and courses—the core of the core, as it were—implies that something essential is missing from any curriculum designed purely on the basis of the most current and "up-to-date" pedagogical, philosophical, and literary texts. What is lost in a curriculum that lacks a core is the rich perspective offered by a solid grounding in the Western intellectual tradition,[2] a perspective that splinters off into a refracted variety of approaches and readings that deepens the most current texts and intellectual debates and allows their aesthetic, ethical, and philosophical significances to be more fully engaged by teacher and student alike. Forming a core curriculum thus springs from a desire for what is not inherently present in any pedagogical practice rooted solely in the contemporary scene, namely, the fertile, shared context that canonical texts can offer. Conceiving of core classes, and teaching them, are activities that long to re-present the canonical in the present (just as Whitman's poetic voice re-presents the bird's memorial song in the present texture of his poem) so that the innumerable echoes set off by allowing a cultured memory a place in an educational curriculum can sound the depths of our present intellectual ground. A core curriculum is essentially a dynamic form of cultural memory that both interrogates and helps define the characteristics of the contemporary culture.

Further, recognizing that memory is fundamentally poetic and that poetry is inherently memorial suggests that one of the ongoing tasks of forming and teaching a core curriculum is continually making and re-making (recall of course that *poiesis* originally referred to a kind of *making*) the core, since a core text or class must be fashioned (sung, as Whitman would put it) anew based on the particular promptings and contingencies of the present. The rich paradox that sounds through Whitman's poem—that what is present in the poet's song is precisely what is absent—is equivalent to the following paradox that beats in the heart of any core curriculum: canonical texts ostensibly fixed in the past are best engaged by in effect *making them new*, reading them in such a way that, though their original historical and social contexts are engaged as part of their overall meanings, they can be unfixed from dogmatic historicist reductionism so as to speak to present concerns. Paradoxically, core texts are canonical precisely because they remain current. Establishing which canonical texts remain most current, though, must be a constantly ongoing endeavor taking place both in the classroom and in departmental conversations. Creating and nurturing a core curriculum of canonical texts is in effect a memorial engagement with the present, and it requires a poetic sensitivity attuned to likenesses—how is this canonical text like this present concern or debate—and to metaphorical equivalences—how can present concerns and "truths" perhaps be re-visioned in engagement with past texts as equivalent to what, on the surface, they appear not to be: canonical texts both provide complex metaphors through which present reality can be reconceived, and prompt a clarification of the metaphors and perspectives currently at work in our interpretations not only of texts but of the larger world. That cultural memory must constantly be made (poeticized) anew does not require rewriting the past in a relativistic frenzy. Instead, recognizing memory as inherently poetic encourages one to engage past texts with a poetic ear, a Whitmanian ear ultimately attuned to how the past inevitably re-sounds in the present, and to how the present longs for what is absent so as to sing its full significance.

Notes

1. As Roy Harvey Pearce persuasively argues, the later Whitman seeks rather unsuccessfully to transform his poetry from "archetypal autobiography" into literal prophesy. See Pearce's "Whitman Justified: The Poet in 1860," as reprinted in *Walt Whitman: Modern Critical Views*, edited by Harold Bloom.
2. I see no inherent reason why Eastern traditions cannot also be engaged as part of a core curriculum. Though in the West the notion of a liberal arts curriculum, and thus the basic structure of higher education, overtly stems from a Western context—particularly the Western philosophical and rhetorical traditions—there is by now a long history of Western engagement with Eastern traditions, a history that has been construed in a number of ways within Western academic discourse.

Works Cited

Bloom, Harold. *Walt Whitman: Modern Critical Views*. New York: Chelsea House, 1985.

Hillman, James. "Image-Sense." In *Working with Images: The Theoretical Base of Archetypal Psychology*, ed. Benjamin Sells. Connecticut: Spring Publications, 2000.

Hirsch, Edward. *How to Read a Poem and Fall in Love with Poetry*. New York: Harvest, 1999.

Whitman, Walt. *Poetry and Prose*. Library of America Edition, 1996.

The Burning Deck:
Elizabeth Bishop's Modern Parable

David Southward
University of Wisconsin-Milwaukee

Let me start with a confession. There are days when I walk out of my classroom feeling discouraged, wondering whether it really is important for my students to know about Plato's theory of forms, the nuances of Milton's theology, or the biblical subtext of *The Sound and the Fury*, when most of them will don their iPods the moment they leave the building, catch a bus to their jobs in retail and service, and, after writing a competent paper about one of the esoteric subjects I am trying to teach, never give them a second thought. Are core texts *truly* relevant and essential to my students' humanity, or have I simply convinced myself that it is so, because I have felt these texts to be essential to mine?

A poem that deals with this question, albeit in a circuitous way, is Elizabeth's Bishop's "Casabianca." Bishop's poem may not be regarded as a "core text" in the way that Plato's and Milton's are, but it reflects deeply on the process of cultural transmission via canonical literature. It is certainly about core texts, in other words, as well as about our motives for teaching them. The poem's meta-textual perspective is made apparent in the opening lines, where a young boy foolishly persists in reciting verse while standing on the deck of a burning ship:

> Love's the boy stood on the burning deck
> trying to recite "The boy stood on
> the burning deck." Love's the son
> > stood stammering elocution
> > while the poor ship in flames went down.
>
> Love's the obstinate boy, the ship,
> even the swimming sailors, who

> would like a schoolroom platform. too.
>   or an excuse to stay
>   on deck. And love's the burning boy. (Bishop. 5)

The poem that the boy recites is Felicia Hemans's nineteenth-century ballad of the same title, an anthology standard in Britain and the U.S. well into the twentieth century (Hemans, 348). The brave lad in Hemans's poem is no faltering schoolboy; he embodies a national ideal, the princely seaman whose loyalty to ship, captain/ father, and empire knows no limits. Recitation of this poem by generations of schoolchildren, one presumes, was meant to instill in them a similar virtue, through their empathy with the boy's dutiful suffering.

Bishop's poem does something more complicated than her predecessor's: it superimposes on the literally burning deck of the original a figuratively "burning" classroom dais, on which Hemans's lines are recited. The technique resembles that of dreams, where scenic shifting or fusion occurs by means of a metaphoric hinge. One effect of Bishop's technique is to disorient her reader, a point I will return to. Her more obvious purpose is to highlight an irony of education, specifically its insistence on preserving and transmitting the literary past. Cleverly juxtaposing the heroic death of Casabianca with the humiliating performance of the burning boy, Bishop invites scrutiny of the damaging effects of rote learning on impressionable children (Robson 158). What's more, she draws our attention to the schoolboy's struggle to get the poem right while the ship and its sailors confront their fate, thus underscoring the futility, if not outright absurdity, of clinging to a tradition that may threaten one's very survival. How can our reverence for the past, Bishop seems to ask—reverence for the parents and teachers who assured us of its importance and measured us by its exalted standard—save us from a sinking ship, literal or metaphoric? Might our obstinate devotion to tradition have no practical value at all? Perhaps the sailors are right to see the boy's recitation as an "excuse." It relieves him from diving into the world's shifting currents and making his way through them unaided, as all must do outside the classroom.

It is not hard to see in Bishop's "Casabianca" a familiar strategy of the modernists: to expose sentimental Victorian ideals to the unpleasant realities those ideals served to screen. Bishop's stammering boy may bring to mind the similarly flawed heroes of Conrad's *Lord Jim* or Joyce's *Portrait of the Artist as a Young Man*. who find it equally hard to live by or "recite" ancestral platitudes with ease. In Samuel Butler's classic attack on Victorian mores, *The Way of All Flesh*, the protagonist is actually drilled by his father on the meaning and moral of Hemans's "Casabianca," which leads him to the depressing conclusion that "he should never never have been like Casabianca. and that Casabianca would have despised him so much if he could have known him that he [Casabianca] would not have condescended to speak to him" (Butler, 111). The ironic lesson of this boy's catechism is much like that of the burning boy's recitation: children who are taught to ape impossible ideals will only end up ashamed of their inadequacy.

Yet there remains an element of mystery in Bishop's poem that does not strike one as modernist irony, and this is her repeated use of the word Love. The entire poem is cast as a definition of love, which on the one hand Bishop characterizes as an all-encompassing force or feeling (taking in boy, ship, and sailors as the poem proceeds) yet on the other hand attributes an almost weirdly specific meaning: love is a boy burning with shame while he tries to recite a poem ... and includes everything else in his vicinity?! Nowhere in the long history of love's allegorical representation, from Greek mythology to the Renaissance emblem, is there an image quite like this. Its incongruity not only adds to the effect of dreamlike disorientation I mentioned earlier, but it constitutes (in my opinion) the real power of Bishop's "Casabianca," confronting readers with the task of imagining *how* this burning boy can be Love. At the same time, the incantatory repetition of the word "love" holds out the possibility that the poem is not ironic, or not merely ironic, but an effort to reclaim for modernity some vestige of transcendent meaning.

If I am right about these puzzling features of the poem, perhaps a better way to conceive of it is as a parable of love. In his book on biblical hermeneutics, *The Genesis of Secrecy,* Frank Kermode explains that parables are comparisons used to illustrate important moral truths but in a dark or ambiguous manner that demands interpretation. Jesus was fond of reciting parables, the opacity of which appears to have stumped most of his followers. But for those who gleaned their meaning, the parables acquired what Kermode calls "radiant obscurity," an aura of spiritual depth and suggestiveness. In modern times the parable form is comparatively rare; when used at all, it tends to have a political or satirical edge, as in Orwell's *Animal Farm,* published the year before "Casabianca." Bishop's use of parable to communicate an obscure truth about love seems almost archaic by comparison, and it raises the question: what exactly is this obscure truth?

One possibility is that Bishop seeks to broaden the conception of filial duty in Hemans's elegy by including all those stammering schoolboys and swimming sailors who, however eager they may be to please their superiors, achieve no glamorous martyrdom. Or perhaps the love Bishop refers to is more romantic: love is a burning attachment to some longed-for union (here symbolized as a successful performance) which everyone, including the lover, knows to be impossible yet cannot help but covet. While both readings seem warranted by the text, neither fully addresses the prominence given in Bishop's parable to the act of *recitation.* What sort of love is like a recitation, specifically a recitation that can't be completed in time or to anyone's satisfaction?

The answer, I will venture, lies in the self-reflexive opening of Bishop's poem, "Love's the boy stood on the burning deck/trying to recite 'The boy stood on/ the burning deck.'" If we forget about the source in Hemans for a moment, it becomes suddenly clear what this boy is doing: he is trying say what is happening to *him* at this very moment, struggling to express his condition—perhaps thinking thereby to master it—in the short time he has "on deck." In a sense, this boy is a poet. And as is true for all poets (all human beings, for that matter), his sole means of articulating the life burning within and around him is the borrowed language of his ancestors, which even under the best circumstances will be imperfectly suited to his needs. Although Hemans's lines may seem perfect for the burning boy's situation, his obstinacy suggests an unconscious resistance to them, as if only the most exacting "elocution" could possibly imbue those lines with *his* meaning, *his* existence. Viewed in this light, the poem is about the struggle to integrate the cultural past with one's own unique circumstances, the difficulty (yet necessity) of understanding oneself through the lens of tradition—because it is the only lens available. The terms of Bishop's parable now become legible: the boy is any one of us; the burning deck is the ceaselessly changing world we live (and die) in; the recital is our baffled attempt to save all that we are losing by putting it into the only transmissible form we know. And Love is the whole order of defiance this implies. An obstinate love for life prevents us from simply letting it burn, though burn it must.

None of us is immune from the burning deck. Even that most hard-nosed critic of Western cultural traditions, Michel Foucault, once acknowledged how in his era "the immense and proliferating criticizability of things, institutions, practices, and discourses" had induced "a sort of general feeling that the ground was crumbling beneath our feet, especially in places where it seemed most familiar, most solid, and closest to us" (Foucault 6). So it remains in our own time: although the concrete and carpet we stand on are regularly mended and replaced by the powers that be, the deck burns beneath our feet as fiercely as it did beneath Foucault's and Plato's and Milton's. Getting my students to feel its heat may be the best way to interest them in authors with whom they appear to share little else. What "Casabianca" affirms for me is the ineffable, abiding love that sends me back to the schoolroom day after day to rehearse the impossible act of salvation.

Works Cited

Bishop, Elizabeth. *The Complete Poems 1927-1979*. New York: Noonday Press, 1983.

Butler, Samuel. *Ernest Pontifex, or The Way of All Flesh*. Boston: Houghton Mifflin, 1964.

Foucault, Michel. *"Society Must Be Defended": Lectures at the Collège de France 1975-1976*. Trans. David Macey. New York: Macmillan, 2003.

Hemans, Felicia. *The Poetical Works*. New York: R. Worthington, 1884.

Kermode, Frank. *The Genesis of Secrecy*. Cambridge, MA: Harvard UP, 1979.

Robson, Catherine. "Standing on the Burning Deck: Poetry, Performance, History." *PMLA* 120.1 (2005): 148-62.